Watch This!

RELIGION, RACE, AND ETHNICITY
General Editor: Peter J. Paris

Watch This!

The Ethics and Aesthetics
of Black Televangelism

Jonathan L. Walton

NEW YORK UNIVERSITY PRESS

New York and London

NEW YORK UNIVERSITY PRESS
New York and London
www.nyupress.org

Library of Congress Cataloging-in-Publication Data

Walton, Jonathan L.
Watch this! : the ethics and aesthetics of black televangelism /
Jonathan L. Walton.
p. cm.
Includes bibliographical references and index.
ISBN-13: 978-0-8147-9417-3 (cl : alk. paper)
ISBN-10: 0-8147-9417-3 (cl : alk. paper)
ISBN-13: 978-0-8147-9452-4 (pb : alk. paper)
ISBN-10: 0-8147-9452-1 (pb : alk. paper)
1. Television in religion—United States. 2. Evangelistic work—United States—History—
20th century. 3. Evangelistic work—United States—History—21st century. 4. African
Americans—Religion. 5. United States—Church history—20th century. 6. United States—
Church history—21st century. I. Title.
BV656.3.W35   2008
269'.2608996073—dc22   2008037033

Manufactured in the United States of America
c 10 9 8 7 6 5 4 3 2 1
p 10 9 8 7 6 5 4 3 2

Contents

Acknowledgments

I would like to acknowledge a collection of individuals, groups, and organizations that have assisted me over the past few years while I was researching and writing this book. I begin with the two wonderful sages of love that created my first university classroom around the dinner table inside my family home: my parents, John Henry and Rose Marie Walton. They and my supportive sister, esteemed grandparents, and many other family members to whom I am connected by blood and love have enveloped me with words of prayer, encouragement, approval, and admonishment. Their love animates me.

This book began at Princeton Theological Seminary. Here I was blessed with what could be considered a "dream team" of scholars of African American religion and cultural theory. It was my privilege to sit at the feet of Peter J. Paris and witness *phronesis* in the flesh. Peter and Adrienne will always remain near and dear to me. The computer-like mind and critical eye of Mark L. Taylor always kept me honest. Finally, the indefatigable commitment of Eddie Glaude to my work and the incomparable insights of Cornel West to this project have endeared me to them in ways that only the language of love could describe. Brother Eddie's "golf course intervention" altered the trajectory of my academic career, and Cornel's spiritual genius shared at the "Church of the Annex" taught me not to be ashamed of the gospel. To these dear persons I am indebted.

I have to extend my deepest appreciation to the Fund for Theological Education (FTE) and Dr. Sharon Watson Fluker, FTE vice president for doctoral programs and administration. Without the support of the FTE, I could not have completed my degree, let alone this project. I must also acknowledge the Center of African American Studies as well as the Center for the Study of Religion at Princeton University. Both provided valuable financial resources that allowed me to travel the country in order to conduct interviews, attend megachurch conferences, and purchase more televangelism videos than the law or the Lord should allow. This sentiment also extends to the Department of Religious Studies at University of California, Riverside, which also provided essential resources and valuable writing time to complete this project. I could not have asked to be a member of a more supportive department than that to which I belong at UC Riverside. This includes Professors Sterling Stuckey and Emory Elliott, who have been more than generous with their time and knowledge since my arrival. Thank you.

In researching this book I have encountered warm and welcoming personalities. I would like to extend my appreciation to Frederick and Eula Eikerenkoetter, "Rev. and First Lady Ike," for opening up their beautiful home in Miami to my wife and me. The Eikerenkoetters, along with their courteous staff, particularly Carolyn Jackson, were as hospitable as the heavenly hosts. I am thankful for Rev. Ike's willingness to share his story, and I pray this project represents it fairly. I was also fortunate to spend time with Bishop Carlton D. Pearson and the wonderful people of New Dimensions Ministries of Tulsa, Oklahoma. Bishop Pearson and his staff—Pastor Jesse Williams, Tonielle Bent, David Smith, and the legendary gospel singer Sara Jordan-Powell—have a spirit of grace and love that is infectious. I hope more congregations will catch it. I appreciate the assistance of Mr. Assif Reid in the Holy Spirit Research Center at Oral Roberts University, who helped me dig through the stacks on multiple occasions. The ministry of Bishop T. D. Jakes and the Potter's House deserves special mention for their willingness to enter into dialogue with members of the religious academy. I would thus like to note the gracious spirit of Bishop Jakes and his beautiful family during their time in Princeton, as well as the professional and organizational excellence of Tina Polite and Beverly Robinson, who orchestrated the bishop's visit. And I will always be grateful to Dr. Jamal Harrison-Bryant for our candid conversations concerning the world of African American religious broadcasting. Despite our theological disagreements, which have made for instructive and entertaining dialogue, Brother Jamal has remained a friend and intellectual interlocutor for over a decade, and I continue to be impressed by his immense talent and gifts.

I want to also express my appreciation to a larger community of scholars who helped shape this book. James Cone, A. G. Miller, Noliwe Rooks, Bill Gaskins, Darnise Martin, Edward Blum, Wallace Best, and Stewart Hoover all provided insight and useful comments at different times. Graduate students Lerone Martin (Emory) and Ryon Cobb (Indiana) provided invaluable assistance (and laughter) at the most opportune moments. Leslie Wingard, with her remarkable writing ability and keen eye for detail, was particularly helpful in overcoming my homiletic tendencies. Professor Wingard definitely took some pressure off my brilliant editor, Jennifer Hammer, who has been more than a joy to work with at every stage of this project. Ciara McLaughlin, Gabrielle Begue, and Despina Papazoglou Gimbel at NYU Press have also been of great assistance at varying junctures of this process. And despite their busy schedules, Marla Frederick, Shayne Lee, and Anthony Pinn all closely scrutinized the manuscript, pushing my analysis in more constructive directions and encouraging clarification at the appropriate times. That they each read this project with such care endears them to me not only as colleagues in the academy but as friends.

Speaking of which, without the support and camaraderie of friends, in and outside of the academy, none of this would matter. I am so thankful for the Marshall, Owens, Logan, Gilbert, Ellison, Quick, James, Samuel, Sorett, Sanders, Johnson, Gerald, Pierce-Cortez, Jackson, and Drake families for adding sunshine to my family's life. (And a special shout-out to Geddes and Carye Lou Hanson, a.k.a. Momma "G.G." and Grandpa Doc.) This also includes faith communities such as Rev. William Smith and the Israel Baptist Church family in Atlanta, Georgia, the members of the Victory Baptist Church of Stone Mountain, Georgia (particularly the ushers' ministry), and the beautiful people at the Union Chapel A.M.E. Church and Memorial West Presbyterian Church in Newark, New Jersey. I am because you are!

I have reserved my final sentiment for the ones most deserving. None of this would have been possible without the care and support of my wife, Cecily Cline Walton, my life partner, confidante, mind regulator, and love. I am at times embarrassed by her superhuman amenability with regard to my professional pursuits. I so appreciate her grace, beauty, and keen insight into life in general and my personality in particular. And my beautiful twins, Zora Neale and Elijah Mays, are the center of my joy and the source of my continued maturation. They have helped me to discover what life is all about as they impel me to engage in Socratic reflection on a daily basis. Thus each day I pray that I will be more for them than I was the day before. My family and the grace of God are the best things that have ever happened to me. They both "look beyond my faults and meet me at my needs"!

Prelude

A charge to keep I have, A God to glorify,
A never dying soul to save, And fit it for the sky.
To serve the present age, My calling to fulfill;
O may it all my pow'rs engage, To do my Master's will!
— "A Charge to Keep I Have,"
in *African American Heritage Hymnal*

Two decades after the public scandals of Jimmy Swaggart and Jim and Tammy Faye Bakker introduced many to the lavish and often lurid subculture of evangelical Christian broadcasting, the gilded world of televangelism recently made its way back into the national spotlight. In November of 2007, Senator Charles Grassley, ranking member of the Senate Finance Committee, sent personal letters to half a dozen evangelists questioning their extravagant lifestyles and budgetary practices. The senator's main concern was whether select ministries were abusing their tax-exempt status to subsidize their aggrandized lifestyles. Recalling Jim and Tammy Faye Bakker's matching Rolls-Royces and air-conditioned doghouses, the senator wanted evangelists Benny Hinn, Kenneth Copeland, Joyce Meyer, Paula White, Creflo Dollar, and Eddie Long to provide detailed statements that would explain ministry spending. The six individualized letters questioned excessive cash payments, multi-million-dollar mansions, private jets, and even a $23,000 toilet.

To be sure, it was of little surprise to many that the vast majority of those under scrutiny proclaim some variant of the prosperity gospel— the belief that material wealth is God's desire for the faithful. Thus the luxurious lifestyles of many evangelists are socially accepted and, for some, theologically expected as the material rewards of a life committed to spiritual discipleship. And while it was unclear at that point where the investigation would lead, it brought the world of Christian broadcasting back into the public eye.

This new publicity, however, was restricted to the issue of exorbitant spending. Little attention was directed to the ways many televangelists are regarded by their followers as role models of effective ministry and the standard-bearers of a particular Christian identity—an identity defined, for the most part, by theological, cultural and political neoconservatism. For the vast majority of televangelists, commitments to hyper-American patriotism, free-market capitalism, and patriarchal conceptions of the ordering of society are regularly transmitted through mass-mediated images and "Christian" discourse. And in this media-constructed Christian realm, American flags drape the cross of Christianity, material wealth is divinely ordained, and hypermasculinity models God's power just as female docility signifies purity and virtue. Thus it is intended to come across as natural that these sorts of political and cultural commitments exemplify what it means to be a devout Christian and a loyal American.

These are just some of the reasons that many are suddenly curious concerning this popular expression of the Christian faith, especially among African American communities, where the phenomenon of televangelism has some of its most successful practitioners and ardent supporters. Questions abound. Is it the message of the Gospel or a message of greed? Does it represent the "authentic" voice of the black church, or is it the Christian Right in blackface? Is it orthodox "Christianity" or an ethnocentric "Americanity" wrapped in religious language? Yet despite such polarizing inquiries and assertions, one would be hard-pressed to deny televangelism's mass appeal in the African American community. It is incontestable that the most artistically gifted of these preachers, who in my opinion include Bishop T. D. Jakes, Bishop Noel Jones, and Prophetess Juanita Bynum, embody the rhythmic syncopation, kinetic orality, and emotional physicality of the African American preaching tradition.[1] From the depths of their experience, they are able to evoke, awake, and encourage their listeners' faith, hope, and self-love. For this reason alone, it makes sense that persons dehydrated by doubt, despair, and dejection would flock in mass to baptize themselves in this transformative encounter. Persons who willingly participate in this experience—whether by worshipping on Sunday morning, seeing a video of a service, or attending one of the oft-held mass events—not only are made to feel beautiful but also are given a glimpse, through their existential angst, of an alternate kingdom where the "first shall be last and the last shall be first."

Also, televangelism's recurring themes of social and financial empowerment seem to be attractive to many African Americans, particularly

African American women and the new black middle class. Via participation in varying "women-only" events and engagement with other forms of literature targeting female audiences, many black women see themselves as throwing off the multiple stereotypes that are projected upon black female bodies in America.[2] No longer reduced to the image of "single mother," "divorcee," "Auntie," "bitch," or "nappy-headed ho," they become "God's leading lady," "anointed woman of God," and "Daddy's little girl."[3] Similarly, the emphasis on economic advancement, which pervades the message of African American televangelists, appears to be particularly attractive to post–civil rights generations with middle- and upper-class aspirations. A God-sanctioned message of financial liberation and prosperity resonates with many blacks who have seen their parents and grandparents stay at the bottom of America's capitalist economy because of this country's history of racial apartheid and who themselves desire a larger slice of America's economic pie.

So this explains why, in part, African American televangelists have attained increasing societal acclaim and political clout. On September 17, 2001, T. D. Jakes made the cover of *Time* magazine under the heading "Is This the Next Billy Graham?" and in the past few years select African American televangelists have been afforded entrée to the White House through the Office of Faith-Based Initiatives instituted by President George W. Bush. Thus it is imperative that scholars concerned with black religion and culture take televangelism seriously as an influential form of popular and political culture.

My own research interest in African American religious broadcasting came in part from what I perceived to be the gaps in my academic religious training. I was working too hard to reconcile what I learned in the classroom concerning black religion Monday through Friday with what I was experiencing, and had experienced, attending church on Sunday. Armed with my Bible in one hand and a copy of James Cone's *God of the Oppressed* in the other, and poised to combat the pernicious "isms" of racism, classism, sexism, and militarism, I soon discovered that my academic embrace of the God of the "freedom-fighting black church" did not necessarily jibe with the Jesus that black people in suburban Atlanta desired to know firsthand. Though in my mind my God offered liberation from racial and gender injustice and capitalist exploitation, I saw other preachers seemingly get further with a Jesus who provided the keys to the Kingdom in the form of a four-bedroom house and a Mercedes-Benz.

Moreover, among my former ministerial colleagues, there was very little discussion concerning the intellectual contributions of prominent African American theologians like Dwight Hopkins, Katie Cannon, and Cornel West. However, the names of C. L. Franklin or T. D. Jakes could evoke spirited responses of all kinds in pastors' quarters, ministerial conferences, and any other context where clergy typically converse. I was thus forced to ponder why persons having such a profound impact, good or bad, on local ministers and congregations were never studied in the classroom.

This form of black Christian expression has seemingly not made its way into the academic realm. For the most part, scholars of African American religion in general and black theology in particular theorize about the black church in America according to a particular historiography that excludes and ignores certain "pop culture" voices. This statement reflects my experiences as an undergraduate student at Morehouse College and as a seminarian and then a doctoral candidate at Princeton Theological Seminary, as well as my engagement with the published academic literature on forms of black Christian expression. Many professors and scholars seem to think that if they either ignore the phenomenon long enough or denigrate it loudly enough these televised acts of "buffoonery and chicanery" will simply disappear.

On the other hand, I have noticed that many African American students embrace the phenomenon as a guilty pleasure. Influenced by the social pressures and sense of shame imposed on students by the academic environment, they stash away Bishop Noel Jones and Reverend Jamal Harrison-Bryant videos in dorm rooms like some sort of spiritual porn collection that can be viewed only in privacy. The videos offer a fantasy (of mass appeal, public acclaim, luxurious living) that many who have received a "call" to ministry privately indulge but refuse to admit that they will probably never experience. All the while, both professors and students contribute to the resounding silence, particularly in African American theological education, where the black liberal Protestant theologies and a black theology of liberation make a poor fit with the sensibilities of the increasing number of students informed by Trinity Broadcast Network and StreamingFaith.com. Thus I have chosen to examine African American religious broadcasting in order to begin filling in some major gaps in the study of black religion in general and African American theological education in particular.

Those who want this book to be a dogmatic treatise that reads like either a hagiographic celebration of celebrity preachers or an outright dismissal of the phenomenon will be sorely disappointed. I am not interested in adding my voice to the choir that uncritically sings the praises of charismatic figures like Bishop T. D. Jakes and Pastors Creflo and Taffi Dollar. They have their share of ecclesial cheerleaders. Neither am I interested in rejecting these ministries outright as unworthy of scholarly analysis and devoid of intellectual import. Scholars of religion do not have the luxury of dismissing a religious phenomenon that has captivated the hearts of such a large segment of the African American faith community. For me to do so, as a Christian ethicist, would be to lock myself within the ivory tower of academe and isolate myself from their spiritual strivings and religious sensibilities.

Rather, this project seeks to critically unpack and ethically evaluate all forms of dogmatism, parochialism, and provincialism, including those of the black Christian community and the academy, that preclude intellectual innovation in relation to this form of African American Christian expression. As one informed by the creative potential, rhythmic sensibility, and imaginative appropriation of hip-hop culture, I am committed to looping and sampling across genres to create an emergent and danceable bricolage. My hope, then, is that by applying the scholarly methods of investigation to the cultural mores and practices of technologically driven and mass-produced religion of the postmodern moment we will move toward identifying a new mode of discourse and communicative exchange that will benefit all involved. In this regard, *Watch This!* is not simply an ethical and cultural critique of African American religious broadcasting. It is the first step in a call for dialogue among those in the pulpits, pews, and classroom who are committed to vanquishing the forces of injustice that impinge upon human flourishing and fulfillment.

Time to Tune In

The Phenomenon of African American Religious Broadcasting

Shine on me, shine on me.
Let the light from the lighthouse
Shine on me.
— "Shine on Me," in *African American Heritage Hymnal*

At the dawn of the twentieth century, W. E. B. Du Bois described the black preacher as "the most unique personality developed by the Negro on American soil."[1] For the majority of the century, because of societal constraints regulating the movement of persons of color in America, these spiritual poets were largely confined to preaching to their own racial and residential communities. Today, however, with the victories of the civil rights era and the emergence of advanced forms of media communication, many of these dynamic personalities have gained wider visibility both nationally and internationally. To channel-surf from BET to TBN to MBC to the Word Network is to witness the creative genius and artistic imaginations of these religious figures. And it would be virtually impossible to enter any African American Christian congregation and find someone who had not heard of such televangelists as Bishop T. D. Jakes, Bishop Eddie Long, and Pastor Creflo Dollar. These preachers seem to have become ubiquitous in black popular culture as a result of their constant television broadcasts, mass video distributions, printed publications, gospel stage plays, musical recordings, and gargantuan congregations. With an astute marketing consciousness, these preachers and their style of ministry have found an enduring place in the African American religious imagination.

Televangelism and the Black Church in America

Any discussion of televangelism and the black church involves an engagement with two distinct areas of religious expression that have grown
exponentially in the post–civil rights era: religious broadcasting and the
megachurch movement. By *religious broadcasting* I am referring to the
broad-based use of electronic media as a primary tool of proselytization.
Religious broadcasting includes evangelists who broadcast their services
on radio, television, and/or Webcasts as well as the organizations from
which these persons develop, package, and promote ministry-related
products like CDs and DVDs, books, conferences, and citywide crusades
throughout the world. The organization can be the church where the
evangelist serves or a separate entity established with the sole purpose of
distributing the televangelist's message.[2]

The term *megachurch movement* refers to congregations with mem-
berships of at least two thousand. Megachurches are characterized by
colossal edifices that house not only sanctuaries that seat thousands of
people but child care centers, gymnasiums, bookstores, and a host of
other business ventures. The seven-day-a-week, one-stop-shopping design
has proven itself attractive to baby boomers, "buppies" (young black
urban professionals), and "unchurched" populations.[3] These facilities,
like suburban shopping centers, create a space for many to participate
in pseudoanonymity, much as they might view a religious broadcast in
the privacy and comfort of their own homes, yet remain connected to the
community, "blending in" amid the thousands who show up to worship
on any given Sunday. In major metropolitan areas like Atlanta, Houston,
and Los Angeles, megachurches have become both a standard-bearer and
a staple of African American religious life. As a result, megachurch pastors have become spiritual icons and national celebrities within the black
community.

Religious broadcasting and the megachurch movement are different
religious phenomena but not mutually exclusive. Being involved in religious broadcasting does not mean that one must pastor a megachurch,
and vice versa. But with regard to leading African American televangelists, religious broadcasting and megachurches, though perhaps theoretically distinguishable, are inseparable in praxis. Unlike the principal
players among the Christian Right and white evangelical broadcasting—
James Dobson, the Crouch Family, and Pat Robertson—who control

media empires apart from a local congregation, the major producers of religious broadcasting in the African American community emerge from and remain rooted in the parish context. Thus evaluating the ministries of prominent African American televangelists requires viewing their media efforts and congregations, though distinct in principle, as symbiotic. The megachurch serves both as a site of worship and as a recording studio for television broadcasts.

The increasing occurrence of this latter dynamic in the larger evangelical world has led more astute media theorists to identify the megachurch phenomenon as religious broadcasting incarnate. This is to say, megachurches provide the mass-mediated features of televangelism that participants find attractive. Such features include TV-styled worship through the reconfiguring of traditional pulpits into theater-like stages and the installation of movie screens in the front of the sanctuary that project live footage of the worship service, the words to the congregational hymns, Bible verses, and the pastor's main sermonic points in Power Point fashion. Even church announcements and other aspects of the worship service are aired during Sunday morning service. Bishop Jakes, for instance, will dim the lights during worship service and broadcast the "Potter's House News," in which a white man behind a news anchor desk announces upcoming church events, interrupted by commercial breaks advertising Bishop Jakes's latest sermon series. Also, the majority of contemporary worship services in megachurches borrow from popular musical genres like rock, rhythm and blues, and hip-hop in a televisual manner that is clearly influenced by mainstream music videos.[4] As I will elaborate more explicitly throughout this book, the megachurch context offers the sort of high-tech entertainment one would expect from a professional theater company or a television network. These are the reasons this book holds African American religious broadcasting and the megachurch movement in tension as it seeks to evaluate the religious world that televangelists and their viewers occupy.

To be sure, all ministers who take part in varying forms of religious broadcasting are not considered televangelists. From the number of black churches that record and sell their worship service, air their broadcast on local cable access channels or use the Web to provide streaming broadcasts of service, it is fair to conclude that the vast majority of black churches participate in some form of religious broadcasting. But there are qualitative and quantitative differences between ministries that broadcast their worship service and religious broadcasters. As stated earlier, religious broadcasters are those who employ varying mass-mediated forms as the *primary* tool of proselytization. Numerous roaming television cameras, photographers, and media soundboards that serve as focal points in the sanctuary, as well as multiple broadcasts on national television networks such as TBN, CBN, BET, and Word Network, are just a few markers that distinguish bona fide televangelists from their ministerial colleagues. This is why, for example, this book features the ministry of a Bishop Eddie Long at New Birth Missionary Baptist Church but not Rev. Kirbyjon Caldwell and the Windsor Village United Methodist Church in Houston. The latter's Sunday morning broadcasts on StreamingFaith.com pale in comparison to Bishop Long's *Taking Authority* broadcasts on nineteen different national and international television networks throughout the week.[5] Yes, Rev. Caldwell may broadcast his Sunday service, but Bishop Long is a religious broadcaster.

The Overarching Characteristics of African American Religious Broadcasting

In his classic essay "Of the Faith of Our Fathers," W. E. B. Du Bois identifies three salient characteristics of black Christian worship. There is the preacher, whom Du Bois describes as "a leader, a politician, an orator, a 'boss,' an intriguer, an idealist."[6] This gifted personality, according to Du Bois, combines "adroitness," "earnestness," and "consummate ability" toward obtaining and maintaining preeminent status within the community. Next is the music, which, for Du Bois, "remains the most original and beautiful expression of human life and longing yet born on American soil." With and through the music of the black church black people are able to express "sorrow, despair and hope."[7] Then there is the frenzy, which Du Bois also refers to as "shouting." The frenzy is believed by many to be a visible manifestation of an invisible God, an audible praise of an ever-present God operating in the life of the believer. It is commonly articulated in many black Christian circles that "I couldn't worship a God that I couldn't feel." Whether in the form of a shout, hand clapping, or low murmurs and moans, this expression of transcendent joy rises above life's troubles to kiss the divine.

I cite Du Bois's descriptions here because they remain appropriate in relation to the world of African American religious broadcasting—a dynamic personality, a Broadway-like theater production, and a frenzy of activity that envelops the worship experience.[8] This is true on multiple levels and in varying ways. Both the amphitheater-like atmosphere and the mass-mediated form expand and amplify the preacher, music, and frenzy. For instance, the frenzy does not always take the form of persons "catching the Holy Ghost" and running up and down the aisles. It can also take the form of intensive buying, selling, and advertising of ministry-related products in the shopping mall–like atmosphere of the multiple concession areas that crowd the vestibules of many megachurches. Further, it can be created through pre- and postproduction editing of the television broadcasts. Slow-motion images of a pastor laying hands on the heads of parishioners and zoom-in shots of a parishioner feverishly taking notes during the sermon all express the spiritual activity taking place. For some, marking up a Bible full of sermon notes supplants participating in the ring shout. Nonetheless, in my view, these are all physical responses to a spiritual encounter, however mediated. They illustrate how African American religious broadcasting is consistent with preceding forms of black Christian practice but gives them a new mass character in this historical moment through advanced forms of media technology. Consequently African American religious broadcasting today can be defined as having the following three overarching features: it is personality driven, crowd dependent, and entertainment oriented. These features sum up the phenomenon as a whole regardless of the ecclesiastical, theological, or political perspectives of the individual ministries.

To assert that the phenomenon is personality driven is to say that the ministry is wholly developed around the charismatic authority of a particular pastor, preacher, evangelist, or revivalist. The form and function of the ministry often wholly reflect the personal narrative—real or constructed—of its leader. This is observed in the ways that viewers and parishioners often reify the charismatic leader as the church or ministry. One might notice that when people speak of a particular congregation they do not say "the Potter's House," "New Birth Missionary Baptist Church," or "World Changers Church International" but "T. D. Jakes's church," "Eddie Long's church," or "Creflo Dollar's church," respectively.

Like movie stars, popular musicians, and athletes, these charismatic figures are seemingly transformed in the minds of their parishioners into living and breathing religious icons. Those who handle the publicity and marketing for the ministry are careful to place the physical image of the leader anywhere and everywhere so that their faces are indelibly etched upon the psyche of their followers. As a marketing technique, such a strategy is intended to create a sense of comfort, familiarity, and intimate connection between parishioners and their "pastor," even though, for the majority of those who purchase video series and books and pack into cathedrals and arenas, the relationship will never be more than one-sided.

Second, the phenomenon is crowd dependent. In discussing the preceding characteristic I employed Max Weber's designation of charismatic authority as representative of the leadership style. Weber defines charisma as "a certain quality of an individual personality by virtue of which he is set apart from ordinary men and treated as endowed with supernatural, superhuman, or at least specifically exceptional qualities."[9] Weber situates the operational function of charisma in the societal context. In Weber's view, if a particular society is likened to a stage play, the individual possessing the charisma is the captivating main character who by virtue of his or her presence drives the production. Nevertheless a dynamic personality alone is insufficient. Charisma stems from the cooperation of the group population as much as it is projected by a particular personality. There is always a dialectical and dialogical relationship between the gifted personality and the people whom he or she seeks to engage. The people place the sacred stamp of approval on a particular personality, thus validating whether the message conveyed is a gift of God's grace or of human origin. This is why the audience plays a critical role in religious broadcasting. Images of the crowd listening attentively, affirming sermonic points with nodding heads or raised arms, are vital to a successful broadcast.

Also, to put it bluntly, radio and televangelism are expensive. There are ministries that spend millions per month. And, for the most part, pastors derive their financial support from their congregation (if they have a church), their broadcast audience, and maybe a handful of wealthy supporters.[10] On the basis of our previous definition of what constitutes a megachurch, the life and vitality of the congregation, whether in terms of membership numbers or quality of services, depend on mass attendance. The more people the ministry can attract, the better the financial contributions that can subsidize and expand the television ministry or the services provided throughout the week at the church. Moreover, we live in a culture in which "might is right." Religious phenomena are often measured quantitatively rather than qualitatively. Whenever preachers are gathered together, the response to the question "How is the church coming?" is normally followed by a numerical figure. This is why cameras with wide-angle lenses and panoramic shots that exaggerate the size of the crowd are common. Such broadcasting techniques demonstrate that a particular preacher's message resonates with the masses.

The final feature of African American religious broadcasting is its entertainment orientation. Whether in the sanctuary on Sunday morning, packed into Madison Square Garden at a "Partners' Conference," or sitting at home in a living room, people come to be entertained. Worship services combine drama, amusement, and suspense, all carefully orchestrated and premeditated in such a way that persons actually witness their own lives being acted out in the pulpit. T. D. Jakes is well known for having trained actors upon the stage acting out the parts of various biblical characters or sermon illustrations during the delivery of his sermon. Doing this—and employing other physical props for visual effect—helps viewers identify with the drama of the human condition on stage. Further, the perfectly orchestrated sermonic soundtrack via the organ response adds to the aural sense of the experience throughout the delivery of the message. As in a movie, the music of a talented organist working in collaboration with the preacher can help create tension, build suspense, and initiate celebration at the appropriate times. This tool is effective in spurring enthusiastic crowd participation.

As I make this claim, I do not employ the term *entertainment* pejoratively. Entertainment has always been a fundamental means of beating back black people's demons of nihilism. This is true of all forms of black entertainment, whether the sultry soul rhythms of Aretha Franklin, the captivating, kinetic performance of James Brown, or the compelling, cathartic whoop of Rev. C. L. Franklin. C. Eric Lincoln and Lawrence Mamiya have rightly described the black church as the first black theater.[11] Characterized by its dramaturgical sense of excitement, entertainment value, and efficacious release, its services enabled black people to act out, and in many cases imagine themselves overcoming, the tragic dimension of being black in a white supremacist society. The cacophonous guttural cries and mourning songs that emanated from victimized black bodies were mixed into a rhythmic symphony of joy as participants both sang and felt, "Up above my head, I hear music in the air."

But beyond serving a cathartic function the entertainment orientation of black religious broadcasting has great commercial appeal. In a media age driven by style and sensory stimulation, the performative dimensions of the black preaching tradition are of great import. The aesthetic is essential. Bishop T. D. Jakes's captivating storytelling ability, Creflo Dollar's seemingly photographic memory for scripture, and Bishop Eddie Long's Bentley in the parking lot resonate with a generation trapped in the oxymoronic matrix of reality television. Just as the televisual dimension of the music industry has forced record executives to package and promote their artists as visually tantalizing as well as vocally titillating, the same is true for African American televangelists. An outfit like a hip-hop star and sexually charged sermon titles such as "Foreplay, How to Make Your Woman Climb the Wall" and "I'm Gift Wrapped" can propel some preachers into pop culture status.[12] The performance aspect, then, plays a critical role. In describing the ministry of Creflo Dollar, one CNN reporter asserted that Dollar was "integrating show business into his business."[13]

The Scope and Aims of This Book

This book is first and foremost a scholarly work in Christian social ethics. Its primary purpose is to evaluate ethically the social implications of African American religious broadcasting as a religious and cultural phenomenon against the professed theological commitments, ecclesial agendas, and social aims of leading African American televangelists. This book is interdisciplinary, drawing on the history of both the black church and evangelical revivalism in America, philosophical and theological insights into the role of religious experience, and the work of sociologist and cultural theorists regarding class, race, and gender in America. My questions are informed by the intellectual and political tasks of cultural studies insofar as this project attempts to posit a historiographical argument, provide a theological and phenomenological account, and offer an ideological critique of the dominant themes of African American religious broadcasting. These three tasks will help us to identify and understand the production of religious meaning(s) that extend from African American religious broadcasting and their possible implications concerning how participants (both televangelists as producers and congregants as viewers) may come to interpret their world and understand themselves as classed, raced, and gendered subjects. In what follows, then, I will lay out my objectives while demonstrating how each task enables us to better appreciate the artistic import and liberating aims of black religious broadcasting while holding the phenomenon accountable for its role as an ideological apparatus that potentially reinforces injustice and inequality in America in general and African American Christian communities of faith in particular.

Historiographical Argument

The first task of this book is to stress that African American religious broadcasting, though having flourished in the post–civil rights era, is by no means new. The electronic media have been a salient and essential part of African American Christian practices for multiple generations. The modern history of the black church includes the production of religious race records in the 1920s, radio revivals of the postwar era, and the broadcasting of worship services on television and streaming Webcast in the contemporary moment. Yet there is a lacuna in the academic literature concerning black religious broadcasters. Scholars in the fields of media and religious studies have largely failed to "tune in" to these creative men and women who have used the airwaves to influence and inform the African American religious imagination. Among media theorists and sociologists of religion who have examined religious broadcasting, it seems that African American religious broadcasters are victims of racial invisibility. Their stories have simply not been recognized. As in the case of Ralph Ellison's classic protagonist, the very skin color that classifies people as highly visible also renders persons of African descent invisible, a categorized afterthought or addendum to the narratives of white identity and agency. And among scholars of African American religion black religious broadcasters have been seemingly rendered aberrant according to the rules of racial respectability, since their stories have not been considered consistent with the culturally accepted character of the "true black church." Considered hucksters and ecclesiastical charlatans, figures like Prophet James F. Jones, the Detroit minister who earned national acclaim when the *Saturday Evening Post* referred to him as the "Messiah in Mink" because of his signature mink coat and lavish lifestyle, and Rev. Ike, the New York–based televangelist who was a forerunner to contemporary prosperity gospel preachers, have been buried in the shameful graveyards of black cultural memory.

The book begins, then, with an attempt to tell a different story about African American religion in the twentieth century. My purposes here are not necessarily to supplant but to problematize as well as expand the prevailing narratives concerning the form and function of the black church in America. Chapter 1 examines the dominant historiographies offered by media and religious scholars concerning the development of religious broadcasting and the black church in America. It confronts, first, media scholars and sociologists who have presented American religious broadcasting as predominantly the domain of conservative, Anglo evangelicals and Christian fundamentalists while ignoring the contributions of African American radio and television evangelists. Then it illumines the possible reasons that most scholars of African American religion, particularly black liberation theologians, have excluded African American religious radio and television personalities from their analyses. Finally, this chapter briefly introduces the long-standing tradition of African American religious broadcasting by describing a handful of black religious broadcasting forerunners who gained national prominence through the recording and radio industries in America. Their ministries provide prototypes for the confluence of African American religious expression and mass-mediated forms.

Chapter 2 focuses on the cultural sources that informed the theology and praxis of a principal figure in the tradition of African American televangelism, Rev. Frederick J. Eikerenkoetter II, commonly known as "Rev. Ike." Rev. Ike was one of the first African Americans to use an amphitheater as a place of worship, build an in-house video production center, and package and distribute his teachings to a national audience via television and radio. Known for his custom-tailored suits, fleet of Rolls-Royces, and charismatic and captivating ability to inspire the most socially downtrodden to walk with the confidence of a millionaire, Rev. Ike blazed a trail that black televangelists currently tread. To be sure, the point of this chapter is not merely historical. One of its primary concerns is to understand the contemporary religious phenomenon as a by-product of converging cultural practices of the past.[14] Therefore, it seeks to show that the cultural and existential sources that informed Rev. Ike's ministry have cultivated ways of thinking and practice that have become naturalized over time. I believe this examination will offer a partial explanation as to why the dominant themes of Rev. Ike's message seemingly resonate with both preceding and successive generations in particular African American communities. And the "naturalization" of select religious ideas and customs proves to have ideological import, a discussion that will be taken up in chapters 7 and 8.

Theological and Phenomenological Account

The book now turns to providing a theological and phenomenological account of black religious broadcasting's constitutive traditions. Here my aim is to engage the phenomenon on its own terms by showing its diversity and resisting heavy-handed judgments against its leading producers. In this regard, I attempt to provide a "thick" description of black religious broadcasting while presenting the leading ministries according to their own self-understandings.

What is more, informed by a cultural studies approach, the descriptive task includes a semiotic analysis of the aesthetic dimensions of the phenomenon. This is a jazzy way of saying that this project takes seriously the fact that we live in a video age. Televangelists understand well the maxim that a picture is worth a thousand words. And if this is true of a still photograph, how much more true is it of a live broadcast? A recorded video? A streaming Webcast? Televangelists are master communicators who realize that they are talking loudly even when they are not saying anything verbally at all. Conspicuously placed diamond rings, custom-tailored suits, and state-of-the-art postproduction graphics are loaded with potential meanings. So those of us concerned with analyzing the theological reflections of the most popular religious voices in the black community today must consider both the visual and aural dimensions of their message. And for a social ethicist, focusing simply on the doctrinal correctness or systematic consistency of a televangelist's theology is insufficient. This would be comparable to trying to figure out why a highly sensual and sexualized musical performer can sell more records than a vocally trained artist. In an MTV age, the erotic aesthetic of the former typically outshines the classical ability of the latter. The same holds true for African American religious broadcasting. We must isolate and interpret the multiple signs and symbols of leading televangelists with the aim of understanding their possible attraction and cultural resonance.

Chapter 3, then, illumines the internal variety in the phenomenon of black religious broadcasting. Analytically, this chapter moves beyond the catch-all categories that do not appropriately accentuate the distinctiveness found among contemporary black televangelists. In the recent literature, the broad use of terms like *neo-Pentecostal, Charismatic, prosperity gospel,* and *new black church* to describe black religious broadcasting in its entirety has obliterated this phenomenon's numerous ecclesiastical identities and differences.[15] African American religious broadcasting is distinguishable as a cultural phenomenon but far from monolithic. For instance, Bishop T. D. Jakes, a neo-Pentecostal pastor, and Pastor Creflo Dollar, a Word of Faith pastor, have different conceptions of God, the church, and the church's role in society. It is thus inappropriate to describe the ministries that make up the phenomenon of black religious broadcasting according to terms that impose a fictitious uniformity on the widely varying theological, ecclesial, and social views of African American televangelists and megachurch pastors.

The particular aim of this chapter is to classify the diversity within African American religious broadcasting. African American televangelism is composed of and rooted in diverse (sometimes competing) theological orientations, ecclesial traditions, and political sensibilities. I propose that three representative perspectives constitute African American religious broadcasting in America: neo-Pentecostal, Charismatic mainline, and Word of Faith. To be clear from the outset, I am not arguing that *all* African American religious broadcasters fit neatly into one of these respective categories. There are exceptions to every rule. I also understand the potential dangers of drawing rigid boundaries around black Christian practices, so I would like to refrain from declaring these categories as exhaustive or absolute. But I do believe that these categories assist us, conceptually and analytically, in assessing the predominant theological traditions and ecclesial perspectives in contemporary African American religious broadcasting. Moreover, I believe that it is possible to situate the majority of current African American religious broadcasters within one of these three camps. The classification will help us examine the ministries of the foremost African American televangelists against the historical and cultural backdrop of the traditions that inform their theology, ecclesiology, and personal understanding of the church's role in society. From this we can evaluate individual ministries ethically according to their own professed ministerial objectives and intent.

Chapters 4, 5, and 6 present the leading producers of African American televangelism who are among the most influential voices of the phenomenon and who typify the three aforementioned perspectives: Bishop T. D. Jakes (neo-Pentecostal), Bishop Eddie Long (Charismatic mainline), and Pastor Creflo Dollar (Word of Faith). Each chapter begins with a biographical sketch. Televangelists' autobiographical stories offer insight into their personal conception of God, ministerial aims, and social outlook. This is why the biographies provided in each chapter draw from the constructed and sometimes contradictory narratives that each figure has presented of himself through sermons, writings, and rare interviews with the media. I then proceed to outline the theological thought, ecclesial outlook, and political and social orientations of Jakes, Long, and Dollar accordingly. Such questions as how they view God, God's activity in the world, and the role of the church in society and how they address the social realities of class, race, and gender drive my analysis. I particularly focus on and emphasize these questions, as the answers provide the core of my subsequent ethical critique.

I would like to address two important issues concerning chapters 4, 5, and 6. First, my reasons for focusing on the three televangelists under consideration have to do with their national prominence and popularity as religious broadcasters. They all broadcast nationally and internationally, and all three have attained a pop culture status within the African American community. Further, as already stated, I believe that their ministries epitomize the neo-Pentecostal, Charismatic mainline, and Word of Faith perspectives. This does not mean that any one of their individual theological orientations is interchangeable with that of any other televangelist coming from the same perspective. I consider both Bishop T. D. Jakes and Bishop Noel Jones to be neo-Pentecostals, but I do not claim that the theological thought of either of them is reducible to that of the other. In the same way, just because Bishop Eddie Long promotes a particular theological commitment at New Birth Missionary Baptist Church does not mean that Bishop Paul Morton adheres to the same conception of God at Greater St. Stephens Full Gospel Baptist Church, though both are Charismatic mainliners. The broader perspectives I set forth provide an ecclesial etiology of sorts so that we may account for the individual thought and practices of televangelists within a particular tradition. There is a reason that Bishop Jakes is ambivalent about active political involvement, while Bishop Long interprets his ministry and active political engagement as continuing the work of Martin Luther King Jr. and the civil rights movement. It can be found in the ecclesial perspectives from which their ministries extend, Pentecostal and black mainline, respectively. Similarly, Rev. Frederick Price's and Pastor Creflo Dollar's emphasis on positive confession and divinely ordained health and wealth is grounded in the larger Word of Faith perspective, even though the two men may not agree on every theological, ecclesial, or social matter. So although I want to be clear that each televangelist under consideration is speaking for himself and his ministry only, I do contend that his thoughts are informed by a larger tradition and ecclesial perspective of which his ministry is a part.

The second matter involves my decision to examine only male televangelists as the representative voices of each perspective. It is no secret that although every facet of African American Christian practice is dependent on the labor of women, black Christian congregations remain predominantly headed by men.[16] Black religious broadcasting is no different. Male televangelists continue to serve as the dominant producers and leading personalities. And the role of women in this phenomenon, unfortunately, continues to be sanctioned and conferred by patriarchal male authority. A cursory examination of the leading female televangelists shows that they continue to minister under subordination to a male pastoral figure, a husband, or, in the apparent majority of cases, both (their pastor is their husband).[17] Moreover, the dominant theological orientations and ministerial themes of leading female evangelists are largely indistinguishable from those of the men to whom they are subordinated (i.e., their "coverings"). And while the gendered bodies of female televangelists are often used by their male colleagues in the ritual performance to reinforce and reify certain cultural understandings in ways that male bodies cannot, women are still largely reduced to proverbial props according to the rules of hegemonic masculinity and femininity. This is true even though the nontraditional religious airwaves have afforded women a level of freedom not readily conferred in the denominational churches. This is why I feel justified, if not comfortable, in focusing upon predominantly male leaders in chapters 4 through 6.

Ideological Critique

The last two chapters of this book offer an ideological critique of African American religious broadcasting. I seek to show that many of the prevailing messages and belief systems illumined in previous chapters may assist viewers to obscure reality, flatten internal contradictions, and ignore constructive alternatives for attaining desired spiritual and sociopolitical ends. I do, nevertheless, realize that no ideological critique can take place without acknowledging and analyzing the human interests that causes persons to gravitate toward the dominant themes televangelists transmit. Simply put, black people have spiritual, psychological, physical, and financial needs. And they would not embrace the message of a particular televangelist, either in part or wholesale, unless they felt certain needs were being met. As ethicist Jeffrey Stout contends, ideology critique is a hermeneutical ambulance. If called upon too quickly, it can treat fellow citizens as patients rather than as moral subjects worthy of mutual respect.[18] Therefore, instead of throwing out the baby of human experience with the bathwater of ideology, I wish to pay proper attention to the former.

Chapter 7, then, provides possible reasons that viewers of African American televangelism appear to gravitate toward the phenomenon. Though chapters 4 through 6 point up the internal diversity among black televangelists, the various African American religious broadcasters do express certain common identifiable themes. These dominant themes—economic advancement, the minimizing of race, and Victorian ideals of the family—have historically been offered by elites and interpreted by the masses as viable means for African Americans to integrate into mainstream culture. Despite different strategies, varying points of emphasis, and competing conceptions of divine and human responsibility among televangelists from Rev. Ike to Creflo Dollar (and everyone in between), the messages of religious broadcasting seem to strike a chord with viewers because televangelists all sing a familiar tune. The songs of immense wealth, instantaneous racial equality, and a divinely ordered family life make up the soundtrack of African American spiritual longing. And by modeling this worldview for their viewers on the screen, televangelists encourage persons to create themselves anew by imagining a world that instead of being encumbered by the realities of class, race, and gender discord expresses only possibility and potentiality. Whereas the material world of viewers may be defined by economic anxiety, discrimination on the job, or normalized attacks against black female identity in popular culture, televangelists allow persons to participate in a constructed space, if only for a moment, where they are no longer defined by their circumstances. Insofar as this is the case, this chapter encourages the reader to view televangelism as a ritual of self-affirmation for its participants.

Yet this chapter also contrasts televangelism's role as a ritual of self-affirmation against its role as a ritual of social accommodation. It reveals that televangelists rely heavily on pervasive cultural myths to garner mass acclaim. The logic is simple: the larger the crowd that televangelists seek to attract, the more they must refer to collective ways of thinking and cultural myth systems that are often used to bond otherwise diverse communities. Moral in scope and romantic in outlook, cultural myths help us to cope with otherwise grim aspects of a society. And preachers and politicians alike appeal to these myths in order to communicate in a common language that smooths over competing worldviews and internal contradictions between a society's ideals and realities.

By referring to the theological thought, ecclesial outlook, and political and social orientations of Jakes, Long, and Dollar as set forth in chapters 4, 5, and 6, I argue that African American religious broadcasting promotes the following three cultural myths: the myth of American success (economic advancement), the myth of black victimology (the minimizing of race), and the myth of the "Strong Black Man" as savior of the race (Victorian ideals of family). While these enduring cultural myths and national ideals resonate with a cross section of Americans and are often called upon to assist us in making sense of our world, they also obscure the systems of relations operative in American society.

Here lies the link between cultural myths and ideology. The French cultural theorist Roland Barthes has argued that when cultural myths become naturalized over time and become that which is taken for granted, they serve a legitimating role.[19] Whatever systems of relations are in place are deemed natural and legitimate—what has always been will always be. Appeals to the cultural myths of American success, black victimology, and the Strong Black Man legitimize conservative and anecdotally based views of wealth distribution, racial discrimination, and gender hierarchy that contradict the liberating intent of televangelists. They may also serve to anesthetize participants to the unjust ordering of the larger society even as persons seek to revolutionize their own world. So while the ritual of self-affirmation may inspire hope and optimism about achieving the ends of individual liberation, the competing ritual of social accommodation can frustrate the televangelist's professed aims by encouraging viewers to appeal, adjust, and adapt to ideological conceptions of an unjust society.

The eighth and final chapter evaluates and unpacks the three operative myths of African American religious broadcasting in relation to Jakes's, Long's, and Dollar's explicitly stated aims of economic and social empowerment for viewers. It lays out the inconsistencies and incongruities of these myths when measured against the historical and social scientific data concerning the lived realities of black people. Though images of the self-made individual inspire persons to "dream the impossible dream," they are also fuel for America's capitalist economy, which has a parasitic relationship to America's under- and working classes. It thus appears that televangelists are prescribing business enterprise and entrepreneurship as a viable means of economic empowerment at a moment when the economic ladder of mobility is being held up away from, rather than climbed up by, the vast majority of Americans. The myth of black victimology argues that African American perceptions of racism in America are more a mind-set to be overcome than a reality to be fought against. This understanding of the social functionality of race, however, belies statistical data demonstrating that the systemic effects of white supremacy and gender discrimination continue to foster racial and gender caste systems in American society. And the myth of the Strong Black Man as savior of the race, which promotes the patriarchal ordering of society, was historically constructed out of the relational model of preindustrial slavery. In every epoch of African American history black men have sought to assert their humanity through hypermasculine displays of machismo. But rather than saving the race, movements based on masculine power have only proven to thwart the overarching aims of freedom, justice, and democracy for all. In a nutshell, the previous chapter demonstrated that televangelism has the capacity to help participants confront and temporarily endure the storms of life. This final chapter shows that televangelism also has the capacity to recreate and perpetuate the storms. In the process, the liberatory aims of leading televangelists such as Bishop Jakes, Bishop Long, and Pastor Dollar are frustrated. The functions of African American religious broadcasting as a ritual of self-affirmation and as a ritual of social accommodation conflict as the latter extinguishes the former. Thus the producers and participants of African American religious broadcasting may find themselves reinforcing the very social systems that they believe themselves to be dismantling.

1

We Too Sing America

Racial Invisibility, Respectability, and the
Roots of Black Religious Broadcasting

There's room at the cross for you, There's room at the cross for you;
Tho' millions have come, There's still room for one—
Yes, there's room at the cross for you.
                    —"There's Room at the Cross for You,"
                         in *African American Heritage Hymnal*

Religious broadcasting is an essential proselytizing tool of
American evangelical Christianity.[1] This fact is undeniable. Many have
addressed the intersections between the mass media and religion as they
relate to the development of the Christian Right (read conservative, white
evangelicalism). But televangelism in the African American community
has been largely ignored. This is unfortunate. There is a widespread misconception among the dominant society that religious broadcasting in
America was and remains the sole domain of white men with shellacked
hair, the grin of a car salesman, and a gaudily adorned spouse. I have discovered this to be particularly the case among those in academe. In sharing the subject matter of this book with many of my progressive, creden-
tialed, and mostly white colleagues, I often received responses like "Oh, I
didn't know there were African American televangelists." This comment
was often followed by a head-scratching query: "I thought members of
the black church opposed the Religious Right?"

Now I realize that such responses have to do, in part, with the prevailing image of televangelists in popular culture. The 1980s and 1990s
introduced the larger American public to the subculture of Christian
religious broadcasting in precipitous and problematic ways. The drama-
laden world of Christian broadcasting supplied national news outlets

with the types of shocking exposés—replete with sex lies and scandals—found in supermarket tabloids. Who can forget Jimmy Swaggart's tearful public repentance(s) for sex solicitation? Or Tammy Faye Bakker's trail of mascara tears after her husband was federally indicted for racketeering? Or former Moral Majority leader Jerry Falwell's failed attempts to expose one of the Teletubbies as a "closet queen" in need of Christ?[2] But there is something else. The attention garnered by the public shaming of celebrity preachers and ultraconservative causes is not the only reason many have a one-sided view of American religious broadcasting. My contention is that the stories that scholars tell, about both religious broadcasting in America and African American religious life, contribute to and corroborate prevailing biases about the former and the latter. A thorough examination of the academic literature on each subject reveals an unsurprising trend. Religious broadcasting is presented as representative of the white Christian Right, and African American religion is presented as a typically left-leaning, more progressive religious orientation embodied by the civil rights movement in America.

In reality, though, the electronic media have been a primary component of African American Christian practices for nearly a century. Ever since the rise of acoustic media revolutionized and reorganized the dissemination of information and entertainment in the 1920s and 1930s, African American preachers have taken advantage of the expanded social, political, and religious functions assigned to mass media. From the explosion of the "radio age" in the 1920s to the commodification of electrically recorded works in accessible and affordable formats such as the phonograph record, radio and record producers eagerly took advantage of these means to capture the aural vividness of black preaching. It can be argued that aside from the Bible, nothing has been more central to the circulation of the black church tradition than the recorded and/or mass-transmitted sounds of the worship experience. Whether in the form of gospel recordings or coveted "preaching tapes," mass-mediated distribution of the "Word" via electronic formats has been underanalyzed and omitted from the historiographies of American religious broadcasting and the black church.

Religious Broadcasting in America and Racial Invisibility

To date there are no comprehensive historical studies of religious broadcasting. There are, however, several scholarly articles and texts in media studies and sociology that contribute to our understanding of the historical development of the electronic church.[3] Quentin Schultze, Peter Horsfield, and media theorist Stewart Hoover have presented the emergence of religious broadcasting as one of contestation between mainline ecumenical organizations and conservative white evangelicals.[4] On the heels of the Scopes trial of 1925, where John Thomas Scopes was placed on trial for teaching evolution in his Tennessee public school classroom, evangelical fundamentalists were commonly presented as militant antimodernists who were out of touch with the American mainstream. Journalists and social critics such as H. L. Mencken often satirized Christian fundamentalists as "bigots and ignoramuses" desperately clinging to an antiquated theology in a modern age. Rather than evoking Protestant traditions predominantly located in the urban North, as was factually the case, the term *fundamentalist* came to signify a rural, backwater Christian contingent lacking education and social respectability. Contributing to this social stigma were the reactionary tactics of fundamentalists themselves. As historian George Marsden states, the movement began to assume in reality its pejorative image that was circulating throughout popular culture.[5] Fundamentalists became embroiled in all sorts of seemingly fanatical groups and causes like the Ku Klux Klan, antievolution laws, and extreme Prohibition protests, causing many conservative Christians among the mainline denominations to disengage.

Conservative evangelicals, especially Baptists, embraced the radio early on as a means of both evangelizing and advancing their cultural agenda. Church historian Dennis Voskuil describes the few years after the first religious broadcast in 1921 as a "frenzied frequency free-for-all."[6] Obtaining a federal license was not difficult, and radio transmitters were relatively inexpensive. Thus conservative evangelicals, militantly committed to what they considered to be their "Kingdom agenda," entered the fray full throttle. But in 1927 the Federal Radio Commission passed down a ruling strictly regulating the radio industry. One of the regulations restricted the issuing of frequencies to "propaganda stations." *Propaganda* was broadly defined to include Christian preaching on matters of doctrinal dispute or other controversial matters. Seemingly put off by what they considered the ideological agenda of groups like Christian fundamentalists, the commission established principles of "nondiscrimination" that sought to create "well-rounded" commercial programming. Coupling this regulation with expensive operating equipment and licensing that were now required by the FRC (later to be renamed the FCC), the commission literally silenced Christian fundamentalists and conservative evangelists.[7]

In this same ruling the FRC also made it one of the public service obligations of the commercial networks to carry what the commission deemed to be "acceptable religious broadcasting." By offering sustaining time to religious organizations, radio networks could fulfill their government obligations to the community as imposed by the FRC. Religious groups were required to pick up the tab only for their production costs as a result of the free on-air time. Consequently, ecumenical advisory councils such as the Federal Council of Churches of Christ, the National Council of Catholic Men, and the Jewish Theological Seminary in America began forming cozy relationships with major radio networks such as NBC and CBS.[8] Tacit and formal agreements between these councils and networks shored up sustained airtime for the religious "Big Three," mainline Protestantism, Catholicism, and Judaism. This mainstream hegemony over the religious airwaves, then, disproportionately afforded free airtime to mainline denominations while pushing conservative evangelicals further toward the margins. By 1948, Methodists, Presbyterians, and Catholics paid for less than a third of their broadcast airtime while Baptists and members of the Pentecostal and Holiness traditions purchased more than two-thirds.[9]

Since early television stations were owned and operated by the networks that controlled the radio, the same dynamic was in effect with regard to early religious television broadcasts. The early years of religious television were no different in terms of the mainline monopoly. Television producers conferred with the same ecumenical groups that were advising religious radio. Religious television shows like CBS's *Look Up and Live* and *Lamp unto My Feet*, ABC's *Directions,* and NBC's *Frontiers of Faith* dominated through the 1950s. For the most part, these shows expressed broad religious themes with little pointed engagement of any social or theological debates.[10] Yet all one has to do is look across the landscape of religious broadcasting today to see that there was evidently a sea change. Though the unleveled playing field forced conservative evangelicals and fundamentalists to the margins, their marginalization proved to work in their best interest. This claim can be made for several reasons.

For one, conservative evangelicals and fundamentalists, as producers of paid-time, audience-supported programming, were forced to develop creative proselytizing and innovative fundraising techniques. As mainline groups coasted along the airwaves of the national networks at limited cost, independent Protestant groups scratched and clawed for their existence on local stations appealing to particular niche groups for financial support. By 1950, as radio stations began to lose advertising dollars to television, major radio stations like ABC became more amenable to carrying paid-time religious broadcasting. Conservative groups, by now having established local bases of support, were thus in a secure position to acquire the increasing number of paid-time radio slots offered by local radio affiliates. Many conservative Christian broadcasters had the audience and the money already in place.

Moreover, in the previous decade, the National Association of Evangelicals and the National Religious Broadcasters had been formed to promote the rights and increase the exposure of evangelical broadcasters.[11] The latter organization even adopted codes of conduct regarding program content and ethical fundraising standards for its members. Leaders of these groups, which included Carl McIntire and Billy Graham, sought to transcend the negative images often associated with evangelical broadcasters of being religious racketeers and hucksters. Thus, after decades of wandering in the radio-wave wilderness, conservative broadcasters were unwittingly primed for the FCC ruling to come. In 1960 the FCC ruled that no public interest was being served by the distinction between sustained and paid programming.[12] As a result, local radio and television stations could sell religious airtime and still receive credit for serving the public interest.

This new ruling had deleterious consequences for mainline religious organizations that had once thrived on a subsidized basis. With networks no longer having any reason to afford free airtime to any particular religious groups, an ecclesiastical bidding war erupted in which conservative evangelicals were much more adept at fundraising, religious creativity, and energizing their local bases. As Christian conservative broadcasters watched their stock rise, mainline ecumenical power quickly fell. A case in point: before the 1960 FCC ruling, 53 percent of religious television was paid time, but by 1977, this figure had increased to 92 percent, with conservative groups controlling the lion's share.[13] The entrepreneurial and ingenious broadcasting techniques that these groups were encouraged to develop by their status as cultural outsiders is what many argue led to their ultimate success in America's religious broadcasting marketplace.

But some contend that creativity and ingenuity spurred by marginalization account for only part of conservative evangelicals' success within the broadcasting marketplace and that something endemic to the ecclesiology and theology of conservative evangelicalism accords well with mass-mediated forms. Sociologist Razelle Frankl argues that we cannot understand the contemporary electronic church phenomenon apart from the highly rationalized, technically orchestrated, and entrepreneurially informed impulses that constituted late nineteenth- and early twentieth-century urban revivalism.[14] For this reason, Frankl, like sociologists Jeffrey K. Hadden, Charles Swann, and Bobby Alexander before her, traces the ancestral line of religious broadcasting to the proliferation of Protestant evangelicalism during the period some refer to as the Second Great Awakening during the mid–nineteenth century.[15]

Evangelists of this era, such as Charles Grandison Finney, Dwight L. Moody, and Billy Sunday, turned the effective and efficient techniques of industrial expansion toward the industry of saving souls. Religious revival, as argued in Finney's classic text *Lectures on Revivalism,* is not a metaphysical occurrence. Though induced by the divine, the actual activity of revival "is the work of man. It is something for man to do."[16] The former lawyer and Presbyterian minister taught that there was a method to constructing a revival and saving souls. Ministers needed a clear and coherent argument that would extended from the truth of the Bible, use the common language of the people rather than cryptic theological terms, and appeal to persons' emotions as a means of persuasion. Urban revivalism was both a plan of action and a technology. And by utilizing the formats of highly organized prayer meetings, preaching services, and the mourner's bench (where persons would sit or kneel before the congregation to discuss their soul salvation with the preacher), Finney's pragmatic approach to religious revival had a profound impact on the religious ethos of the era. In fact, *Lectures* can be credited, in part, with shifting the theological and ecclesial terrain upon which American Protestantism had been constructed. The emphasis of American Protestantism was transferred from the cultivation of Calvin's predetermined "elect" to an Arminian outlook that teaches that Jesus's atoning work is intended for all persons, thus expanding God's kingdom to "whosoever will." This, Frankl believes, created a fertile soil, commercially and theologically, for the industry of itinerant revivalism. Dwight L. Moody's self-professed "business-like" approach to revivalism commonly borrowed metaphors from the business world. And Billy

Sunday discovered that quality entertainment made for good business. The former professional baseball player is remembered as one of the great American showmen in the vein of P. T. Barnum. From this tradition of evangelical entrepreneurialism and entertainment, many argue, mid-twentieth-century broadcasters like Billy Graham, Rex Humbard, and Oral Roberts emerged. These practices and preachers were well suited for the profit- and entertainment-driven arenas of radio and television.

This seemingly consensus historical account of the emergence of the electronic church in America is not wrong, just narrow. What the literature on religious broadcasting in America shares is its reliance on the history of white Protestantism. There appears to be an a priori understanding of black evangelicals as always and already outside the field of study such that the vast majority of scholars have not bothered to acknowledge persons of color in the history. Those who did recognize the existence of African American evangelicals were able to quickly isolate and expel them from the history of religious broadcasting without even having to put forth an argument to justify it. British sociologist Steve Bruce, for instance, simultaneously acknowledges and dismisses African American evangelicals and broadcasters from his field of inquiry in the first footnote of his text *Pray TV: Televangelism in America*. Bruce condones his decision to omit African Americans from his examination of the electronic church by stating that he understands Christian broadcasting to be primarily the domain of the Christian Right. According to Bruce, "Televangelism is dominated by whites and attracts a largely white audience." He also admits a sampling bias, noting that "blacks are a small proportion of many of the samples on which quantitative research is based," but immediately links this to the fact that most analysts are solely concerned with investigating the Christian Right.[17]

Because Bruce's text was published in 1990, before the embrace of black televangelists by white evangelical networks like TBN, one might be more willing to understand his point while still noting factual discrepancies. Oral Roberts catered to and relied on black viewers for decades as a critical source of donations. Further, as Steve Bruce points out himself, it is hard to equate ministries such as those of Billy Graham, Oral Roberts, and the Bakkers, the disgraced PTL Network founders, with the Christian Right agenda of James Dobson, Jerry Falwell, and Pat Robertson. Statistical research reveals that the former televangelists kept overtly political agendas at bay in favor of a more inclusive message of salvation, physical healing, and personal prosperity, thus causing a rift among otherwise conservative evangelicals.[18] Bruce's conflation of televangelism with the white Religious Right in order to justify his ignoring of black religious broadcasters contradicts his later attempts to distinguish between the not-so politically oriented evangelists of the airwaves and the conservative, hyperpolitical voices of the Religious Right.

But if Bruce's text was published before the proliferation of black evangelical superstars like Bishop T. D. Jakes and Pastor Creflo Dollar, the same qualification cannot be made for Heather Hendershot's more recent text, *Shaking the World for Jesus: Media and Conservative Evangelical Culture*. Though she acknowledges African American gospel artists like Kirk Franklin and Ce Ce Winans, she too situates black evangelical participation in the electronic church outside not only the scope of her research but the larger phenomenon itself. Hendershot states that people of color are largely absent from Christian media aside from being marked as "the other." Thus she feels justified in studying only white evangelical media participation because, as she puts it, "for the most part, evangelical media are made by whites and for whites."[19]

This sort of crude historical and theoretical reductionism that equates evangelical media with the Religious Right cuts out a host of African American participants who have contributed to the development of religious broadcasting in America. American evangelicalism, though typically conservative with regard to religious broadcasting today, is not ecclesiastically, theologically, or racially homogenous. It consists of multiple denominational perspectives, theological traditions, and racial/ethnic groups. To reduce the evangelical presence on the airwaves of America to the activity of the white Religious Right unduly constricts the history of religious broadcasting. Therefore, scholars of the dominant persuasion have unwittingly rendered African American radio and television evangelists inaudible and invisible. But as we will see shortly, these evangelists, too, sing over America's religious airwaves.

Religious Broadcasting in America and Racial Respectability

The racialized lenses of media scholars and sociologists do not fully account for the marginalization of African Americans in the recorded history of American religious broadcasting. Many scholars of black religion have their own biased lenses. In the case of black Christian practices, there has been a tendency throughout the twentieth century to portray black liberal Protestantism and progressive political action as embodying "true" black religion. Black liberal Protestantism has become the classical norm against which all other forms of Christian expression have been historically evaluated. As a result, other religious traditions in black America, such as the Pentecostal and Holiness traditions, which have disproportionately embraced the mass media, have not been given the same breadth of coverage.

First-generation scholars of black religion, deeply influenced by the theological liberalism and supercilious pseudo-Darwinism of Robert Park and the Chicago School of Sociology, commonly encoded their own social and theological commitments in their treatment of black religious practices. They employed preestablished categories that were thinly descriptive and overtly normative. Benjamin Elijah Mays and Joseph William Nicholson's seminal sociological study *The Negro's Church*, arguably one of the most influential texts to shape the academic approach to black religion, is a classic example.[20] In this book, as in Mays's subsequent work *The Negro's God, as Reflected in His Literature*, expressive demonstrations of worship, a Holiness orientation, and common-folk sensibilities are pejoratively described as otherworldly and compensatory. Mays and Nicholson were unable to move beyond their deeply held beliefs that African American progress was inversely related to the rural "folk" mores of the South. They felt that southern religion, whether as expressed in the rural South or in urban storefronts, was holding back the "civilizing" of the race. Hence their binary categorizations such as otherworldly versus this-worldly, compensatory versus instrumentalist, praise oriented versus protest oriented, and resistant versus accommodationist were innately tied to the implicit assumption that black Christian congregations, in their best manifestations, were socially active and politically progressive, the marks of a civilized and sophisticated faith. As historians Randall Burkett and David Wills assert about the era, "A conviction that the black churches should restrain their 'otherworldly' expressivity and devote themselves more energetically to instrumental 'this-worldly' reform and a reliance on a very simple model of the secularizing effect of urbanization would appear to have played central roles in shaping what became the scholarly orthodoxy about religious life."[21]

While some scholars engaged other forms of black religious expression that developed during the interwar period and within black urbanized spaces, their "objective analyses" were more than partial. Figures such as Father Divine, Daddy Grace, and Prophet Cherry were sardonically characterized in books like *Black Gods of the Metropolis* and *Black Sects and Cults* as manipulative cult leaders at best and "fakers and pikers" at worst.[22] Both Arthur Huff Fauset and Joseph Washington condescendingly claimed that manipulative cult leaders were exploiting the uneducated urban masses. Thus until very recently few scholars have taken seriously the spiritual strivings and theological commitments of African American common people whose religious practices fell outside the "bourgeois mainstream."

To be fair, and out of immense respect for these groundbreaking intellectual giants, it is important to acknowledge the social and political terrain upon which first-generation scholars of black religion were forced to fight.[23] The context in which they wrote was, as it largely continues to be, one of white supremacy, normalized black invisibility, stereotypical representations of black life, and the belief in the intellectual ineptitude of black religious expression. As a corrective, the primary task of this handful of black academics who could ill afford not to engage in antiracist activity became one of countering these negative regimes of representation with positive images of black people. At the same time, they were forced to use the "legitimate" categories of the academy to critique the white supremacist assumptions of the academy. With intellectual creativity and moral fortitude, these scholars engaged in the type of antiracist activity that Stuart Hall calls changing the "relations of representation"— struggling for the right to control and represent one's own experience positively to counter forces of marginalization.[24] The prevailing historiography that reads black Christian practices as a consciously progressive narrative of civil rights activity supports this endeavor. Therefore, it does make sense that normative assumptions of black liberal Protestantism would have great resonance among black religious scholars in such a historical moment and cultural context. But it has had the net effect of presenting the vast majority of African American religious practices as precluding social protest and progress and fostering an "otherworldly" and apolitical perspective among the people.

Succeeding generations of scholars have made minimal progress in expanding the customary narrative concerning the form and function of the black church in America. While important and impeccable work has been done to expound the critical role of social activism in the life of the black church, this is just one side of the story. Yet a small body of scholarship in recent years has pushed the study of the black church in new directions. Social scientists and social historians have driven this new trend, for the most part, perhaps because of the methodologies that social scientists and historians employ. In social science, the trend began with Cheryl Townsend Gilkes's contemporary though already classic essay "Plenty Good Room: Adaptation in a Changing Black Church," which reveals how the economic and geographic shifts of the black church have extended theological boundaries by bringing formerly marginalized religious practices to the mainstream in the post–civil rights era.[25] The work of sociologists Omar McRoberts and Milmon Harrison and cultural anthropologist Marla Frederick shows the strength of ethnography in revealing the lived religious worlds, experiences, and strivings of ordinary people.[26] The same is true for the social history of such researchers as Nick Salvatore and Wallace Best. By analyzing the relationship between urbanization, migration, and black religion, Salvatore's cultural biography of the Reverend C. L. Franklin and Best's in-depth treatment of religion in black Chicago between the wars have already forced us to rethink the neat categories of culture and class composition in the black church.

Unfortunately, this expansion beyond traditional narratives does not seem to have occurred in what many would consider the most productive and popular offshoot of early black religious scholarship, black theology of liberation. As an academic discipline, black theology of liberation was intellectually born in the cultural matrices of the civil rights and Black Power movements of the 1960s. It began with the copious and courageous writings of James Cone, who argued that amid volatile social conditions and terrorist activity directed toward black people white theologians were engaging in intellectual conversations that had little to do with God or God's response to the destruction of black life.[27] With a historicist turn that grounded ideas of God and matters of faith within the lived, material conditions of people of faith, Cone and subsequent black theologians argued that theologians should turn from conceiving static metaphysical notions of God and church to producing a narrative of the spiritual yearnings of oppressed people in America, who are primarily and disproportionately persons of African descent. The formula is simple yet compelling—where suffering is, Christ is; black people are suffering, thus Christ has a special relationship to black people.

The theoretical turn of black theologians that grounds conceptions of God and the role of the church in the lived experiences of the people is, however, stunted by its corollary claims of racial exceptionalism. We see that a theology that identifies God with the suffering of those oppressed by a system of white supremacy—as well as other forms of injustice such as classism, sexism, and heterosexism that subsequent black liberation theologians have appropriately identified—privileges black people who are involved in the fight against injustice. Hence, the members of the American black church are deemed God's special elect. But as social ethicist Victor Anderson points out, this places black theologians in a theoretical predicament. Is black theological thought that distinctive from European Christianity in general and American evangelicalism in particular? If so, black theologians of liberation sever the tradition of black theological thought from black churches, the communities from which black theology is purported to emerge and that it represents. Even a thin historical analysis of the black church in America will reveal the less than serendipitous relationship between white and black evangelicalism dating back to the mid–eighteenth century. Yet if black theologians were to locate black theological thought back in historic black churches alongside the conservative, evangelical theology that informs African American Christian life, it would have to renounce, in part, the claims of black exceptionalism that are salient to the perceived profundity of black theology of liberation as an academic project.[28]

To overcome this conceptual conundrum, succeeding generations of black theologians have had to delimit the stories they tell about the black church in America. It is difficult to reconcile the conservative theology of the vast majority of black evangelicals with the progressive slant of black theology of liberation. This places black theologians in the position of highlighting African American Christian communities and narratives that are more consistent with its Afrocentric and exceptionalist claims. African American religious philosopher Eddie Glaude refers to this problem as the "historical malady" that plagues the black theological project.[29] A particular moment in the 1960s and 1970s, influenced by civil rights and Black Power movements, has become the narrow lens through which many black theologians gaze back into African American religious history. Rather than serving as a telescope that enlarges experiences of the past, it functions more as a kaleidoscope that pieces together historical fragments to serve as an illusion of the whole. Such progressive biases about African American historical and religious experiences function much like the predetermined categories posited by first-generation scholars. A priori assumptions about the form and the function of the black church continue to be analytical traps for many African American scholars of religion. Like previous generations, they tend to dismiss the diversity of African American religious practices in favor of flat descriptions that privilege a progressive worldview. In the process, alternative sources for theological reflection, namely forms of expressive "folk" culture, mass-mediated popular culture, and other unconventional sites of religious experience, are at best given little more than lip service and at worst mentioned only to be dismissed. To support this claim, I can cite the magisterial and otherwise intellectually prophetic work of black liberation theologian Dwight Hopkins.

In his text *Heart and Head: Black Theology—Past, Present and Future*, Hopkins tangentially engages dimensions of the megachurch phenomenon by describing what he refers to as the "life and death struggle" facing African American churches in the twenty-first century. Hopkins describes on the one hand black churches "catering to the conservative forces in the country." These congregations are caught up in the prosperity gospel message, are concerned with the individual self as opposed to the community, and have been seduced by dreams of becoming millionaires via entrepreneurial efforts and corporate accommodation. According to Hopkins, these churches "foster a spirituality that removes the individual from this world in order to feel good in the midst of material suffering and psychological wounds, while avoiding Jesus' mandate to revolutionize systems on earth on behalf of those lacking the resources to impact the direction of the nation or their lives on a daily basis."[30]

Hopkins contrasts these types of black churches to those that he claims practice a black theology. Describing these churches as "prophetic" and living out the "spirit of liberation," he asserts that they are rooted in the community and offer day care, housing for seniors, prison ministries, drug counseling, and a host of other social and community services. These congregations, according to Hopkins, "serve as a prophetic yeast for the rest of the African American community by urging people to remember the tradition of their slave ancestors, their West African forebears, the heroic role played by black churches in the civil rights movements of the 1950s through the 1970s, and the message and practice of Jesus when he walked this Earth."[31]

Though in a more nuanced manner, we see Hopkins describing contemporary popular forms of black Christian expression according to the same preestablished binary categories as Mays and Nicholson. Congregations that would be situated within the religious broadcasting category are judged according to an implicitly constructed either/or dichotomy to be otherworldly rather than this-worldly, prosperity focused rather than liberation focused, individualistic rather than socially oriented, and even Western rather than West African. Hopkins thus relies on the constructed assumptions of many black theologians concerning the true nature of the black church. As a result, the most popular black preachers in America today are too easily deemed anomalous, aberrant, and/or nonblack when measured against black theology's constructed norms.

Besides being theologically biased, Hopkins's rendering of the life-and-death struggle facing the black church is descriptively flawed. From this book's introductory account of megachurch congregations such as the Potter's House or New Birth Missionary Baptist Church, one can easily problematize Hopkins's rigid categories. Congregations that are active in religious broadcasting, as in other forms of black Christian expression, are more both/and than either/or. Some promote the prosperity gospel and Christian entrepreneurial impulses while also offering social and community services such as child care, assisted living, and other ministries to the socially afflicted. Similarly, some self-described prophetic congregations are nationalistic in their theological orientation and African influenced in their ecclesiology but at the same time socially conservative in relation to issues of gender, sexuality, and the traditional ordering of family. (And a "prophetic" pastor may own a house and car as luxurious as those possessed by one of his prosperity gospel rivals.) Glib descriptions do not force theologians to wrestle with the complicated nature of African American Christian forms.

How does one categorize, for instance, Rev. Joseph H. Jackson, former esteemed president of the National Baptist Convention, U.S.A., the largest black denomination of the twentieth century, who promoted a staunch political and economic conservatism and was an ardent opponent of Martin Luther King Jr.? And can such binary categories account for Rev. C. L. Franklin, a socially progressive radio evangelist and ally of Martin Luther King Jr. who unapologetically flaunted his fame and ostentatious prosperity lifestyle? The overriding temptation is to simply flatten these figures' complexity in order to sweep what we consider to be their contradictions into the dustbins of history. Theologians have thus been inclined to obscure rather than clarify African American religious history, thought, and practice. Historical subjects and contemporary religious phenomena fall victim to a parochial racial politics that is blinded by a concern for positive representation and nostalgia rather than informed by a quest for understanding and nuanced interpretation.

Hence the attempt to divide "liberation" and "prosperity" within contemporary African American Christian thought ends up misrepresenting the ambiguous nature of black Christian practice.

The Origins of Black Religious Broadcasting

From our analysis thus far, it is apparent that the history of black religious broadcasting is the history of religious blacks who constituted the hidden and rejected underside of a broader evangelical population already marginalized. For the majority of the twentieth century, these African American men and women were crying out from beneath the pages of recorded history so that they might become visible to the dominant white society and be deemed respectable in the eyes of the African American intelligentsia. The lasting impact of their religious imagination, however, is readily evident in the work of contemporary televangelists. In keeping with a tradition of African American creative capacity to vivify artistic forms through spoken word and song, religious race records and radio broadcasts dating back to the 1920s reveal the ways early preachers capitalized on new media and a growing black consumer culture and sowed the seeds of the contemporary phenomenon.

Religious Race Records

Religious race records are germane to the history of black religious broadcasting. In the 1920s and 1930s, record companies such as Columbia, Okeh, Victor, and Paramount began catering to the new black proletariat by capturing the creative rhythmic ruminations and folk orality of southern religion that were then beginning to fill the storefront churches of the northern urban ghettos. These recordings were in stark contrast to the Europeanized products of the Fisk Jubilee Singers. Alongside the iconoclastic articulations of blues singers strumming the significations of a working-class culture were now the wails of gospel blues artists and down-home preachers informed by the Holiness-Pentecostal tradition known as "Sanctified" religion. In this moment one can readily pinpoint how an ecclesiastical cottage industry originated inside African American Christian houses of worship.

The first preacher recorded on a major label was Rev. Calvin P. Dixon in 1925. Dixon's sermon, "As An Eagle Stirreth Up Her Nest," has proved to be an influential theme within the homiletic history of the black church. Columbia's race series inaugural religious effort, however, did not make a great splash among targeted consumers. Blues and jazz historian Paul Oliver attributes the minimal success of Dixon's record to Columbia's inability to capture the pneumatic quality of the southern black worship experience.[32] The sole emphasis was on Dixon's sermon, yet a preacher constitutes only one part of the Du Boisian descriptive trinity of "the Preacher, the Music and the Frenzy." Oliver's argument is convincing. Subsequent recording efforts encouraged preachers, with the assistance of congregational members, to reactualize the quintessence of the preaching moment on the original synthetic vinyl discs in what came to be known in the vernacular as " putting it down on wax." Record companies thus began to either bring a group into the studio or send a crew out "into the field" as pseudoanthropologists to record worship services on location throughout the South.

One early example is Rev. J. C. Burnett of Kansas City. Burnett's initial studio recording featured women from his congregation lining out the hymn "I Heard the Voice of Jesus Say." "Lining out" a hymn, also known as "Dr. Watts" hymn singing, refers to the singing of hymns according to a limited number of familiar tunes intoned by a leader and then responded to by the congregation in an elongated meter.[33] As Burnett delivered his sermon "The Downfall of Nebuchednezzar" with a rushed staccato, the women continued the hymn while interjecting responses of "Amen" and "Yes" at the appropriate moments. This recording was a commercial success, selling eighty thousand copies in 1926—four times the figure for Bessie Smith, the leading blues singer of the day.[34]

Another pioneer of religious race records was the Reverend A. W. Nix from Birmingham, Alabama. Reverend Nix was well respected within black Baptist circles for his homiletic imagination, exemplary elocution, and soulful, inspiring singing voice. Thomas Dorsey, the legendary "father of gospel music," credited Nix's embellished rendition of "I Do, Don't You?" with spurring his own spiritual conversion at the National Baptist Convention in Chicago in 1921. Recalling it, Dorsey later stated that "my heart was inspired to become a great singer and worker in the Kingdom of the Lord—and impress people just as this great singer [Nix] did that Sunday morning."[35]

Reverend Nix's sermons and songs were known for their vivid imagery and detailed story lines. In his best-known sermon, "Black Diamond Express to Hell," Nix employs the familiar metaphor of a train where "sin is the engineer, pleasure is the headlight and the Devil is the conductor." As the Black Diamond Express starts off, Nix cries out in a raspy voice, "All aboard for hell." Accompanied by the encouraging responses of female congregants serving as liturgical background singers on the record, Nix continues with a detailed sketch of the many station stops that follow:

"First station is Drunkardsville!"
Stop down there and let all the drunkards get on board.
They have a big crowd down there. . . .
some drinking moonshine, some drinking white mule and red horse.
Alllll of you drunkards, you've got to go to hell on the Black
    Diamond train.
The Black Diamond starts off for hell now.

"Next station is Liars Avenue!"
Wait there and let allllll the liars get on board.
Have a big crowd of liars down there,
you got some smooth liars, some unreasonable liars, some
    professional liars,
some bare-faced liars, some ungodly liars, some big liars, some
    little liars. Some go to bed lying, get up lying.
Lie all day, lie on you and lie on me.
A big crowd of liars. You got to go to hell on the Diamond
    Express Train.

"Next station is Deceiversville!"
Wait there and let all the deceivers get on board.
Some of you been deceiving one another ever since you been in the
    world.
Friend deceiving friend, husband deceiving wives, wives deceiving
    husbands,
But you got to go to hell on the Black Diamond Train.[36]

Before Nix, a recorded sermon had allotted the minister only around three minutes for an opening hymn, the introduction of the text, a subject, the main idea, and celebration.[37] This is why the rapid-fire whoop, a rhythmically cadenced style of preaching, became common among early recordings. It was a matter not so much of style as of necessity. This format provides an early example of the ways mass-mediated production affected both the style and substance of the recorded sermon. Whether the format was prescribed by record companies is not clear, but the consistency among early recordings reveals just how common the practice was.[38] It allowed preachers to pace their delivery in order to drive home the message in a concise yet compelling manner. Anyone who has ever heard an elderly deacon lead prayer during a traditional Baptist devotional service understands the aesthetic impact of these short recordings. The hastily delivered singsong of a prayer reflects the tempo, tone, and timbre of these early three-minute sermons.

"Black Diamond Express to Hell," however, was the first recorded sermon to introduce the multipart message. Nix recorded it in two parts over six minutes, recasting the early-established mold. This formula was successful, and subsequent preachers became famous for releasing sermons in parts—a practice that of course caused consumers to anxiously anticipate the release of subsequent parts of their favorite sermons. Thus in 1927 we have the birth of the recorded sermon series.

Consistent with the black church tradition, the vast majority of those who made religious race recordings were men. Only a few women were invited to do so. They emerged not from the black mainline denominations—the wing of the black church tradition that tends to be culturally accepted as more progressive—but from the Sanctified churches. For instance, Pentecostal preacher Rev. Leora Ross recorded on Okeh records in Chicago in 1927, accompanied by a band of fellow female vocalists. Her elocution was similar, if not superior, to that of her male contemporaries. She begins her recordings with a song, then quickly reads the text and moves straight toward her whoop. With her high-pitched shrill and her demonstrated range on the record, Rev. Ross sounds as if she had an instrument in her chest as she often extemporaneously riffs above the other assembled singers.

In her recording "Dry Bones in the Valley," Ross places her theatrical adroitness and vocal dexterity on display while assuming the character of the prophet Ezekiel. Without missing a note from the opening song, "We Shall Run," Ross plays up Ezekiel's charge to prophesy to the dry bones in the valley. She intones, "Ohhhhhh, dry bones. . . . Ohhhhhh, dry bones . . . hear the Word of the Lawd!" She then repeats the prophecy to the wind: "Ohhhhhh, east wind. Ohhhhhh, east wind, blow upon these bones!" And demonstrating this same repetitive cadence throughout, Rev. Ross concludes the sermon by leading her respondents into an upbeat closing tune, "Ohhhhhh, Will You Come? Ohhhhhh, Will You Come?"[39]

Rev. Ross's recordings show little difference in cadence or content from those of her male contemporaries. Her language is creative and her tone is essentially pietistic. Just as early religious race records share a seemingly prescribed format of song, text, subject, main idea, and celebration, they vary little in their subject matter. The vast majority of preachers appear to elaborate on a biblical story such as Daniel in the lions' den or Ezekiel in the valley of the dry bones so that they may speak to what they consider the sinful signs of the times. The denunciations of drinkers, gamblers, "midnight ramblers" (masculine), and "midnight walkers" (feminine) are all common tropes in the genre. The inordinate emphasis on "fast living" and fire and brimstone was a sure-fire yet simplistic response to the structural realities affecting urban African Americans.

There were rare exceptions. Paul Oliver notes that Rev. Sutton Griggs's 1928 sermon "A Hero Closes a War" was one of the very few to criticize the color line in America. Griggs, a Methodist minister who wrote novels about America's racial divide in the first decade of the twentieth century, eschewed the histrionics and emotionalism of the Southern Baptist and Sanctified traditions and spoke in a vocabulary more "educated" than that of the average listener. Consequently, his style did not accord well with the targeted market, and his record, for the most part, sat on the shelf. Religious records did not allow enough time to build a homiletic argument that encouraged reflective and reasoned responses from listeners. The condensed format forced preachers to strike fire quickly lest they either run out of time or fail to captivate listeners from the outset. Griggs did not even attempt to do so; he simply offered a sermon demonstrating that the height of humanity is manifested in racial cooperation.[40] Second, the success of other ministers who engaged in histrionics from the pulpit signaled to producers that many consumers of religious race records were not interested in purchasing and listening to what they considered to be the bromidic sermons that they associated with black middle-class churches. The producers of religious race records had found their market in the working- and lower-class communities and were committed to them as a consumer base.[41] And it appears that sermons emphasizing pietistic and puritanical responses to the ills of society were more palatable to a mass audience.

Yet religious records did not ignore social issues. By 1930, several preachers began to move toward a greater engagement with black secular culture. No preacher garnered more fame from this than Rev. J. M. Gates. While serving as the pastor of Mount Calvary Church in Atlanta,

Georgia for twenty-six years during the 1920s and 1930s, Gates recorded over two hundred sides on twenty different record labels.[42] When he began recording in 1926, his format was consistent with those of the recordings previously mentioned. He was known for a powerful singing voice and would line out hymns before going into spirited sermons such as "You Mother Heart Breakers," "Straining at a Gnat and Swallowing a Camel," and "Dead Cat on the Line." But as his popularity increased, Gates seems to have redirected his attention beyond the faithful toward a broader audience. No longer confined to the biblical text, he began recording sermons that offered what he considered to be practical advice for daily living. Without reading a biblical text, he would engage members of his congregation in conversation based on relevant themes of his choice. For instance, on a record entitled "Pay Your Policy Man," Gates brings up the topic of life insurance:

> Gates: You know, I am getting tired of begging the church to help bury your dead. You should pay your policy man.
>
> Woman: I know, but the thing what gets on my nerves is that you worry us about paying the policy man but you never do say nothing to the policy men about paying us when somebody die.
>
> Gates: Yeah, but you know, no earlier than this morning I heard a woman muddling and talking 'bout the insurance company not paying her, when I heard her say that "the funeral man is always at my door." And she didn't pay her policy man and she 'spect the company to pay her. So you should pay your policy man.
>
> Woman: Well, I paid mine in September, mine all set.
>
> Gates: Why don't you take out a 5 or 10 cent, 15 or 25 cent policy and pay it by the week, the month, or by the year?
>
> Deacon: Oh, I takes out a policy every week, but I ain't got nothing to pay 'em with.
>
> Gates: Now that is the very thing I want to talk to you about. Why don't you stop taking out policies and pay them you have?
>
> Deacon: Well they keep on running me down, I told 'em I ain't had nothing.
>
> Gates: You ought to have sense enough to know if you 'spect to get anything out of a policy, you must pay your policy man.[43]

The narrative here reveals an early emphasis on personal responsibility and fiscal accountability. Reverend Gates chides congregants, as well as the broader working-class black community, for not being conscientious about their debts. Interestingly enough, Gates diverts the woman's query concerning the unjust practices on the part of insurance companies toward the poor in general and African Americans in particular—practices that are well documented from the dawn of the twentieth century to the swindling of Hurricane Katrina victims along the Gulf Coast. Gates's anecdotal example of a woman's irresponsibility problematically and tragically exonerates the insurance companies of any culpability.

But there are also instances of Gates siding with the proletariat in attacks against the exploitative practices of the powerful. Case in point: he lent his voice and recording time to the anti–chain store movement of the 1920s and 1930s. Many at the time saw the ascendancy of major chains such as the Great Atlantic and Pacific Tea Company (more commonly known as A&P) as a threat to independent retailers and thus local economies. Even before the contemporary debates about Wal-Mart and transnational corporate domination, the growth of chain stores in America was viewed by many as undermining democracy because of their oligopolic control of the market.[44] In fact, the FRC shut down a Louisiana radio station in 1927 under the Radio Act when a Shreveport businessman and station owner referred to chain stores as "damnable low down thieves from Wall Street."[45] But what was banned as propaganda on the airwaves was fair game on wax. Thus around 1930 Rev. Gates and members of his congregation recorded a two-part series entitled "Good Bye to Chain Stores."

Part I involves a series of exchanges with members of Gates's congregation. Gates begins by warning that the rise of chain stores signals the end of jobs for parishioners as well as credit offered by retailers. A deacon then begins to testify, saying, "The place I was working at, the white folks went out of business 'cause the chain stores ruin them. And that's why you ain't been seeing me at the church. If things keep going the way they going now, Brother Pastor, you won't see me soon. But I hope it will change." Reverend Gates then retorts, "It'll never change so long as you stay in the chain stores." Part II begins with Reverend Gates encouraging listeners to spend their money only at the establishments of local retailers in their respective communities—retailers, Gates quips, that will "give you a job." Then he introduces a group of men singing an up-tempo song entitled "Stay Out the Chain Stores." Though it sounds quasi-comedic to contemporary ears, I am sure the lyrics of the song were sincere. The men begin:

Let me tell you people,
Oh, white and colored too.
It's time for you to wake up
And see how they treating you.
You better stay out of them chain stores.[46]

The most interesting shift in Rev. Gates's recordings came with his seeming embrace of the popular culture of the age in the form of vaudeville-inspired radio. The recorded dialogue between Gates and members demonstrates the racist and sexist humor of the era's most popular radio minstrel show, *Amos n Andy*. In one particular message, "Kinky Hair Is No Disgrace," the exchange between preacher and congregants belies the otherwise racially empowering title. Far from James Brown's "Say It Loud, I'm Black and I'm Proud" four decades later, this recording reflects the critical connection between Christian soteriology and white supremacist ideology. Rather than asserting that kinky hair and black skin are attributes to be proud of, it portrays them as features that people should want to be delivered from. The slapstick comedy and stereotypical characterizations employed on the record further indict Gates's purposeful appropriation of the minstrel format. The dialogue's point is that God looks on the inside and man the outside, so people need to focus on getting right with God:

> Gates: Skin and hair don't make the inside of a man or woman good nor bad.
> Woman #1: I know, but bad hair make a fella look so bad.
> Gates: Well, I know it. But you remember that God looks on the inside and man looks on the outside, and a whole lot of this hair straightening is simply so man can see it. . . . Kinky hair and black face is no disgrace.
> Woman #2: (with an exaggerated southern drawl) Look here, Bruh Pastah. You talkin' bout me?
> Gates: Well, yes. I'm talkin' about you. Because you got bad hair and it seems you get along all right.
> Woman #2: Oh but it looks so disgraceful [inaudible] . . . Sister, [inaudible] would you loan me a dollar so I can go get my hair straight. . . . You know how disgraceful my head look, I gotta go to church Sunday.
> Woman #1: Uh, look at the back of mine. . . .

Gates: Yeah, you right now. . . . If you going to straighten your hair you ought to straighten that in the back, it looks so bad. It ain't only kinky, it's knotty!

Deacon: Why don't ya'll sisters be like me? I don't worry about my hair being straightened.

Woman #1: It don't look like nobody been worrying about it either. . . .

Gates concludes the record by saying, "Don't worry about your hair being kinky. . . . Kinky hair and black face reminds me of a coconut. All the beauty and all that is good is on the inside."[47] To be sure, such crude attempts at humor thwart the intended liberatory aim of the message. Appeals to gross stereotypes and minstrel representations for the sake of laughs undercut the underlying theme. This type of religious record, rather than serving as a cultural precursor of black power consciousness, as the title would imply, is more consistent with today's gospel stage plays that display stereotypical and overly exaggerated characters for laughs.

Religious Radio

A key figure in the early years of black religious radio was Holiness preacher Elder Solomon Lightfoot Michaux. Elder Michaux, a former fish salesman from Newport News, Virginia, launched his program *The Radio Church of God* in 1929 on a small radio station, WJSV, near Alexandria. Within a few years, the station was purchased by CBS and became the major outlet broadcasting along the eastern seaboard. The local popularity of Elder Michaux's broadcast caused it to be the only holdover from WJSV, immediately multiplying Michaux's access and audience. Because of his catchy intro theme song, millions in America came to affectionately know Elder Michaux as the "Happy Am I Preacher."[48]

From his early years on WJSV, Elder Michaux was highly touted for his penchant for showmanship and his interracial following. He effectively used his radio broadcast to promote his brand of traveling revivalism. Elder Michaux's open-air revivals at Washington, D.C.'s Griffith Stadium, for example, regularly drew a crowd of over thirty thousand, as many desired to hear the revivalist live and participate in his mass baptisms. And in 1934, *Time* magazine reported that when Elder Michaux arrived for a revival in Philadelphia and requested one hundred female ushers, four thousand girls, black and white, applied.[49] Other white journalists often drew comparisons between Elder Michaux and the famed white evangelist Billy Sunday; some described Michaux as "the world's greatest radio evangelist" and "the best known colored man in the United States."[50] The recorded shows from these mass events and broadcasts were cut and distributed as records from the 1940s to the 1960s. Elder Michaux became one of the first African Americans to go on television when CBS sponsored a television broadcast between 1949 and 1951.

Along with his national acclaim, an additional characteristic of Michaux's broadcast is noteworthy. The Holiness preacher's radio show contradicts accepted characterizations of the conversionist strand of black religious practices as apolitical. This Pentecostal-informed evangelist unapologetically employed his broadcast to address political issues of the day. Elder Michaux's weekly on-air sermons consisted of public praise and rebuke of political leaders. For instance, upset with Herbert Hoover's Depression-era policies, Elder Michaux energized listeners to abandon the Republicans in favor of Democratic candidate Franklin D. Roosevelt. Michaux biographer Lillian Ashcraft Webb contends that despite his self-proclaimed role as a radio prophet to the nation, Michaux's involvement in politics was less prophetic and more pragmatic. Along with his revivalism, Michaux, like Billy Sunday, was a forerunner of evangelical entrepreneurialism and often involved in multiple economic ventures at any given time. Aside from the *Happy Am I* radio show, he had a newspaper, the Happy News Café Restaurant, and Mayfair Mansions, which afforded housing to working- and middle-class African Americans. And Ashcraft Webb states that Elder Michaux learned early in his ministry that being favorable to political leaders enabled him to curry favor.[51] Therefore, rather than serving as a thermostat that influenced the climate of public opinion, Elder Michaux might be viewed as a thermometer. His opinions over the radio merely reflected the sentiments sweeping the nation, thus strategically placing him in support of the victors. Rather than upholding uncompromising moral stances, Michaux most likely demonstrated keen political perception and insight. But regardless of his political stances, one thing remains true: Elder Michaux's proficiency and prominence on the religious airwaves reveal that it was possible for African American evangelical preachers to reach beyond their own racial and economic communities and operate in the larger society.

Another prominent African American radio evangelist of the interwar era was Mother Rosa Artimus Horn. A widowed dressmaker at the outset of the Great Migration, Horn originally relocated from Georgia to Indiana. In Indiana, abandoning her Methodist roots, Rosa Artimus united with the Fire Baptized Pentecostal Church. Her foray into revivalism came honestly, as she was ordained a minister in the Pentecostal Church by the nationally renowned white healing evangelist Mary Woodworth Etter. An acclaimed revivalist of the late nineteenth and early twentieth centuries, Etter is credited with shaping the careers of subsequent female revivalists like Aimee Semple McPherson. Her healing revivals and tent meetings were well-known for persons being slain in the spirit—persons passing out upon Etter's touch—and the sense of excitement and energy that encompassed the event.[52] After marrying William Horn in 1926, Rosa Horn settled in Brooklyn and organized the Pentecostal Faith Church in Harlem.

Mother Horn, as she came to be known, was unlike most Pentecostal preachers of her era. She had attended private school in her native South Carolina and exuded intellectual confidence and erudition. As her ministry began to grow, she was offered a deal to broadcast a radio ministry on WHN. She was labeled the "Pray for me Priestess" by radio listeners, and her Radio Church of God of the Air was broadcast up and down the East Coast. The popularity of her show caused conflicts with the ubiquitous ministries of both Father Divine and Elder Michaux. Managers at WHN actually sued Father Divine, accusing the Harlem-based deity of intimidation in attempts to run Mother Horn and her congregation out of Harlem. This conflict only boosted her ratings. Within a few years, Mother Horn's Pentecostal Faith Church numbered in the thousands, and she counted among her many members a fourteen-year-old James Baldwin. Baldwin's subsequent stage play *The Amen Corner* is based on the life and ministry of the Pray for Me Priestess. Over the next three decades, Mother Rosa Horn and her congregation became a staple of New York City and a cultural attraction for prominent personalities, both black and white, from across the country who desired to experience the fullness of Harlem.[53]

The most prominent religious broadcaster, on record or radio, in the mid–twentieth century was Rev. Clarence LaVaughn Franklin, pastor of the Salem Baptist Church in Detroit. Reared in Mississippi, where he was exposed to both the sacred tunes of St. Peter's Rock Missionary Baptist Church and the secular tunes of the Mississippi Delta's numerous juke joints, C. L. Franklin perfected a chanted style of preaching that made him arguably the most homiletically influential black minister of the twentieth century. Though unlettered, Franklin possessed an inordinate "sanctified imagination," a compassion for the common people, and a powerful, soulful voice that he would pass on to his daughter Aretha Franklin.

In the early 1950s C. L. began broadcasting a Sunday night service at 10:00 p.m. on Detroit's popular black music radio station WJLB. The national success of Franklin's radio show, voluminous record sales, and cross-country gospel tours placed him on a par with such celebrities as Little Richard and Sam Cooke. In fact, Rev. Franklin's $4,000 appearance fee was not far from Elvis Presley's going television rate of $7,500 in 1956.[54] And like his celebrity counterparts, Franklin wholly embraced the lifestyle. A plush home in the elite section of Detroit, a revolving selection of shiny new Cadillacs, expensive tailor-made suits, and beautiful women on his arm (Franklin was a divorced single father for the majority of his ministry) were as much a part of Franklin's mystique as his hypnotic whoop. Rev. Franklin recorded sermons for distribution well into the 1970s, and these recordings continue to be hot commodities for aspiring black preachers who seek to perfect the art of the chanted sermon.

At the height of the civil rights movement, while Elder Michaux and his followers were protesting the civil activities of the Southern Christian Leadership Coalition (SCLC) and the Student Nonviolent Coordinating Committee (SNCC), Reverend Franklin became an ardent supporter.[55] He was an unabashed political progressive who advocated for civil rights legislation, sided with the working class, and promoted equitable socioeconomic conditions for all American citizens. According to Franklin's biographer Nick Salvatore, Franklin demonstrated a deep commitment to democracy and used the power of his pulpit to broadcast what he considered to be edifying political discourse. A host of public intellectuals were afforded a platform at New Salem, ranging from Marxist theoretician C. L. R. James to black congressmen Charles Diggs and Adam Clayton Powell Jr. and Reverend Franklin's close friend Martin Luther King Jr. According to Salvatore, "Franklin was not a political innocent, open to any and all winds that swirled about. . . . But he gave his pulpit to anyone whom he thought had the best interests of his people at heart, regardless of whether he agreed with their analysis."[56] Until the day Franklin's life came to a tragic end from injuries he sustained as a victim of armed robbery, he would seek to reconcile—sometimes not very well—his lavish celebrity lifestyle with his commitment to the cause of social justice in America.[57] This dilemma, unfortunately, has come to define the world of African American religious broadcasting.

The popularity and prevalence of religious race records and black Christian radio compel both media theorists and black liberation theologians to expand the sources of our analysis. The history of evangelicalism and religious broadcasting in America extends beyond the narrow confines of white Christian conservatism. Similarly, black Christian thought and practice in America transcend a definitional identity structured by civil rights and social justice. When media theorists broaden their vision beyond the dominant racial group and black theologians of liberation critically engage alternative black Christian communities, both fields will benefit. The former will come to see African American religious broadcasters as a pervasive influence on the electronic church, and the latter will find a wonderfully rich source that has influenced how black people view God and God's activity in the world.

Rev. Frederick J. Eikerenkoetter II, a.k.a. Rev. Ike, delivering a sermon at "The Palace" in New York City. Source: Rev. Frederick J. Eikerenkoetter II and the United Christian Evangelistic Association in Boston.

2

Something Within

The Cultural Sources of
Rev. Frederick J. Eikerenkoetter II

What can wash away my sin? Nothing but the blood of Jesus;
What can make me whole again? Nothing but the blood of Jesus.
Oh! Precious is the flow. That makes me white as snow;
No other fount I know, Nothing but the blood of Jesus!
      — "Something Within," in *African American Heritage Hymnal*

One could not help admiring the thousands of glamorously dressed bodies as the television cameras panned across the arena. The rows of black faces were as aesthetically attractive as they were demonstrably excited. Older women with neatly "pressed" hair and men with perfectly circumferenced afros clapped their hands jubilantly to the music. Polyester leisure suits and pastel-colored Sunday dresses filled the folding chairs that served as pews. And jewelry-clad men and women adorned in gold punctuated the theme of the evening, "Don't wait for pie in the sky by-and-by when you die. Get yours now with ice cream on top!" To the roar of applause, Rev. Ike nimbly glided to the microphone in a custom-tailored orange tuxedo. As his diamond-encrusted fingers clutched the microphone, he rhetorically raised the questions, "Do you know that God is still God? Do you know that God is still good? Can you feel the presence of God moving in your soul, mind, and body?" Rev. Ike had inundated the local population for weeks with advertising on radio, on television, and in the *New York Times* encouraging them to attend this "International Healing and Blessing Meeting." And on this night over twenty thousand persons responded to his call, making this the largest gathering of African Americans at Madison Square Garden since the famed pan-Africanist Marcus Garvey had graced the stage in

1920. For at least one moment in 1973 Rev. Ike felt on top of the religious broadcasting world as this event was broadcast into the homes of millions across the country.

Biography

Rev. Ike's progression to this point was over two decades in the making. Frederick J. Eikerenkoetter II was born on June 1, 1935, in Ridgeland, South Carolina. His father was a local Baptist preacher and reported "well-to-do" business entrepreneur, and his mother a schoolteacher. Though he was allegedly born with a silver spoon in his mouth, his parents' separation when he was five years old plunged him and his mother deep into poverty, and although he now states that the poverty of his youth was so devastating that he does not allow himself to think of it any longer, in many of his sermons, writings, and interviews he evokes the image of a shoeless and shirtless boy following his mother to the one-room schoolhouse where she was paid $65 a month.[1] The apparent strained relationship with his father did not deter the young Eikerenkoetter from following his father's footsteps into the ministry. Raised in the Bibleway Baptist Church of Ridgeland, at the age of fourteen he began preaching to a local Pentecostal congregation. Within a year, the former Ridgeland juke joint–turned-church appointed the teenage Eikerenkoetter as pastor.

Like millions of African Americans of his own and the preceding generation, the young Eikerenkoetter did not remain in the rural South. Changing economic and social formations in the South and North spurred the northward relocation of millions of African Americans in the first half of the twentieth century. Between 1890 and 1950, nearly three million black people left the South. Extreme forms of labor exploitation and outright violence stemming from increased competition in the dwindling agricultural market began to push many African Americans into northern cities such as Chicago, Detroit, and Philadelphia. This was coupled with the pull of a stimulated industrial economy in the North as a result of the wars and the increased demand for labor. But social and economic conditions aside, there was also a spiritual dimension to the migration. For the generations of African Americans dating back to slavery who had conceived of the North as the "Promised Land" for black people, the Great Migration was framed by the religious imagery of the journey to Canaan.[2]

Rev. Ike claims that between 1953 and 1956 he earned a Bachelor of Theology degree from a northern institution that he will not name. Then, after a two-year term in the air force as a military chaplain, he briefly returned to Ridgeland long enough to organize the United Church of Jesus Christ for All People. But Rev. Eikerenkoetter soon migrated to Boston and established the Miracle Temple. Here the young evangelist attempted to find his niche as a faith healer. Recalling his time in Boston, Rev. Ike later confessed: "Faith healing, that was the big thing at the time, and I was just about the best in Boston, snatching people out of wheelchairs and off their crutches, pouring some oil over them while I commanded them to walk or see or hear. I don't know if I cured many folks—it's a wonder I didn't kill somebody, though."[3]

Within two years, he again relocated, this time from Boston to New York City, establishing himself among the plethora of preachers proclaiming unconventional spiritual tropes from untraditional houses of worship. He renovated a dilapidated movie theater on 125th Street in Harlem. Here he first posted "Rev. Ike Every Sunday," changing his name because Eikerenkoetter was too hard to pronounce. Situated alongside and largely in competition with such dynamic and oracular personalities as Father Divine and Mother Rosa Horn, Rev. Ike began to rise from obscurity onto the ecclesiastical main stages. Wearing custom-tailored suits and expensive jewelry and sporting a polished conkolene hairstyle, he possessed an aura more like that of Johnny Mathis or David Ruffin than the traditional representation of a preacher. *New York Times* journalist Clayton Riley placed Rev. Ike within the tradition of "religious eroticism."[4] This is to say, Rev. Ike's ability to bring parishioners to spiritual ecstasy was aided by his not-so-subtle sexual energy. This tradition of eroticism is representative and constitutive of the sexually charged, masculinist subculture that lies just beneath the surface of many forms of black religious expression.[5] Such Rev. Ike mantras as "I come to you today looking good, feeling good, and smelling goooood!" are in many ways commensurate with Martin Luther King's hypnotic southern charm, Adam Clayton Powell Jr.'s movie-star good looks, and the homoerotic and exotic sensuality of Charles "Sweet Daddy" Grace.

Encouraged by his bourgeoning bank accounts, broadening philosophical perspective, and desire for crossover appeal, in 1969, Rev. Ike decided to move his United Church from Harlem to the Washington Heights area of New York City.[6] He purchased the former Loew's Theater on 175th Street and Broadway. Erected sometime between 1925 and 1930, it was originally intended to serve as a stage theater. But with the decline of vaudeville and the growth of the movie industry, it was soon transformed into a deluxe movie house. Under Rev. Ike the structure underwent major renovations, including the addition of gold-plated ornamentation, crystal chandeliers, and the restoration of the theater's original "Wonder" Morton pipe organ. Upon completion the United Church theater boasted a seating capacity of 3,500, complete with auditorium and balcony, as well as a recording and production studio that enabled Rev. Ike to broadcast his services over television and radio stations nationally.

Rev. Ike's physical relocation was consistent with his new theological and philosophical orientation. Seeming to abandon his evangelical and Pentecostal roots, he embraced and began promulgating a new philosophy that he referred to as "the Science of Living." In his own words, "My philosophy may be described as self-image psychology. The ultimate goal is to teach the individual to be master of his own mind and affairs by changing his own self-image. Through positive self-awareness, the individual can change the conditions and circumstances in his life. I teach the individual that he can be what he wants to be, can do what he want to do and that he can have what he wants to have, through the presence and power of God which is within each person."[7]

Rev. Ike envisages his theological message as a message of self-awareness. For him, considering the nature and being of God takes one to considering the self. The Science of Living maintains, as the previous quote suggests, that the human mind is the only real God in the universe and that consequently God is in the possession of every individual. Rev. Ike promotes the idea that "God is not someone else, somewhere else, sometime else. God is here and now and living, sometimes dormant in everyone."[8]

Rev. Ike's theology and ministerial philosophy place great emphasis on personal and material gain, as embodied in his own ostentatious lifestyle. Shunning traditional conceptions of heaven or hell in the afterlife, Rev. Ike has asserted, "I don't believe in the God in the sky or pie in the sky, bye and bye, when we die. I believe in God as a presence which is within every individual and that the unlimited power is there to help a person be and do all he desires."[9] Therefore, as one of Rev. Ike's classic lines puts it, "Don't wait for your pie in the sky by and by; have it now with ice cream and a cherry on top."[10]

Very few of the other leading African American revivalists at the time ran a media empire with such sophistication. In addition to over 1,400 combined radio and television rebroadcasts a month in the United States, Mexico, Canada, and the Caribbean, Rev. Ike spread his message of health, wealth, and prosperity via printed publications and national, revival-like tours. The first publication, a quarterly, was entitled *The Study Guide of the Science of Living*. It was touted as offering positive strategies to help people take control of their minds to achieve victorious living. The second publication, *ACTION! Magazine*, was printed biweekly to publish the more than one million letters and praise reports that the United Church received each month. Here positive testimonies of the "millions" of followers who had enrolled in Rev. Ike's "Blessing Plan"—persons who committed to send in a designated offering each month to the ministry— were set forth as evidence of Rev. Ike's famous declaration "You can't lose with the stuff I use!" Moreover, a couple of times a month, Rev. Ike would preach to capacity crowds in major cities. Just one month after his successful "International Healing and Blessing Meeting" at Madison Square Garden, he drew a crowd of fourteen thousand people to Atlanta's Omni arena, where Mayor Maynard Jackson gave him a key to the city. While his tax records for that year indicate an annual salary of $40,000, the church's financial holdings exceeded $6 million, from which Rev. Ike was afforded an unlimited expense account.[11]

Other aspects of Rev. Ike's personal life remain shrouded in mystery. We know that today he is still married to Eula M. Dent Eikerenkoetter, whom he wed in 1964. This union bore a son, Xavier Frederick Eikerenkoetter III. But part of Rev. Ike's allure, like that of most charismatic religious leaders, is his enigmatic nature. Like a great character actor, he carefully constructed and maintained his public image. At his peak of fame in the 1970s, Rev. Ike was ubiquitously visible yet highly concealed. He was a cultural character—a walking myth—in the broadest sense of the term, someone who could be considered famous or infamous depending on one's vantage point. It was this larger-than-life persona that was often depicted and/or imitated in movies and sitcoms throughout the decade. Rev. Ike was Fred Sanford's favorite television preacher on the hit show *Sanford and Son*, Richard Pryor's character "Daddy Rich" in *Car Wash*, and James Evan's childhood friend and popular televangelist "Rev. Sam" on *Good Times*, all examples of the many ways Rev. Ike became a staple of black popular culture in the 1970s.

Cultural Sources of Rev. Ike's Thought

The sole academic treatment of Rev. Ike and the United Church, Science of Living Institute, Inc. is Martin Gallatin's doctoral dissertation. Gallatin, a sociologist, investigates how Rev. Ike was able to successfully move the United Church from one religious tradition to another without any major membership disruptions.[12] This project offers wonderful insight into the life-worlds of Rev. Ike's followers—particularly through the numerous firsthand narratives and testimonies Gallatin provides. Unfortunately, Gallatin's description of the religious orientation of Rev. Ike and his following is thin at best. The author reduces Rev. Ike's theological and philosophical development to a progression from traditional Pentecostalism to New Thought. Gallatin bases his claim on Rev. Ike's shifting emphasis to "positive thinking" philosophies and his change in homiletic presentation from ecstatic, experiential Pentecostal-style worship to an increasingly "rational" approach to the faith.

To be sure, there is no denying the influence of either Pentecostalism or New Thought on Rev. Ike. As we will see, the ensconcing of premodern spiritualist concepts in modern scientific language was a central feature of the theological and cultural milieu of America and infused many forms of new religious movements throughout twentieth-century America. This is why one may claim that Rev. Ike's religious thought, from an early age, was steeped in syncretic religious forms that were not reducible to one or two particular faith perspectives. Gallatin is correct insofar as Pentecostalism and New Thought can be classified within two prominent dimensions of African American religious thought: the conversionist dimension, which emphasizes personal conversion and holiness, and the thaumaturgical or magico-religious dimension, which emphasizes using the power of the mind to acquire esoteric knowledge to gain control over oneself and others. But both of these categories encompass a bricolage of religious movements and traditions, thus making Gallatin's treatment too simplistic.[13] Keeping in mind, however, that simplification on some level is unavoidable in this type of analysis, let us now undertake the difficult but necessary task of delicately teasing out the sources of Rev. Ike's religious thought without ignoring the complexity and fluidity of African American religious practices.

Rev. Ike's thought has three major sources: the rural black evangelical Christian tradition that shaped his religious sensibility in the South, the Pentecostal-healing revivalism that flourished in post–World War II America, and the philosophic and religious worldview of the black Spiritual movement that found expression in storefront congregations in the urban North.

Rural Southern Black Evangelicalism

To understand Rev. Ike is, first, to take seriously the ethos of black evangelical Christianity in the rural South. Fashioned and formed under the social and economic conditions of preindustrial slavery, the black church served as a means for people living under this most peculiar institution to make sense of their situation. Syncretizing certain African customs with an evangelical Christian worldview, black people constructed a mode of resistance against natal alienation and other forms of social and civic death.[14]

As a religious and social institution, the rural black church was the community lifeline, the place where social bonds were established and individual identity was constructed. Within the context of the economic and social caste system of Jim Crow, the local congregation instilled a heightened sense of "being somebody" and nurtured the moral virtues. Referring to his formative years in rural South Carolina, Benjamin Elijah Mays recalled,

> Old Mount Zion was an important institution in my community. Negroes had nowhere to go but to church. They went there to worship, to hear the choir sing, to listen to the preacher, and to hear and see people shout. The young people went to Mount Zion to socialize, or simply to stand around and talk. It was a place of worship and a social center as well. There was no other place to go. . . . This was the one place where the Negroes in my community could be free and relax from the toil and oppression of the week. Among themselves they were free to show off and feel important.[15]

For this reason E. Franklin Frazier described the black church as a "nation within a nation."[16] With the merging of the "invisible institution" and the institutional black church after the Civil War, both Frazier and W. E. B. Du Bois judged organized religious life to be the template for African American social life. Over two centuries of slavery and Jim Crow, which precluded viable social opportunities and institutions among black people, made religious enterprise a necessity rather than a choice. Houses of worship became the only locales of collective gathering and relative social control. As a consequence, rural black churches were forced to fulfill roles and responsibilities far beyond their scope, a circumstance that forged what Mays and Nicholson called the "genius of the Negro church."[17]

The rural church, however, is a by-product of southern evangelicalism and revivalism. Though the rural black church had levels of social control and autonomy, it is impossible to discuss black evangelicalism apart from its white religious counterpart. The revivals of the eighteenth and nineteenth centuries brought blacks and whites together into a multiracial, though undemocratic, religious union. Thus, as historian David Wills warns, it is wrongheaded to think of the history of the black church as "black religious history" and the history of white evangelicalism as "American religious history." Rather, the development of American evangelicalism in general and southern religion in particular should be read as an ongoing yet awkward interplay between black and white forms of evangelicalism.[18]

To be sure, southern white evangelicals proved incapable of the moral leadership to break down white supremacist structures of dominance within the church. This is why blacks developed autonomous congregations and denominations in response. But through it all, black churches were forced to struggle with the internal anxieties of theological double-consciousness: though black evangelicalism was theologically oriented toward affirming egalitarian notions of the kingdom of God, it still often measured black equality according to the perceived virtues of black submission and docility and the white supremacist standards of inherent Negro inferiority.

During the era of American slavery and after, blacks had few choices for handling their anger or aggression. According to race theorist S. P. Fullinwider, the only two choices they had to choose from were self-repression or self-destruction.[19] To survive, African Americans had to embrace and publicly perform the character traits of long-suffering, patience, and humility. In the words of poet Paul Laurence Dunbar, "We wear the mask that grins and lies, / It hides our cheeks and shades our eyes." Yet this social defense mechanism was more than simply a public display of racial subterfuge; for some, it united with Christian teachings on how one might emulate Jesus through modeling his demeanor. Many African American Christians began to confuse their forced posture of humility and subservience with living "just like Jesus." What had once been a survival tactic became a perceived moral posture. And according to Fullinwider, a racial strategy became a racial stereotype—so much so that when some African Americans gained more social independence, they still adhered to this ideal of the Christ-like Negro. For many in rural southern America, docility made a person holy and humble submission to the status quo was a mark of faith.

This racial stereotype of the faithful and humble black Christian continued to resonate well into the twentieth century. For the most part, the pronouncements that African American clergy made about the social role and state of the race were consistent with those of white supremacist America. Those who spoke forcefully and protested injustice in America were radicals in the eyes of many black congregations. And those who quietly submitted to dominance were "good and faithful servants." This is not to say that blacks and whites perceived the actions of black Christians on the same terms. While southern whites had a vested interest in a racial caste system, some blacks interpreted their submission as an expression of spiritual and moral exceptionalism. Humility and holiness were interchangeable and worn as a proud garment of self-esteem. Many rural black southerners thus saw themselves as the "true Christians" or a "righteous remnant" in relation to hypocritical whites. Yet despite the motivating belief, the enacted behavior led to the same conclusion, African American submission to white domination. As James Baldwin once described his Holiness preacher father, "He was defeated long before he died because, at the bottom of his heart, he really believed what white people said about him. This is one of the reasons he was so holy."[20]

Many rural African American clergy idealized American society insofar as they accepted white supremacist pronouncements concerning black life. Black preachers in the South commonly denounced African "savagery" while embracing American "civility." This was, in part, a result of northern missionary societies that treated the South as their foreign mission field during the Reconstruction era. Southern black Christians unwittingly embraced a Social Darwinist conception of humanity wrapped inside biblical language. It was the charge of all black Christians to live up to Victorian standards of decorum and morality and European prescriptions of aesthetic taste, knowledge, and beauty.

This latter belief was held even by African Americans who considered themselves racially progressive. When Bishop Daniel Alexander Payne of the African Methodist Episcopal (A.M.E.) Church came to minister in the South, he described recently emancipated worshippers as "primitive, barbaric and heathenish."[21] Rosa Young, an African American educator in Alabama, demonstrated a similar acceptance of black cultural inferiority in a 1915 fundraising letter. Young contacted the Board of Colored Missions of the Lutheran Church to solicit funds for her school in rural Alabama, but her noble aims were undermined by her condescending means. The letter described black children as "dull and backward" and mocked their religious customs by satirizing a Christmas pageant where children sang, "With a joy of molasses and a pan of biscuits in my hand, I'll sop my way to the Promise Land." Young then genuflected to her potential white benefactor with the remark that "such recitations were given on the solemn occasion of the commemoration of the birth of Jesus, the Savior of the world. Gross darkness covered the people."[22]

From a panoramic perspective, this theologically white supremacist and accommodationist view is consistent with the social philosophy of the most influential African American leader at the turn of the twentieth century, Booker T. Washington. Though not a cleric, Washington preached a message of industrial education, economic enterprise, and skillful accommodation to racial and social inequality through Tuskegee, the normal training institution that he founded in 1881.His message that "it is at the bottom of life that we must begin, not at the top," was embraced by many black Christian clergymen as the gospel truth. Thus a significant portion of southern evangelical preachers affirmed that it was the responsibility of black people to inculcate and nurture American "Christian" virtues—virtues that could largely be reduced to whites' idealizing vision of innocence and mythical conception of the race's "progress." This rationale of Negro inferiority, baptized in the waters of sublime white benevolence, surely had the potential to create regenerated beings whose "saved souls" were at war with their own racial identity. Hence, the prayer "Wash me Lord, white as snow" can be read as a heartfelt plea of one who seeks both solace and status in a white-dominated society; more than a prayer, it was, for many, a pathology.

Moreover, while black congregations might ideally be regarded as independent under the exclusive control of African Americans, in southern rural areas like Ridgeland, where Rev. Ike was raised, black control over churches was often restricted by complex systems of white patronage. Adherence to a theological praxis that affirmed black guilt and inferiority and upheld white innocence and benevolence afforded material benefits for black ministers. It was common practice in the rural South for black ministers to engage in a "gift" exchange with influential whites.[23]

Through a hierarchical relationship that codified cultural patterns, black congregations would often receive building materials, financial resources, and other forms of social capital from the white benefactors that Zora Neale Hurston called "Negrotarians."[24] In turn, benevolent whites were able to uphold their own supremacist status while absolving themselves of culpability through this self-interested sympathy.

Sociologist Harry Richardson's interviews with 105 African American rural pastors in 1944 offered insight into such a system. His findings from surveying four southern counties in Alabama, South Carolina, Arkansas, and Virginia demonstrate some general cultural patterns of black ministerial attitudes in response to racial oppression. When asked about the race problem in their respective communities, 79 percent of ministers described race relations as good and 20 percent as fair, and only one minister regarded conditions as bad. To be sure, the researcher was asking how race relations were now compared to what they used to be and was considering only violence and severe mistreatment. And several ministers qualified their use of the term *good* with phrases like "good considering." Nonetheless, even if one takes into account such qualifications or acknowledges that fear of retribution certainly informed the survey responses of some clergymen, respondents may well have been deliberately accepting the status quo as a means of ameliorating otherwise dire racial and economic conditions.[25] In terms of race relations in rural areas, black Christians could better go along if they could get along with their white Christian neighbors.

Richardson's survey findings also clearly spell out the white patronage system in place for black congregations. Ninety-four percent of respondents professed to have friendly and cooperative relations with white clergy. In nearly every instance, the primary form of cooperation was financial contributions to the black church by white congregations. In a handful of cases, white clergy preached from the pulpit of a rural black church, though this action was never reciprocated. And even fewer black clergymen reported an invitation from the white congregation for black members to participate in any form in the white worship service. In other words, the principal form of "racial cooperation" that took place between black and white rural congregations was cash gifts to the former from the latter.[26]

This was the culture in which young Frederick, as the son of a Baptist pastor in rural South Carolina in the 1930s and 1940s, began to develop his own sense of the divine and of ecclesial life. Economic uplift in lieu of social equality and civil rights was theologically sanctioned. And white civility and nobility were idealized and mythologized over and against black inferiority and ineptitude. Rev. Ike's description of his father reveals interesting connections to this ethos of rural black evangelical culture. He now recalls his father as someone who was "well respected by everybody, black and white alike." This respect, according to Rev. Ike, had to do with the fact that the elder Rev. Eikerenkoetter "never pushed, he never shoved, he would have never been a Martin Luther King." Yet Rev. Ike fondly describes his father as a "little Donald Trump," since he reportedly was self-employed, stressed economic advancement, and owned rental properties in Ridgeland—properties that Rev. Ike now reveals his father would rent only to whites.[27] Though the rules of Jim Crow force one to question Rev. Ike's memory that it was actually possible for the elder Eikerenkoetter to economically operate above the color line, the recasting of the narrative remains instructive. An emphasis on economic advancement over social protest was regarded as the foremost strategy for racial uplift.

As a final caveat, it is vital to distinguish rural black evangelicalism in the South, with its opposition to social protest, from urban black evangelicalism in the same region, which developed a tradition of resistance to oppression. It was largely the urban congregations of the South that participated in the civil rights movement of the 1950s and 1960s.[28] Though categorized as black mainline congregations, churches like Wheat Street and Ebenezer Baptist of Atlanta, Sixteenth Street Baptist in Birmingham, and First Baptist Church in Montgomery were distinctively different in constitution and orientation from the Baptist church in Ridgeland where the elder Eikerenkoetter served as pastor. Of course, this is not to essentialize congregations in southern urban centers as paragons of moral courage and counterhegemonic resistance. Many parishioners of "silk-stocking" congregations had little interest in engaging in civil rights demonstrations, and congregations like Montgomery's Dexter Avenue Baptist Church, which rejected the protest activity of its pastor Vernon Johns, or, for that matter, other congregations in the city of Montgomery whose pastors were controlled by the "city fathers" belie any generalized claim. But of the congregations that did choose to openly engage in struggles against white supremacy, the vast majority were in urban areas. Therefore, it is reasonable to assert that southern rural evangelicalism is more consistent with conversionist forms of black Christian practice like the Pentecostal-Holiness tradition than with the black mainline denominations found in urban centers. The former were concerned with personal piety and typically better at attracting and maintaining a sustained following, while the latter were more likely to participate in social protests aimed at reforming the racially unjust practices of the larger society.[29] Noting the commensurability of southern rural evangelicalism and conversionist strands of black religion helps us to make sense of how the fourteen-year-old Frederick Eikerenkoetter could move back and forth between the Bibleway Baptist Church and the Pentecostal congregation that he began pastoring at fifteen.

Oral Roberts and the Post–World War II Healing Revivals

Just as black evangelicalism cannot be discussed apart from its white counterpart, the Pentecostal influence on Rev. Ike must be assessed in light of the emerging national face of Pentecostalism in the post–World War II era. At the very moment Rev. Ike assumed the Pentecostal pulpit in the segregated pocket of apartheid known as Ridgeland, the Pentecostal movement, and the healing revivals that it inspired, were spreading rapidly in the larger society. Gradually moving away from the multiracial, African-influenced Pentecostalism of the first half of the twentieth century, a new cadre of healing revivalists, particularly because of their use of multiple forms of mass media, were being propelled into national prominence and were altering the landscape of Pentecostalism in the second half of the twentieth century. This Pentecostal healing revivalism is the second cultural movement that informed Rev. Ike and his ministry.[30]

Dating back to Charles G. Finney and the Great Awakening revivals, forms of ecstatic Christianity with an emphasis on receiving the gift of the Holy Spirit played a central role among the socially marginalized in America.[31] Tied to the Holiness movement, the Pentecostal movement is grounded in the Wesleyan-Arminian tradition, a precursor to Methodism, and Africanist influences such as the ring shout, conjuring, and spirit possession.[32] Pentecostalism, the most famous manifestation of the Holiness movement in the twentieth century, emerged at the very outset of the century with the competing, racialized partnership of Charles Parham and William Seymour. The major tenet of the Pentecostal faith is that conversion experience—private and public confession of the lordship of Jesus Christ that leads to salvation—is followed by ongoing experiential encounters with God. After conversion, participants are to seek the "second baptism," also referred to as Spirit baptism, which is accompanied by various signs and wonders, the most important being glossolalia, or speaking in tongues.[33] In addition to the second baptism of the Holy Spirit and its evidence of glossolalia, Pentecostalism promotes such spiritual gifts as wisdom, knowledge, faith, miracles, and healings that are viewed as subsequent acts of grace.[34] The belief in this latter gift of healing, as set forth in James 5 and 1 Corinthians 12:8–9, is the doctrinal support for the practice of healing revivalism.[35]

In the first quarter of the twentieth century several healing evangelists emerged in America. There was an apparent shift from the belief that the gift of healing was available to all to an emphasis on the gifted individual's ability to effect healing in others. Persons such as Alexander Dowie, Smith Wigglesworth, E. W. Kenyon, and F. F. Bosworth attained relative levels of prominence. By the late 1920s, largely because of the new medium of radio broadcast, healing evangelists such as Aimee Semple McPherson and her Foursquare Gospel Church in Los Angeles were becoming staples in American popular culture.

Despite this increased fame, for a brief period healing revivalism fizzled in the 1930s. Factors such as the Great Depression and denominational infighting among competing Pentecostal movements and organizations can be credited for the minimal success of independent revivalists during this decade. Nonetheless, along with American economic prosperity, the seeds of healing revival blossomed immediately following the Second World War.[36] The most famous personality associated with this period and movement, someone whom Rev. Ike credits as a great influence in his life, is the Reverend Granville Oral Roberts.

Born in 1918, the son of a poor Pentecostal preacher in Oklahoma, the young Roberts began preaching at the age of seventeen. His call to preach was allegedly intertwined with his own miraculous healing from tuberculosis.[37] For twelve years the young minister toured preaching revivals and pastored a few Pentecostal congregations throughout the South and Midwest, but in 1947 Oral resigned from pastoral ministry to dedicate himself full time to independent revival ministry. Aware of the perceived successes and failures of contemporary evangelists with healing ministries—William Branham, Gordon Lindsay, Jack Coe, and T. L. Osborne—Roberts was convinced that independent ministry would free his vision from congregational control and denominational accountability, both of which restricted the creative capacity and financial profitability of these new ecclesiastical entrepreneurs.[38]

Roberts established Healing Waters, Inc. (renamed Oral Roberts Evangelistic Association, Inc. in 1957) as a nonprofit ministry headquartered in Tulsa, Oklahoma. Beyond Roberts's charismatic appeal, the exponential growth and influence of the ministry can be attributed to his ability to transcend the local church via his citywide crusades, his ingenious use of the mass media, and his creative fundraising techniques.

Roberts's biographer David Edwin Harrell describes his citywide healing crusades as the heartbeat of the ministry.[39] With his traveling five-thousand-person tent, the sheer magnitude of the crusades created a media buzz around the revivalist throughout the country. Oral Roberts never had particularly good relations with denominational leaders, but he was a master of cultivating relationships with local pastors. Six months prior to a crusade, his assistants would travel to a particular city and negotiate arrangements with local pastors. In exchange for encouraging parishioners to attend crusades and acquiring local assistance for the event such as tent construction and ushering, they were granted the honor of sitting on the platform with Oral Roberts during the crusade. The gesture of allowing local ministers to dine with him at a ministers' banquet, coupled with monetary gifts to these local ministries that typically struggled financially, endeared pastors to Roberts in extraordinary ways. The fostering of such relationships, in which Oral Roberts became a "pastor to pastors," afforded Roberts a symbolic bishop status among local clergy. In turn, he cultivated a large following composed of the combined members of local congregations.[40]

After the sermonic address and invitational call, hundreds of persons could pass across the platform to receive a touch from Roberts. These "prayer lines" were far from spontaneous. Potential attendees were informed either by local sponsors or by Roberts's various publications that an afternoon "faith-building service" prior to the evening crusade was required of all who desired healing. Persons filled out a card that included a release form stating that participation in the healing line did not guarantee healing and granting the Roberts organization the rights to publish the results of the healing. The prayer cards were color coded to determine the order in which ushers would organize persons in line. The seriously ill were granted white cards and placed in a separate area referred to as the invalid room. Critics believed the card system was a means to prescreen the ill while partitioning the visibly ill away from spectators and media.[41] Whether this claim is true or not, it did not deter a critical mass of people who believed Roberts possessed healing powers in the palm of his hand. The prayer lines became the most famous aspect, and some would say the greatest crowd draw, of the early healing crusades.

But if the crusades were the heartbeat of Roberts's ministry, the *Healing Waters* radio and television broadcasts were its oxygen. The name *Healing Waters* was derived from the story of Jesus offering healing at the pool of Bethesda in the fifth chapter of John's Gospel. No stranger to the religious airwaves, Roberts began dabbling in radio while pastoring congregations in the early 1940s. In 1947, along with the crusades and magazine publication, he began to perfect what would be the nationally syndicated *Healing Waters* broadcast. Initially Roberts's program was broadcast only in parts of Oklahoma and Durham, North Carolina, but to expand his influence Roberts instituted the "partners for deliverance" system. This system was twofold. First, the ministry solicited individuals or congregations throughout the country to serve as initial radio sponsors until local listening audiences would come to support the broadcasts. The ministry's offer to patrons was "If you can see your local radio station, secure time on Sunday between 8:00 and 9:00 A.M. or 12:00 to 2:00 P.M. and if you are willing to pay for the station time only for the first three months, then we will sign the contract for one year and trust that others will hear the program and will contribute regularly to its support so we may remain on station indefinitely."[42] Roberts utilized the citywide crusades to enlist financial partners. Small brown envelopes were distributed at crusades preprinted with "I will pledge $10 a month to help you get on the radio."[43] In a period of four years (1949–53) the radio network expanded from around twenty stations to two hundred stations across the country. Because of their success and magnitude, Roberts was able to sign a contract with the American Broadcasting Company that instantly doubled the number of stations carrying the broadcast.[44]

At the outset, largely following the format of Billy Graham, Roberts purchased thirty-minute time slots and recorded his show inside a television studio. Television producers wanted Oral to simply enter a studio and act out his part of the tent revival crusades without an audience or the energy of the crowd. But finding this virtually impossible, Roberts inverted the formula, bringing the television cameras to the tent.[45] The success spurred exponential growth that resulted in significant changes to the form and function of Roberts's ministry. These changes, of which I identify three, were reflected in Rev. Ike's ministry as well as countless others since.

First, the format of the crusades altered to adjust to television. For instance, there was a newfound emphasis upon order in the crusades. The sense of frenzy popularly associated with Pentecostal style camp meetings was lost in the transition. Roberts discouraged speaking in tongues and other spontaneous, ecstatic expressions of worship in attempts to heighten his religious respectability and aesthetic appeal. Certainly his sense of the dramatic and performative remained consistent. But aside from an occasional "amen" or hand clap, congregants were to remain participant-observers. It was not uncommon for ushers to remove persons deemed "out of order," as nothing was to detract from or disturb Oral Roberts, the main performer.[46] The people were his props, and it was his prerogative to decide how they would be used.

This was especially clear in the reconfiguring of the healing lines. Gone was the assembly line approach; Roberts began singling out attendees and providing them with special, individualized attention. His assistants would usher persons to the front of the stage or platform and announce to the crowd their condition. Televised footage shows Roberts compassionately conversing with believers about their condition and methodically laying hands on them while praying fervently; apparent miraculous healings took place on the spot. Persons witnessing this on television flocked to healing crusades seeking this same experience from the man with the divine healing touch. But because of time constraints on the crusades that were filmed for television, only a handful of cards were selected for or by Roberts. The television cameras kept the vast majority of crusade attendees who believed in the healing power of Roberts's touch from obtaining access to him.[47]

In response to expressed disillusionment from many revival attendees, the organization began to downplay what had once been the major draw of the crusade—the healing power of Roberts's hands as a point of contact. In his magazine and broadcasts, Roberts started to dissuade persons from participating in the line by saying such things as "You can be healed in the audience before I touch you—or if I never touch you. If you touch God by your faith, you may be healed wherever you are."[48]

This example speaks to the ways television and television producers mediated the crusade experience for at-home viewers and adjusted the service for physically present participants. Televised crusades were prerecorded, and extensive preproduction editing took place prior to broadcast. As a result of postservice editing, Roberts was able to broadcast the more favorable cases and events. What is more, Roberts's organization used P. T. Barnum–like creativity and Hollywood production techniques to make the seemingly impossible instantly possible. Anything that was missing in the live performance could be generated for television audiences. Defending his organization's postservice editing tactics, Roberts stated, "I was trying to establish in the minds of people the possibility that a healing can take place in this century. And that's why that [sic] I brought people who were [sic]. Now I admit there are disadvantages to this, but I had to weigh the advantages over the disadvantages and think of the viewer and his need."[49]

Finally, to meet the exorbitant production costs of television, Roberts's fundraising techniques became ever more creative. The case can be made that creative fundraising often took precedence over or drastically transformed Roberts's theological commitments. For example, to subsidize the initial television pilots Roberts instituted an expanded financial partnership program referred to as the "Blessing Pact"—not to be confused with Rev. Ike's later "Blessing Plan." Persons were encouraged to send in money to the ministry according to their faith, and Roberts would pray for its tenfold return. Drawing on metaphors of seed time and harvest, Roberts professed that making financial offerings was like sowing seeds: according to the natural order of God's law, believers would reap materially in tenfold proportion to what they had sown materially by faith.[50] This notion at the heart of the Blessing Pact proved quite successful for the Roberts organization and remains a central component of their fundraising and theological orientation. Milmon Harrison shows that what began as a fundraising strategy for Roberts is now a salient theological principle for the contemporary Word of Faith movement.[51]

It is clear that Roberts's ministry served as the prototype not only for Rev. Ike but for a whole expanding class of revivalists in the twentieth century. In severing ties with official denominations, establishing radio and television ministries, and even developing biblical training schools, Roberts remains a source of envy, attraction, and emulation. In the 1950s, his ministry presciently drew the outlines of what would be the future of Pentecostal healing revivalism—television would outshine radio, the message of financial prosperity would supplant the promise of divine healing, and swank hotel conferences would replace dusty-tent revivals. As I argue in the next chapter, the neo-Pentecostal perspective was brought into being.

Oral Roberts and his brand of healing revivalism had a profound influence on Rev. Ike. From when he was a young man in Ridgeland,

South Carolina, tuning in to the *Healing Waters* radio broadcast, to when he was a Boston storefront pastor attending Oral Roberts and A. A. Allen healing crusades, Rev. Ike saturated himself in this tradition and embraced its choreographed sensationalism. According to his own testimony, he became quite proficient in the healing crusade technique. Combining this with the communication patterns of the black sermonic tradition, in which language is a shared commodity that preachers can freely borrow from each other, Rev. Ike's ministry shows both Oral Roberts's indelible influence and Rev. Ike's own creative genius.

For example, in sharing the moment when he became cognitively and intuitively aware of the "God potential" within himself, Rev. Ike elaborates on his father's supposed wealth and respect in Ridgeland. The son's hierophanous moment is intertwined with the father's purchase of a new car. The elder Eikerenkoetter brought home a "1940 Chevrolet off the showroom floor" so he could pick up Ike and his mother to drive them around town. Ike now recalls "the pride I felt in my heart that day in that brand new green Chevrolet." He believes that it was through this experience that he opened himself to the opportunity that the God in him wanted him to have more, do more, and be more.[52] However, this testimony is very similar to an experience of Oral Roberts recorded in his biography—a story that Oral often recounted on his radio and television broadcasts. While economically struggling as a pastor in Enid, Oklahoma, in the early 1940s, Roberts came across 3 John 2, which reads, "I wish above all things that thou mayest prosper and be in health, even as thy soul prospereth." Then, in an unrelated turn of events, Roberts was approached by a neighbor, Mr. Gustavus, who owned a Buick dealership. Noting the condition of Roberts's car, Gustavus worked out a deal that enabled Roberts to acquire a brand-new one. Roberts's biographer records that after driving to Detroit to acquire the automobile, "they [Oral and Evelyn Roberts] drove back to Enid in their brand new . . . long, green, slick, Buick." According to Roberts, the "new car became a symbol to me of what a man could do if he would believe God." Then Roberts credits his neighbor Gustavus with encouraging him to move his ministry beyond the confines of the local congregation: "Son, the message you are preaching is too big for one town. The world is waiting to hear it. . . . Someday, Oral, you'll be the biggest man for God this country has ever known."[53] Beyond the obvious similarities, there is an underlying theme in Rev. Ike's appropriation of this story. The story conflates luxury goods, the Spirit of God, and sense of divine call in one unified narrative, a narrative that has become a leitmotif in contemporary African American religious broadcasting.

The Black Spiritual Movement

The third cultural influence on Rev. Ike is associated with the proliferation of widely varying forms of black religious expression in the first half of the twentieth century, particularly in cities. In conjunction with the mass exodus northward, as African Americans were "transformed from an agrarian peasantry into a diversified urban proletariat," they encountered syncretized forms of religious expression that greatly altered and diversified black religiosity.[54] As I have already alluded, the young Rev. Eikerenkoetter was not exempt.

This upsurge of diverse religious phenomena loosened the stronghold that black mainline denominations maintained upon the black community. Many established congregations in the North, if they accepted rural and lower-class blacks at all, believed it their role to integrate new migrants into northern society. Often southern transplants felt uncomfortable with such congregations, not to mention the second-class status they were accorded there. Persons who had once held leadership positions such as deacon or even reverend in the South were now considered spiritual neophytes and indoctrinated into a foreign value system and a bourgeois religious sensibility. In response, in urban centers across the country, southern blacks began joining with like-minded friends and family members to establish their own religious communities. Referred to as storefronts because of the untraditional rented spaces that served as their meeting places, these churches organized their own congregations, appointed independent leadership, and, in many cases, established their own religious rituals and belief systems.

Storefront churches were of varying kinds and denominations—Baptist, Methodist, Pentecostal, Holiness—but were markedly different from the traditional black mainline congregations in the North. Sociologist J. A. Harrison believes that the storefront church phenomenon may be seen as a southern revitalization movement. It was a conscious effort on the part of African Americans in a strange land to recreate their rural religious behavior in an urban environment.[55] But some feel this theory does not adequately articulate the motivations driving the phenomenon. Jill Watts points out in her study of Father Divine that if southern blacks had merely wished to recreate their past religious experience they would have populated the churches of the traditional denominations located in the poorer neighborhoods. Thus she, like E. Franklin Frazier before her, claims that the establishment of storefront churches was not just about recreating the past; rather, persons found the freedom within storefront congregations to construct a new identity that would enable them to forge into the future.[56]

Another popular misconception of storefront churches is that they were principally the domain of the lower classes. The Great Migration did lead to occupational differentiation and thus economic stratification within the black community, and, as in the society at large, blacks ranked themselves and each other according to social status. This does not mean, however, that the religious stratification within the black community followed a descending hierarchy in which white mainline denominations (Episcopal, Presbyterian, and Lutheran) were at the top, established black mainline denominations (Baptist and A.M.E.) in the middle, and a collection of southern transplant storefronts of varying affiliations at the bottom. Wallace Best's study of black Chicago undercuts the assertion that the storefront movement was solely the religious domain of ghetto dwellers. As we will see shortly, several prominent storefront congregations in major urban areas were "large, wealthy and well attended" by people of all classes.[57] And while it is impossible to reduce the storefront movement to a single religious persuasion, one form of African American religion was especially likely to find dynamic expression within the storefront movement and to attract an economic cross section of African Americans: the black Spiritual movement.

The black Spiritual movement is a religious movement that derives from a cross-pollination of esoteric belief systems such as New Thought and Christian Science as well as forms of black Pentecostalism, Voodooism, and Hoodooism. These congregations exhibit many of the attributes of African American Protestant expressions but place particular emphasis on the manipulation of the physical world through magico-religious rituals and psychic phenomena.[58] Little is known concerning the origins of the black Spiritual movement. Developing alongside white Spiritualist churches at the dawn of the twentieth century, predominantly black Spiritual churches were originally identified in locales as disparate as Chicago and New Orleans, but they spread to many cities throughout the North and South during the 1920s and 1930s.[59] And according to Mays and Nicholson's original sampling, 85 percent of black Spiritual congregations were located in storefront complexes.

Anthropologist Hans Baer characterizes and distinguishes the black Spiritual movement as highly syncretistic—not in the sense that it has fallen away from a particular "orthodox" Christian tradition but in the sense that it draws on multiple religious orientations and practices ranging from Islam, Judaism, and Catholicism to astrology.[60] Because of the magico-religious dimensions of the movement and its use of sacred objects to tap into the spirit world, including but not limited to the holding of séances, negative stereotypes have attached to black Spiritual congregations. Often their practices have been pejoratively pigeonholed as witchcraft or black magic. But research has revealed that the dynamism and vibrancy of the Spiritual faith have had an impact even on surrounding houses of worship that do not describe themselves as Spiritual.

Social historian Allan Spear's assessment of black congregations in urban Chicago noted that many congregations that belonged to traditional mainline denominations adopted popular Pentecostal and Holiness practices. For instance, several churches that self-identified as Baptist had a demonstrative worship style more typical of Pentecostal and Holiness groups.[61] Moreover, such practices as faith healing, conjuring, and even root-working that were common in black Spiritual congregations could sometimes be found in other congregations as well. The adaptability of black Spiritual congregations proved both attractive to participants and instructive for competing congregations. In the competitive religious marketplace that the Great Migration produced, this movement was all too aware that it was important to adjust to the structural, cultural, and psychological conditions of black urban life. The religious practices of surrounding churches, the socioeconomic position of the membership, and the charisma and religious sensibility of the pastor were all factors that black Spiritual congregations seemed overtly willing to take into consideration. Joseph Washington believes that this utilitarian approach to religion was part of the movement's attraction. In his description of its syncretism he states, "Magical amulets in the form of charms or amulets were used to guard against any possible evil or attain some cherished good. Spiritualists combined the instinct of voodooism with Roman Catholic holy objects; Baptist and Methodist hymns were borrowed but not their fever-pitched preaching; their spiritual healing was taken over from the Holiness, Pentecostal groups, as well as their ritual of jubilant worship through swinging gospel tunes driven by the beat of secular rhythm and blues."[62] Like Rev. Ike during his faith-healing days in Boston, Spiritual churches were willing to adjust and adapt their practices to stay attuned to the popular trends and desires of the community and potential congregants.

An additional distinguishing characteristic of the black Spiritual movement is its positive orientation to the world. Unlike the mainline black denominations or Pentecostal and Holiness groups, Spiritual leaders tend to reject strident puritanical morality and aesthetic sensibilities and to instead embrace a joie de vivre. The traditional prohibitions against drinking, smoking, dancing, and premarital sex are not present in the black Spiritual church. This is not to imply that any of the above would ordinarily be encouraged. Rather, topics that are generally taboo among black church people, like unwed pregnancy, adultery, or homosexuality, are met with trite responses or silence. The objects of human desires stemming from the cultural context of black people in cities—romance, financial success, physical healing, even a win from playing the numbers—are not shunned according to purist ideals but considered God-ordained blessings. Though acerbic in his characterization of Spiritual leaders as "fakers and pikers who ignored the social conditions," Joseph Washington was accurate in his assertion that Spiritual religion has all of the trappings of a traditional mainline denomination without its negativism.[63]

The First Church of Deliverance, a black Spiritual congregation organized by Father Clarence Cobb, typifies this reality. What began as a small storefront in Chicago expanded into an ecclesial powerhouse and political force in the city. Best describes the congregation's pastor as a man who "was known to smoke the finest cigars, drive a 'flashy car,' and wear clothes of the 'latest cut.'"[64] And Father Cobb's sexual orientation was an unspoken but badly kept secret among the First Church of Deliverance congregation. His annual church-sponsored vacations with his male secretary did not appear to shake the belief of those who were committed to his spiritual qualities as long as what was implicitly understood was never made overt. According to Best, the laissez-faire nature of black urban culture during the early years of the migration allowed the freedom and creativity that Father Cobb and other unconventional Spiritual leaders needed to rise to prominence.[65]

For all these reasons, the Spiritual tradition fits well into the thaumaturgic category of black religious life. Like the established mainline denominations, thaumaturgic congregations believe that society is inherently good; thus they embrace the cultural patterns, value systems, and belief orientations of the larger society. But unlike the more progressive urban mainline denominations, thaumaturgic congregations do not seek reform via protest from within or against systems of injustice. Rather, while seeking to embrace the good life, they believe that they can bypass society's traditional means of social advancement by participating in certain magico-religious ritual behaviors such as mind science, positive confession, and other forms of divination. Thaumaturgics typically hold individuals responsible for their present well-being or lack thereof.[66] Though conceptually flawed in terms of an individual's relationship to social and economic systems, the black Spiritual movement does serve as a means for persons to positively think their way out of adverse situations.

Another premier personality of the black Spiritual movement was Prophet James F. Jones. The Alabama native, who preferred the official title "His Holiness the Rt. Rev. Dr. James F. Jones, D.D., Universal Dominion Ruler, Internationally Known as Prophet Jones," received national acclaim in the 1940s and 1950s because of his flamboyant and recrementitious ministry. Jones came to Detroit to work as a missionary for a southern-based Pentecostal fellowship known as the Triumph the Church and Kingdom of God in Christ. From the moment of his arrival in the Motor City, Jones revealed a flair for the dramatic and an ability to attract media attention. He also wasted little time getting his message on the religious airwaves. It was a blend of personal prosperity, hyperbolic political prophecies, and varying forms of psychic healing and divination. By 1940, around the same time as many religious broadcasters were being driven off the airwaves by antipropaganda laws, Jones began broadcasting over a Canadian radio station whose signal spanned several Midwestern states. As his reputation, radio presence, and relationship with the media grew, his congregation increased into the thousands. He soon severed his ministry and megachurch congregation from his previous Pentecostal affiliation and organized the Universal Triumph, the Dominion of God, Inc.[67]

The pomp of Jones's ministerial title was consistent with the monarchical model of his ministry. His congregation, members of which he referred to as "Ladies," "Lords," "Princes," and "Princesses," worshiped at the old Oriole Theatre, a former movie house in the city. Jones spent $300,000 to renovate the facility, which included plush seating for three thousand people, gold ornamentation throughout the building, and a $5,300 gold chair in the pulpit, an attempt to replicate King Solomon's throne. The former movie marquee in front of the building read, "Universal Triumph, The Dominion of God, Prophet Jones Dominion Ruler," while large portraits of the prophet hung framed outside the building in the spaces once occupied by movie posters. Jones led worship up to four or five times a week, but the main service was on Sunday night at 10:00 p.m. Holding worship at such an unconventional hour allowed his congregation—10 percent of whom were white—to remain affiliated with their own, often more traditional, congregations throughout the city.

Whether Jones was a healer or not, his place in popular culture in the 1950s is indisputable. This self-proclaimed seer and radio evangelist was favorably featured in such publications as *Ebony, Time, Life, Newsweek,* and the *Saturday Evening Post.* The only thing that rivaled Jones's burgeoning popularity was his vast wealth, though many would credit the latter with augmenting the former. It is an understatement to say Prophet Jones lived like a millionaire. In a way that stereotypically underscored his sexual ambiguity to observers, Prophet Jones resided with his mother, who was known as Grace Rev. Lady Catherine Jones, and his private secretary and longtime partner, James Walton, in a three-story, fifty-four-room mansion. Journalists' reported that the house was furnished with a "$7,000 grand piano, $8,000 worth of silver, a stained glass window installed at a cost of $1,200 and rooms of expensive furniture."[68] Prophet Jones is also said to have had "12 servants, five Cadillacs, each with its own chauffeur, a wardrobe of 400 suits, a white mink coat, jewelry and thousands of dollars worth of perfumes."[69] The mink coat, which Jones had received as a gift from two Chicago schoolteachers who said that Jones healed their mother, was stated to have been worth $13,500 in 1953. This piece of the Prophet's attire inspired the *Saturday Evening Post* journalist to headline Prophet Jones as the "Messiah in Mink."[70]

But Prophet Jones was not all about mansions and minks. During the Truman-Eisenhower years he attained political acknowledgment, if not respect, on the local and national levels. Like Elder Michaux, Prophet Jones actively ingratiated himself with elected officials through his own brand of creative spiritual fawning and obsequious support. Presenting himself as a devout American patriot, he opened his radio broadcasts with the national anthem and pledge of allegiance. During World War II his congregation sold twelve thousand dollars' worth of war bonds, and many of his on-air political prophecies were nothing more than nationalist propaganda of the Cold War era.[71] After prophesying that General Dwight Eisenhower would win the 1952 presidential election, Prophet Jones received an invitation to the inauguration. His perceived position as a prophet to the white power structure only added to his allure and mystique among a large number of African Americans. The fact that publications such as *Life* and *Saturday Evening Post* would cover Prophet Jones and that he would receive an invitation to the White House served as a source of divine validation among his members that God had ordained and anointed Prophet Jones's ministry.

To be sure, Jones's meteoric rise to prominence ended with an equally public and media-worthy fall. His ever-increasing publicity in print, radio, and television angered many African Americans. His ostentatious dress, bravado, and quixotic theology undercut increasing efforts to put a religiously sober and politically respectable face on African Americans at the dawn of the civil rights era. His cross-town radio rival C. L. Franklin said that Jones was "a setback of hundreds of years to the integration of all races who are at this time seeking democratic as well as Spiritual brotherhood."[72]

But attacks from fellow African Americans were the least of Prophet Jones's concerns. In a foreshadowing of the prominent sex scandals of later televangelists like Jimmy Swaggart, Jim Bakker, and Ted Haggard, Jones was jailed in 1956 on a morals complaint and charged with gross indecency. The charges stemmed from an undercover police officer's allegation that Prophet Jones had attempted to perform fellatio on him. A media circus ensued. Jones was eventually acquitted, since the police officer's participation in the act rendered it a case of induced entrapment, but the public spectacle hampered his ability to make a successful comeback. His homosexuality, which, like that of Clarence Cobb, had been implicitly understood and accepted by followers, became harder to accept when unveiled in graphic detail as a result of the trial and sensationalized media coverage.

Tim Retzloff, who researches queer life in post–World War II Michigan, argues that the very thing that was a part of Prophet Jones's allure, his gender-ambiguous aesthetic, eventually became his downfall. Retzloff locates Jones in the tradition of the "freakish man," whom he describes as "a flamboyant, sissified entertainer" whose roots go back to the African American vaudevillian era. For the first half of the twentieth century, according to Retzloff, the "freakish man" as entertainer was a prominent part of black working-class culture and was regularly commodified by the predatory and voyeuristic white media. As sacred alternatives to their rock-and-roll contemporary Little Richard, Prophet Jones and Clarence Cobb "destabilized sexual norms and defused sexual tensions among African American men and women caught in the social stresses of migration and urbanization."[73] This "freakish" or effeminate representation of black masculinity, Retzloff argues, was what made Prophet Jones attractive to the white mainstream media. He was nonthreatening, and his persona failed to rub against the American sexual mores that sought to isolate black male heterosexuality from the larger body politic. But as the mid-1950s ushered in the McCarthy era and the image-conscious civil rights movement, the otherwise vibrant and visible aspects of African American gay culture were forced underground as segments of the black community sought to "divorce homosexuality from the African American body" within the popular imagination of the larger society.[74] Thus the public "outing" of Prophet Jones could not have happened at a less opportune time for someone who had built his career, in part, on veiled references to his sexual orientation.

Nonetheless, we cannot deny Prophet Jones's mass acclaim, affluence, and influence on the African American religious landscape in cities. The image of Prophet Jones in 1955 sitting upon his throne, with a gold-handled cane in one hand and a golden goblet in the other, seems to have had an aesthetic impact on a twenty-year-old Rev. Eikerenkoetter. One can add to this the flamboyantly hued suits, the jewelry, and the monarchical posturing before a cohort of male "armor bearers" (guards) and adjutants, as Rev. Ike also embraced the homoerotic posturing that was perceived as giving black men more crossover appeal.

In sum, Rev. Ike stands in the history of African American religious broadcasting as a connectional figure. He links the converging religio-cultural practices of the first half of the twentieth century with the social and technological advances utilized by African Americans in the post–civil rights era. Rev. Ike represents the theological double-consciousness of rural southern evangelicalism, as well as the professionalism and technological savvy of post–World War II healing revivalism. And he embodies the syncretic dimensions of the black Spiritual movement that was nurtured within the black and urban spiritual marketplace of the interwar period. Therefore, Rev. Ike is not only a connectional figure but a pivotal figure. His ministry, as well as the cultural sources that informed his theological and philosophical outlook, are of vital importance for understanding the aesthetic style and ecclesiastical substance of contemporary African American broadcasters. The parade of preachers on TBN, the Word Network, and StreamingFaith.com continue to show Rev. Ike's

3

Standing on the Promises

Diversity and Change within
Contemporary Black
Christian Practices

Anointing fall on me.
Anointing fall on me.
Let the power of the Holy Ghost fall on me.
— "Anointing," in *African American Heritage Hymnal*

The frenzy associated with the experiential and entertainment-oriented dimensions of worship prevalent in today's black megachurches is commonly described as neo-Pentecostalism. C. Eric Lincoln and Lawrence Mamiya used this term to describe what was then considered black mainline denominations' newfound emphasis on experiencing the Holy Spirit in worship. Neo-Pentecostalism, for Lincoln and Mamiya, served as a bridge connecting the experiential worship practices of traditional Pentecostals and the more middle-class mainline emphasis on education and social activism. But when Lincoln and Mamiya employed *neo-Pentecostalism* as a descriptive category to describe forces of change within the A.M.E. Church, they were admittedly unclear about the extent of its influence on black Christian practices. They knew neo-Pentecostalism posed a real challenge for the black church but were unaware of its radical transforming power throughout the 1990s. The influence of this experiential form of religious expression over the past twenty years has proven long and lasting. Neo-Pentecostalism has saturated varying ecclesial traditions in ways that have accentuated the postdenominational qualities of black Christian life.

Despite this, I feel it necessary to more accurately qualify *neo-Pentecostalism* as a descriptive term. Its analytic usefulness has been over-extended. The prevalence of ecstatic exuberance as a worship style and the renewed emphasis on spiritual gifts have overshadowed other salient characteristics that distinguish the different black televangelists. Let us remember that Lincoln and Mamiya defined neo-Pentecostalism in the A.M.E. Church as a "combination of deep Pentecostal spiritual piety and the A.M.E. tradition of involvement in progressive politics and political activism."[1] Neo-Pentecostalism was thus a category that combined an exuberant worship style with progressive political ideology or involvement. We should not, however, assume that these two characteristics of churches are necessarily found together. Most recent scholars of African American religious broadcasting and megachurches have simply labeled as neo-Pentecostal any ministry that has a charismatic leader or meets in a megachurch. But as Cheryl Townsend Gilkes contends, in many ways neo-Pentecostalism is nothing more than a revitalization of traditional black worship.[2] And since a demonstrative, experiential approach to encountering the divine extends across numerous forms of traditional black worship, Christian and otherwise, Gilkes argues that the term, when used in this way, flattens distinctions in ecclesial traditions, theological orientations, and political sensibilities.

For instance, should we expect Bishop T. D. Jakes, who emerges from a Sanctified tradition, to think about God and the role of the church in the same way as Reverend Jamal Harrison-Bryant, the son and grandson of A.M.E. bishops? We may determine that both are Pentecostal inspired in worship (in that they emphasize experiential encounters with the Spirit as continued demonstrations of God's grace), but they are informed by divergent theological orientations, ecclesial traditions, and political sensibilities. The Sanctified tradition is different from the black mainline tradition from which the A.M.E. Church extends. The latter's tradition of social engagement and political empowerment is in stark contrast to the individualist conversion orientation of Sanctified culture.

The same can be said for comparing Bishop Eddie L. Long, a Baptist preacher, and Creflo Dollar, a Word of Faith teacher. Is preaching a message of financial liberation or economic empowerment the same as the prosperity gospel, which affirms that God desires only physical health and abundant material wealth for the faithful? Should we equate the American cultural practice of conspicuous consumption with a theological orientation of divinely promised health and wealth? Though the strategies and aesthetic dimensions of black religious broadcasting may appear uniform to the casual observer—and indeed are very similar—

certain ecclesiastical antecedents structure the numerous variants of the contemporary phenomenon.

Instead of using a single defining term, I posit three dominant ecclesiastical perspectives that make up this contemporary religious phenomenon: the neo-Pentecostal, Charismatic mainline, and Word of Faith perspectives. These are based on the three waves of Pentecostal-influenced Christian expression in the twentieth century as set forth in Stanley Burgess and Eduard van der Maas's introduction to *The International Dictionary of Pentecostal and Charismatic Movements*—the classical Pentecostal, Charismatic, and neo-Charismatic movements.[3]

According to Burgess van der Maas, classical Pentecostalism can be traced back to the multiracial alliance of Holiness fellowships organized in the late nineteenth and early twentieth centuries. This includes but is not limited to the revivalist activities of Charles Parham and William Seymour. Specific to the African American context, this tradition is composed of religious organizations, denominations, and fellowships that arose in the post-Reconstruction era. Some black people associated with what Zora Neale Hurston referred to as the Sanctified Church movement as a means of resisting the acculturating tendencies of the black mainline denominations. The Sanctified Church is composed of the traditional Holiness, Pentecostal, and Apostolic movements. These three movements have their differences. Pentecostals and Apostolics affirm glossolalia as a sign of salvation. The Holiness church does not. The Holiness church emphasizes personal holiness while the other two emphasize spiritual power. And, most notably, the Apostolics reject the doctrine of the Trinity, while the Holiness and Pentecostal churches adhere to it. But as noted in the previous chapter, they have the same origins, and they share an emphasis on the experience of Spirit baptism and ecstatic worship. This is why Holiness, Pentecostal, and Apostolic fellowships are often grouped under the broader category of classical Pentecostalism— affirming a deep appreciation and seeking of a New Testament Pentecost experience.

The Charismatic movement of post–World War II America is defined by an increased interest in spiritual gifts, such as second baptism, glossolalia, and healing, among more affluent mainline congregations in America. This trend flew in the face of deprivation theories that had connected Pentecostalism and other experiential forms of worship with the lower classes. Occurrences such as Oral Robert's temporary move into the United Methodist Church and the embrace of demonstrative expressions of spiritual gifts among select Catholics exemplify the diffusion of charismatic renewal throughout the larger religious matrix in America. This movement has also been called the transdenominational movement of American Christianity, since its emphasis on gifts of the Spirit in private and public worship has sprung up across denominational lines.

Then there is the neo-Charismatic movement, a classification that includes a broad array of independent fellowships and congregations that came into full expression in the final quarter of the twentieth century. The most prominent example of the neo-Charismatic perspective is the Word of Faith movement in America. Though the Word of Faith's professed founder, Kenneth Hagin Sr., began preaching his message of health and wealth as a part of the larger Charismatic movement in the postwar era, it was not until the 1970s that Word of Faith became viewed as a critical and credible force in the Charismatic world. Its adherents emphasize Pentecostal-like encounters with the Holy Spirit in a way that overlaps with the two preceding categories, but neo-Charismatic groups often lack the Pentecostal terminology or denominational structure. Like the syncretic black Spiritual congregations, neo-Charismatics show more creativity and originality in their approaches to engaging life's pragmatic demands and meeting material desires and needs. This movement also exemplifies the postdenominational climate in America, as groups like the Word of Faith movement have no ties to either classical Pentecostal fellowships or traditional denominations.[4]

I find Burgess and van der Maas's categories of classical Pentecostal, Charismatic, and neo-Charismatic movements useful in sorting out the complexities within African American religious broadcasting. My own labels, *neo-Pentecostal, Charismatic mainline,* and *Word of Faith,* represent slight adjustments to these categories to make them more appropriate to the world of black religious broadcasting. And though my aim is to provide a broad classificatory schema, none of these categories should be regarded as mutually exclusive. Instead, the three perspectives should be viewed as partially overlapping circles. What typifies one religious perspective directly may signify another indirectly. But all three groups are in theological and ecclesial conversation as well as culturally homologous with regard to the broader characteristics of the black religious broadcasting.

Neo-Pentecostals

The term *neo-Pentecostal* describes contemporary ministries that origi-nated from one of the recognized classical Pentecostal movements. Inso-far as televangelists' ecclesial affiliation can be traced back to a Pentecos-tal fellowship or denomination such as the Church of God in Christ, they are Pentecostal. But they are neo-Pentecostal if their ecclesial practices unashamedly integrate traditional Pentecostal beliefs with the cultural characteristics of the contemporary moment. This ecclesial and cultural correlation has three interrelated features.

First, neo-Pentecostals have their finger on the pulse of society. Wit-tingly or unwittingly, they blur the line that for Pentecostals tradition-ally separated the sacred and the secular. According to Cheryl Sanders, classical Pentecostalism was based on a dialectical identity that por-trayed believers as being "in the world but not of it." Congregants were self-defined "saints," an ethical designation.[5] This self-definition placed them in opposition to other African American Christians of the mainline denominations who chose not to travel what Pentecostals understood to be the road of biblical purity and holiness. Neo-Pentecostals, in contrast, are "in the world but not of it, unless it is in the name of Jesus." Rather than denounce the devil's media, music, and movie industry, they are will-ing to participate in these various arenas with the aim of converting the culture to Christ. This is not to say that neo-Pentecostals have an easy relationship with the world. They have blurred the line between sacred and secular, not erased it completely. Many remain like the woman who loves to sing in the insulation of her own shower but dares not join the community choral group.

A major impetus of the neo-Pentecostal Christian cottage industry that has emerged in recent years is toward constructing viable "hip" options that are considered saintly alternatives. Many neo-Pentecostal congrega-tions, parachurch organizations, and broadcast networks afford contem-porary "saints" the luxury of participating in all of the activities of "the world" as long as they do so "in the name of Jesus." Many megachurches hold Christian dances for teenagers, develop singles ministries for young adults, and even form co-ed athletic leagues for all ages. Churches with bowling alleys, movie theaters, coffee shops, and health clubs become a sanctified oasis for neo-Pentecostals who want to enjoy the cuisine of commercial culture for the sake of the Gospel but are not quite ready to dine with tax collectors and publicans. This embrace of commercial culture extends even to church-based record companies that produce everything from gospel gangsta rap to sacred love songs for the saved couple.

Second, for neo-Pentecostals, the value system of the culture industries supplants traditional social mores. This is particularly true with regard to the accumulation of luxury goods and participation in the capitalist economy. Sanders points out that, historically, Pentecostal churches preached a message of asceticism, forbidding the use of alcohol, gambling, secular dancing, and immodest apparel. But today the ascetic dimensions of traditional Pentecostalism are eschewed, for neo-Pentecostals do not necessarily fear consumer culture. The realized eschatology of classical Pentecostalism, which promoted experiencing in this life the power of the Holy Spirit many had reserved for the afterlife, now includes consumer goods. Mansions on high, streets paved with gold, and riches laid up in heaven can also be realized in this world. Unlike traditional Pentecostals, neo-Pentecostals are known for having lavish sanctuaries, dressing flamboyantly, and taking an unapologetic attitude toward wealth. In recent years, the classical Pentecostal emphasis on healing and deliverance has shifted to financial blessings for neo-Pentecostals. Describing the turn from traditional Pentecostal revivalism to what I describe here as neo-Pentecostalism, author David Harrell states that "the revival also became much more diverse in style. Even the recent tent campaigners could not recapture the uniform and spontaneous milieu of the early meetings. In general, the campaigns became more stereotyped, more staged, and more professional. Among the sophisticated, the revival moved into Hilton Hotels and ornate churches; and revival services were replaced by charismatic conferences and seminars."[6] As a result of this shift in perspective, leading neo-Pentecostals are now known for their financial prosperity rather than the economic deprivation of their Pentecostal forebears. Posh hotel "conferences" have replaced dusty tent revivals, and major cable networks have supplanted local AM radio stations.

Third, neo-Pentecostals emphasize personal experience over communal concerns and even doctrinal authority. This is not to say that neo-Pentecostals do not appeal to the Bible as the authoritative source. Indeed they do. They just tend to cite, more often than not, scriptural texts that support personal blessings and deliverance as opposed to judgment and responsibility. Neo-Pentecostals affirm the experiential encounter with the Spirit, divine healing, and deliverance from demonic forces without the negativism commonly associated with doctrines of hellfire and brimstone. 3 John 2 has become a commonly quoted text among neo-Pentecostals: "Beloved, I wish above all things that thou mayest prosper and be in health, even as thy soul prospereth." For this latter reason, I agree with Shayne Lee that neo-Pentecostalism puts less emphasis on the baptism of the Holy Spirit and glossolalia and more on the other gifts of the Holy Spirit, which include healing, vibrant worship, prophetic utterances, and prosperity for believers.[7]

To be clear, this neo-Pentecostal emphasis on participation in the capitalist economy, culture industries, and wealth attainment should not necessarily be confused with the prosperity gospel. The telos of the aforementioned activities for neo-Pentecostals is transforming the culture toward Christ. Luxury goods are not considered the guaranteed right of all Christians according to their faith. The neo-Pentecostal perspective retains a teleological blues sensibility that regards pain and suffering as having a perfecting role in the life of the believer. In the words of one neo-Pentecostal superstar, "There are multiplicities of fiery trials but thank God that for every trial there is a faith that enables us. He [Christ] knows what kind of heat to place upon us to produce the faith needed in the situation."[8]

Ecclesiastically, neo-Pentecostal congregations vary. There is an episcopal hierarchy in place among many of the Holiness, Apostolic, and Pentecostal fellowships. It includes ecclesiastical positions like bishop, overseer, senior pastor, and elder. Congregations may or may not embrace traditional Christian ordinances and iconography. And some congregations embrace traditional rites of the Christian faith such as baptism and communion more than others. The West Angeles Church of God in Christ under the leadership of Bishop Charles Blake, for instance, serves communion regularly the first Sunday of each month. This is in contrast to Bishop T. D. Jakes's Potter's House in Dallas, where the Lord's Supper is only offered a few times per year. The same holds for ecclesiastical garb such as robes, collars, and cassocks. It seems to be a matter of personal preference for neo-Pentecostals. However, whether embracing or resisting traditional clerical attire, neo-Pentecostal preachers are highly stylized and fashionable. Today, aesthetically, neo-Pentecostals are fashionable to the extent of trendy. Many men of the neo-Pentecostal perspective enter the pulpits as if they just had an encounter with a professional stylist. From their prominently dyed and primped hair to their manicured fingernails, their style evokes fashion runways more than traditional Pentecostal storefronts. They are known for their custom-made zoot suits with matching colored alligator shoes as well as conspicuous jewelry. Often these outfits are worn with clerical collars, striking the perfect balance between tradition and style. Similarly, it is standard to see women evangelists in sequined outfits, four-inch heels, and custom-fitted ecclesiastical robes. For women with a constant television presence, notable facelifts are not uncommon. The style and overt femininity of Prophetess Juanita Bynum or Paula White, a white female televangelist who has risen to prominence in certain African American faith communities, trump traditional stereotypes of the asexual female Pentecostal preacher. While T. D. Jakes has been compared to a sanctified Barry White, Prophetess Bynum is an ecclesiastical and cultural cross between the fiery spirit of Mother Mattie Poole and the sex appeal of a Hollywood actress.[9]

Doubtless, some would argue that my criteria for distinguishing neo-Pentecostalism from classical Pentecostalism are not useful, since Pentecostals have always had their finger on the pulse of society, have always engaged with America's culture industries, and have always placed great emphasis on experiential encounters. Of course, there are examples of culturally savvy Pentecostals throughout the twentieth century. Previous chapters have highlighted the showmanship of radio evangelist Elder Michaux and the creative homiletic ability of Rosa Horn. They have described how Rev. F. W. McGee and Rev. Leora Ross recorded albums that engaged the blues and other forms of popular culture and how the Pentecostals have always emphasized a realized eschatology in which faith bears the fruits of demonstrable spiritual gifts. But these previous examples are more illustrative of the impact of mass media on any given religious form than representative of the Sanctified tradition of which Pentecostalism is a part. The evangelists who recorded sermons with Columbia and Okeh Records and early radio pioneers built upon but moved far beyond their Pentecostal roots. Classical Pentecostalism is known for its contentious relationship to the "world" and its ambivalence about Christians who seek mainstream acceptance in the larger society. Listening to secular music, going to movies, and accumulating luxury goods were all frowned upon by denominational leaders, ministers, and local elders. To be sure, radio and later television evangelists, with their neo-Pentecostal sensibilities, have helped to weaken the control of classical Pentecostalism in each given era. But until the post–civil rights era, with its proliferation of mass-mediated forms of religion, culturally attuned Pentecostals like Rev. Leora Ross and Rev. F. W. McGee remained more the exception than the norm. The full shift to mainstream

Bishop Carlton Pearson delivering a sermon at one of his annual AZUSA Conferences in Tulsa, Oklahoma. Considered a forerunner of Neo-Pentecostalism, Bishop Pearson can be credited with launching the careers of several prominent African American televangelists, including Bishop T. D. Jakes. Source: Bishop Carlton D. Pearson and New Dimensions Ministries of Tulsa, Oklahoma.

acceptance of what I refer to as neo-Pentecostal attributes did not take place until the 1990s. It was then that a young protégé of Oral Roberts named Carlton Pearson ascended to become the Pied Piper of the neo-Pentecostals.[10]

The Pied Piper of Neo-Pentecostals: Bishop Carlton Pearson

From a young age Carlton Pearson was exposed to the best in his ecclesiastical circle of Pentecostalism. Born a fourth-generation classical Pentecostal, Pearson was raised as an active member of the Church of God in Christ in San Diego. Bishop Julius Augustus Blake, then pastor of Jackson Memorial Church of God in Christ in San Diego, and father of contemporary famed neo-Pentecostal pastor Bishop Charles Blake of West Angeles Church of God in Christ, took the young Pearson under his wing. When Pearson was in the eighth grade, his mother took him to hear a gospel choir from Tulsa, Oklahoma, named the Collegiates—later known as the World Action Singers. The Collegiates were in San Diego recruiting students to attend the recently organized Oral Roberts University (ORU). Pearson now testifies that at that moment both he and his mother were sold on his attending ORU.

In 1971, with the blessing of Bishop Blake and S. M. Crouch, state bishop of the Church of God in Christ (and uncle of the famed gospel singer Andre Crouch), Pearson headed to Tulsa to attend ORU. In his first year on campus, he was recognized by Oral Roberts as a gifted vocalist and bright student. Roberts immediately asked Pearson to audition for the World Action Singers. This was Pearson's introduction to televangelism. The World Action Singers would accompany Oral on his many prime-time television specials. Among fellow World Action Singers members like Kathy Lee [Gifford], and celebrity guests such as Pearl Bailey and Elvis Presley, Pearson stood out. Roberts would often allow Pearson to testify or sing a solo on these television specials.[11]

At the time, 25 percent of Oral Roberts's income came from African American viewers. Thus a savvy business sense, if not solely genuine admiration, led Roberts to highlight Pearson. It is well documented that over the course of Pearson's collegiate career he became like a son to Oral Roberts. He toured in Roberts's private jet, was whisked around in his limousines, and swam in Roberts's family pool. This exposure encouraged Pearson. In reflecting on how he negotiated the two worlds of classical Pentecostalism and the glitz and glare of Oral Roberts's form of Charismatic consumerism, Pearson says he always remembered Bishop J. A. Blake's admonition, "Don't you forget about us." Pearson says that he felt a deep longing to be a bridge between the Church of God in Christ community of his upbringing and the new world of Charismatic revival in which he now participated. Thus he now reflects, "I wanted my church to have ORU. . . . I wanted to make [black] Pentecostalism pretty!"

Before Pearson could earn a degree from ORU, the Pentecostal world was opening up for him. In 1977 he formed his own evangelistic organization, Higher Dimensions Inc. He followed this four years later by organizing his own congregation in Tulsa, Higher Dimensions Church. Fueled by Roberts's insight and wealth, Pearson became a Pentecostal superstar in his own right. He was the first African American to serve as a guest host on PTL (Praise the Lord Network—the leading force in Christian broadcasting at the time) and soon became the first African American to host his own show on TBN (Trinity Broadcasting Network). Also, Pearson became the first African American appointed to the Board of Regents at ORU.

To understand the significance of Pearson as a trailblazer, one must understand the arena of Christian television at the time. White televangelists controlled the airwaves. In the 1980s, Black Entertainment Television was in its infancy, and the current stations that direct their programming primarily toward the African American community, like the Word Network, MBC, and TV One, were inconceivable.[12] Pat Robertson, Jimmy Swaggart, Jim and Tammy Faye Bakker, and Paul and Jan Crouch emerged alongside Oral Roberts as leading voices and/or owners of privately owned television networks.

But because their audiences contained large numbers of African Americans, white televangelists realized it was good business to cultivate black people as a donor base. Roberts, Bakker, and Crouch sought out African American preachers and singers that held or at least appeared to hold similar theological and political beliefs. Pearson fit the mold. With the singing voice of an angel and an affinity for Reaganomics, Pearson found himself on the 700 Club, PTL, and TBN as a regular stand-in host and contributor. Depending upon your perspective, Pearson became a Pentecostal power broker or an African American gatekeeper. But indisputably he was able to introduce black Pentecostals to wealthy white television barons like the Crouches.

Toward the end of the 1980s, Pearson decided to organize a conference for black Pentecostals. In a sense, this was his way of making official his role as a bridge builder between Oral Roberts's Tulsa-based Pentecostals and traditional black Pentecostals, like members of the Church of God in Christ, who sought to bypass denominational networks by connecting with the figures who controlled the religious airwaves. Named after the Pentecostal revival led by William Seymour in 1906, the AZUSA Conference was Pearson's way of making "black Pentecostalism pretty." Within a few years, Pearson named this interracial but predominantly black cluster of congregations the AZUSA Fellowship. Yet the most significant aspect of the fellowship remained the annual conference. The AZUSA Conference was an interdenominational event that brought thousands of preachers and gospel singers to Tulsa to witness the best and brightest of the emerging neo-Pentecostal class. Within a few years it became an honor to preach or sing at AZUSA. The honoraria were enormous, but the exposure was the real draw. Keynoting at AZUSA could guarantee a preacher an extra $200,000 a year in preaching fees. Sociologist Shayne Lee provides an account of the AZUSA Conference that likens it to a heavyweight championship fight. The author paints a vivid picture of what I am arguing neo-Pentecostal culture represents:

> Part of the thrill of attending the nightly meetings was to gaze at the VIP section and get a glimpse at what the prominent preachers and famous gospel singers were wearing. Expensive suits and dazzling dresses were on display as an air of elegance imbued the arena. Those who had the good fortune of attending this grandiose affair could not avoid the feeling that they were part of something exceptional. The glamour and panache at AZUSA meetings did much to give black Pentecostalism a facelift as a movement no longer relegated only to the disenfranchised but appealing to more privileged African Americans.[13]

It appears from this description that Pearson had succeeded in his goals. He had effectively reached back to black Pentecostals with the wealth and resources of the larger Pentecostal community and provided Pentecostalism with a social facelift.

Charismatic Mainlines

The term *Charismatic mainline* is used to describe ministries that individually derive from one of the traditional black mainline denominations. Insofar as a ministry belongs to one of the six associations that constitute the two black mainline denominations (Baptist and Methodist), it is mainline.[14] But it is considered Charismatic mainline if its ecclesiastical practices integrate a Pentecostal-like experiential encounter with the divine in worship. This latter dynamic may be evidenced in at least one of the following ways.

First, Charismatic mainline churches encourage members to seek levels of spiritual encounter and expression that may include experiencing a second baptism of the Holy Spirit. Like Pentecostals, Charismatic mainlines seek evidence of this experiential encounter. This evidence may include but is not limited to glossolalia, healing, and prophecy. Second, Charismatic mainline churches encourage ecstatic worship. Traditional organs, anthems, and hymns have been replaced with full band ensembles, upbeat praise and worship songs, and even hip-hop-influenced gospel like that of Kirk Franklin. This charismatic style of worship can create an environment that feels more like a nightclub than the A.M.E. Zion Church you may have attended with your grandmother. Third, traditional titles and denominationally accepted structures have been reoriented. In some cases, titles such as *Reverend* or *Minister* have been replaced with *Elder*. Moreover, in the case of Baptists, the traditional democratic structures of the local congregation have taken a more hierarchical shape. In extreme cases, deacon and trustee boards are dismantled in favor of unilateral decision making on the part of the pastor. Even within the interconnected structure of the A.M.E. system, where ministers are appointed by the bishop for one-year terms, certain prominent personalities have unofficially transcended itinerant status.

One of the more notable shifts among the Charismatic black Baptists is that loosely organized networks have replaced autonomous local congregations. These networks are not unlike those of the traditional Pentecostal fellowships. Reflecting postdenominational life in American religion, congregations are choosing to unite with other like-minded ministries despite denominational affiliation. Thus we have witnessed the emergence of bishops among black Baptists.[15] These networks have increasingly embraced a hierarchical episcopal structure.

Ecclesiastically, Charismatic mainlines embrace traditional ordinances and Christian iconography. Sanctuaries are laden with crosses, doves, and symbols of the Eucharist. These congregations regularly participate in the practices of baptism and communion. Clerical garments such as ecclesiastical robes, collars, and stoles are regularly worn. The Charismatic mainlines tend to be a little bit more traditional ecclesiastically than their neo-Pentecostal counterparts, and, as we will see, extremely different from the Word of Faith churches. But this is not to say that the attire of Charismatic mainlines lacks the flair of the neo-Pentecostals. In many ways they are similar. This is particularly true for the younger evangelists, among whom clerical pulpit attire has given way to more elaborate prints and flamboyant colors in recent years. Ministerial robes now come in array of designs, colors, and styles that range from papacy-like vestments complete with sash to sleeveless cassocks. Moreover, many preachers do not mind donning hip clothing for their pulpit appearances, such as silk shirts, baggy wide-bottomed pants, and pseudo–zoot suits.

Like all aspects of this phenomenon, these recent developments are representative of forces that have been at work for decades. They did not appear out of nowhere in the 1990s. The Charismatic influence and neodenominational climate in America both reflect and spur the decline of mainline Protestantism. The frenetic activity of Charismatic congregations is on the rise, while the institutionalized structures of the Presbyterians and Lutherans have increasingly declined in the larger society. This is indeed part of the issue at hand. But the Charismatic mainline perspective can also be regarded as the culmination of a class and culture war that has been raging for over a century among the black mainline denominations. More than an embrace of something new, the Charismatic mainline perspective can be interpreted as a renewed level of appreciation and accentuation of ecclesiastical activity from below.

Mainline Diversity, Conflict, and Cultural Change

The Great Awakening revivals of the eighteenth and nineteenth centuries contributed to the mass conversion of blacks to Methodist and Baptist denominations. The extemporaneous preaching and worship style coupled with the seemingly democratic nature of autonomously controlled religious bodies suited black converts well. The worship style, particularly among southerners, was compatible with traditional African religious practices, and initially the denomination afforded leadership to blacks. As Cornel West states, "The uncomplicated requirements for membership, open and easy access to the clergy and congregation-centered mode of church governance set the cultural context for the flowering of Africanisms, invaluable fellowship, and political discourse."[16] What one would consider black mainline denominations developed, for the most part, from two religious movements: free blacks who separated from Methodism prior to the Civil War and black Baptists who organized their own conventions in the post–Civil War era.

But not long after these conventions were established, the freedom of extemporaneous and demonstrably emotional worship that originally attracted blacks to Methodists and Baptists fell under attack. As noted in the previous chapter, when northern missionaries began promoting alternative value systems among former slave communities and newly established black schools in the South, Victorian morality with an emphasis on temperance and narrow definitions of rationality came into direct conflict with the cultural practices of the recently emancipated. These new values were linked to advancement and upward mobility. At the same time, many black leaders and organizations uncritically denounced the old standards of black culture as vestiges of slavery and the backwardness of the race. In the closing decades of the nineteenth century, the dim outlines of a class and culture war within the black community were forming, and the black church became a prime battleground in that war.

For instance, a new class of educated black clergy equated the spiritual advancement of the race with the expansion of the reading public.[17] Print discourse came to the fore as a tangible expression of black progress and upward mobility. The oral tradition that had characterized the black worship experience was being replaced in prominent denominational sectors with an emphasis on literacy. The use of hymnals replaced the practice of lining out, which was criticized by an emerging group of middle-class mainline leaders. In conjunction with the placement of hymnals in the pews were stylistic changes in the pulpit. Extemporaneous preaching was supplanted by the use of a prepared manuscript. Preaching "off the cuff" or as the "Spirit moved" was abandoned for what many ministers thought should be a rational homiletic exercise.

By the beginning of the twentieth century, W. E. B. Du Bois's concept of a guiding "Talented Tenth" began to resonate with the black mainline elites. Educated black Baptists and Methodists encouraged church members to eschew "superstitious" and "emotional" faith in favor of a cerebral approach that was not expressed through physicality in worship. Formally educated clergy and congregations distinguished themselves as the exceptional members of the race by tying the salvation message of the Gospel to higher education and race uplift. To be saved meant to be socially empowered as a people; this included educational, political, and economic empowerment.

Though such cultural imperialism is problematic on varying levels, one cannot deny the positive impact these mainline congregations had on black life. They may be credited with the development of civil society in the South in the decades following the failures of Reconstruction. The church of Ralph Ellison's boyhood, Avery Chapel A.M.E. in Oklahoma City, stands as a stellar example. A bastion of black respectability, Avery Chapel hosted educational and political activities that attracted the black middle and upper classes to its sanctuary. Promoting virtues such as thrift, sobriety, and industry, such community institutions threw a spiritual lifeline to families that, like the Ellisons, were drowning economically. Biographer Lawrence Jackson describes Avery Chapel in the life of Ellison's young widowed mother, Ida, as "the source of the faith that she and her boys would survive."[18]

To be sure, the black mainline churches' exaggerated emphasis on black refinement and probity contributed to the unjust marginalization of blacks' own rich vernacular culture. But fortunately the expressive and experiential dimensions of black religion continued to be cultivated by spiritual geniuses who understood the sorrowful joy of the spirituals and the rhetorical wonder of the chanted sermon. Once record industries elected to capitalize not only on blues and jazz but also on the singing and preaching of African American working-class churches, the aesthetic sensibility of Afro-conversionist southern religious life was sure to be retained.[19] As we saw in previous chapters, this development marked the advent of black religious broadcasting.

This is an important point both historically and descriptively. Among the traditional black mainline denominations, charismatic, Spirit-filled worship has always dominated the electronic medium. Educated "Morehouse men" who were considered pillars of pulpit respectability may have led the various denominational conferences and civic organizations, but down-home Baptist preachers who could whoop and sing controlled the religious airwaves with their appeal to the black working-class masses. This, unfortunately, led to a class and culture war that contributed to class and culture differences between the black mainline churches.

For example, from the late nineteenth century onward there have been congregations regarded as the prominent "silk stocking" churches. These churches have traditionally known for academically trained clergy and are composed of black lawyers, doctors, and educators. In Atlanta, for example, they would include the historic First Congregational Church, the Ebenezer Baptist Church, and Big Bethel A.M.E. In terms of the worship experience, services were typically characterized by order and decorum. The choir sings hymns, anthems, and Negro spirituals with Mozart-like precision. Further, these congregations are congruent with Hans Baer and Merrill Singer's understanding of black mainline denominations. They historically have promoted what the authors refer to as a reformist strategy of social activism that enables parishioners to better integrate politically, socially, and economically into the larger society. Their social activism includes lending support to community protest, organizing against racial discrimination, and sponsoring college scholarships.[20]

Then there are the black mainline congregations of the working class. The pastors of these congregations often lack formal academic training. The preaching is more vibrant and extemporaneous, ending in a rhythmic whoop. The communal activity of call and response is encouraged, and parishioners are lively in worship. Hymns are "raised" by a deacon or pastor rather than read from a hymnal, and services are led by a spirited gospel choir. Parishioners are not ashamed "to make a joyful noise" in worship and are even prone to catch the Holy Ghost. Dancing, running the aisles, and audible moaning are just a few tangible expressions of parishioners' experiential encounters with the divine. Insofar as this is the case, such congregations among the Baptist denominations have been playfully tagged as "Bapticostal."

These congregations may participate in community affairs like their silk-stocking counterparts, but this is not their common modus operandi. They are better known for creating a safe place of ecstatic worship. Through vibrant preaching and singing, congregants can be cleansed from a society that dirties and debases black and poor bodies. In Atlanta during the 1970s and 1980s, Salem Baptist Church, pastored by Jasper Williams Jr., and Israel Baptist Church, under the leadership of William H. Smith, are two examples of such churches.

In the late 1980s, however, building upon processes of blending styles that began during the migration and interwar eras, a new class of preachers emerged in the black mainlines that bridged the class and cultural divide. These preachers were formally educated but promoted ecstatic worship. They were civic and socially minded yet concerned with the individual soul. They had the ecclesiastical probity of Gardner C. Taylor with the charismatic flair of C. L. Franklin. As noted earlier, Lincoln and Mamiya trace this transformation among the black mainlines to the ministry of Rev. Dr. John Bryant Jr., who was then pastor of Bethel A.M.E. Church in Baltimore.[21] In the course of his tenure at Bethel from the mid-1970s to 1988 he took the congregation from about five hundred to over six thousand members. This impressive growth can be attributed to the church's adoption of a Charismatic mainline–style encouragement of deeper levels of spirituality among members through experiential, ecstatic worship. Bryant developed his emphasis on encountering the Spirit while working on a Peace Corps mission in Africa. He reports that he witnessed persons being healed and exercising spiritual power even though they lacked any understanding of Jesus Christ. This led him to reexamine the scriptures in order to tease out the power of the Spirit in the life of the believer.[22] Through this experience Bryant, the son of an A.M.E. bishop, gained a deeper appreciation for the Charismatic wave of Pentecostal influence.

Today the most prominent Charismatic mainline ministries are following the example set by John Bryant, now bishop of the fifth district of the A.M.E. Church. In fact, several leaders in the contemporary megachurch phenomenon are directly tied to Bishop Bryant. They include Dr. Floyd Flake, pastor of Allen Temple A.M.E. Church in Jamaica Queens, New York; Dr. Frank Reid, current pastor of Bethel A.M.E. in Baltimore; and Bishop Bryant's son Dr. Jamal Harrison Bryant, pastor of Empowerment Temple A.M.E. in Baltimore and an emerging televangelist on the national scene. All these persons share characteristics that place them squarely in the Charismatic mainline perspective. They all pastor megachurches, have vibrant television and media ministries, have advanced theological degrees, promote civic involvement, and encourage a realized eschatology that promotes experiencing gifts of the Spirit. Flake is the current president of Wilberforce University, Reid is Harvard and Yale trained, and Jamal Bryant holds degrees from Morehouse College, Duke Divinity School, and Graduate Theological Foundation. Each of their ministries is heavily involved in community outreach that includes but is not limited to community development corporations, primary schools, and low-income housing programs for the community. And to walk into any one of these congregations on Sunday morning is to enter an "old-school Pentecostal" revival service.

In Baptist circles the growth of this perspective over the past decade can largely be attributed to Bishop Paul Morton. Besides being the senior pastor of the Greater St. Stephens Baptist Church in New Orleans, Paul Morton is a Stellar Award–winning gospel artist, an author, and a nationally recognized televangelist. Building upon the success of Pearson's AZUSA Fellowship, Morton seized an opportunity when the Baptists found themselves at an ecclesiastical crossroads.

In the mid-1990s the National Baptist Convention U.S.A. was mired in scandal and internal dissension. The convention was locked in internal turmoil for years as result of an old boys' network that rewarded fidelity to leadership.[23] Morton became increasingly disillusioned with the way emerging congregations with bourgeoning membership rolls, thriving media ministries, and innovative styles of worship were being locked out of National Baptist leadership. He was also aware of how many black

Baptist ministers were foregoing the National Baptist Convention annual meeting in September to attend Carlton Pearson's AZUSA Conference in April. Therefore, in April of 1994 Morton called together over twenty-five thousand Baptists to the Louisiana Superdome to organize the Full Gospel Baptist Church Fellowship (FGBCF).[24]

Three characteristics distinguish Morton's fellowship from the traditional black Baptist denominations. First, the FGBCF was organized on the belief that the church had to recognize the free expression of the gifts of the Holy Spirit. According to its mission statement, "The Full Gospel Baptist Church Fellowship builds upon the traditional Baptist Church as its foundation. That Baptist heritage is embraced yet balanced with more charismatic influences."[25] Second, the FGBCF challenges traditional black Baptists by affirming the role of women in ministry. Gender inclusion is promoted on all ministerial levels within the fellowship. Third, the FGBCF is structured according to an episcopal hierarchy. The "Tiers of Leadership" include the Bishop's Council; the College of Bishops; general, state, and district overseers; a Financial Assistance Council; and senior pastors. Morton was appointed international presiding bishop at the first FGPCF organizational conference in 1994.

Not all Charismatic mainlines of Baptist affiliation are members of the FGBCF. The FGBCF is just one example of a larger movement among Charismatic Baptist megachurch congregations; a plethora of such fellowships have arisen over the past decade. Like their A.M.E. counterparts, the leading Baptist personalities that fit into this perspective are, for the most part, formally educated and promote civic involvement. They include Bishop Kenneth Ulmer of Faithful Central Bible Church (formerly Baptist Church) in Los Angeles; Bishop Joseph Walker III of Mount Zion Baptist Church in Nashville, Tennessee.; and Bishop Donald Hilliard of the Cathedral of the Second Baptist Church in Perth Amboy, New Jersey.

Word of Faith

The label *Word of Faith* is used to describe an emerging, loosely organized fellowship of churches that belong to the larger neo-Charismatic movement. It is referred to as neo-Charismatic because it has no official ties to any of the classical Pentecostal fellowships or any other ecclesiastical denominations. Known by many names—Word of Faith, Word-Faith, faith formula theology, positive confession theology, and the prosperity gospel—this ecclesiastical perspective emerged from post–World War II charismatic revivals. It shares many characteristics with other popular contemporary religious movements, but it is a distinct neo-Charismatic subculture. In this historical moment, the emerging Faith movement cannot be reduced to its ecclesiastical antecedents and interlocutors.

To date, sociologist Milmon Harrison has provided the sole academic study of the Word of Faith movement in the African American community. His exceptional and insightful work posits three core beliefs and practices of the Faith message. First, to live the higher Christian life, persons must know who they are in Christ. This true understanding of Christian identity is premised upon the professed spiritual laws of the scriptures. The scriptures are viewed by Faith adherents as a contract between believers and God. Since God is understood to be faithful and just, it is up to the believer to hold up her end of the covenant relationship in order to receive all of God's promises.[26] This type of faith allows persons to exercise spiritual authority and walk in divine favor. The end result of such faith is the capacity to "name" whatever one wants and "claim" possession of it by faith.

The act of "naming it and claiming it" is an exercise of positive confession. This is the second core belief and practice of the movement. Once believers have a clear understanding of who they are in Christ, they are able to "speak the same words about themselves that God has spoken about them in the Bible."[27] The "Word of Faith" name refers literally to the act of positive confession. The aim of such a pragmatic theological orientation is to bring into existence that which is believed by faith through the spoken word. Faith is a confession, and the power of faith is made manifest by the tongue. For this reason, believers are encouraged to speak only positively concerning their situation in life, regardless of what their circumstances may be. Faith teachers say that negative speech indicates a lack of faith and resignation to one's condition. For example, the pastor of Faith Christian Center in Sacramento, California, does not employ terms such as *poor* to describe the economically underprivileged but instead refers to them as "persons between blessings."[28]

Finally, for believers to "know who you are in Christ" and then to positively confess what God desires for them is to unlock prosperity: divine health and material wealth. For the casual observer, this is the most recognizable aspect of the Word of Faith movement, the prosperity gospel. The prosperity gospel affirms that God desires everyone to live a life of health and wealth. Faith teachings reject traditional notions of

Jesus as poor. The prosperity gospel teaches that Jesus was financially prosperous and that he desires the same for all believers.

Two things are important to note concerning the prosperity gospel. First, the prosperity gospel asserts that everyone has the capacity to be a millionaire and never get sick. Divine health and wealth not only are the fruits of the higher life but are synonymous with the higher life. Thus one's faith in Christ can be measured by one's prosperity because faith and prosperity are directly proportional. Conversely, to be poor or sick is an indictment against one's faith in Christ. People are locked in the world's system of poverty and illness because they are not clear on who they are in Christ. Poverty and illness are not social realities for individuals in Christ but a mind-set, a spiritual curse. Developing a poverty mentality is the negative consequence for Christians who fail to uphold their contractual agreement to God as set forth in scripture.[29]

Second, at the core of the prosperity gospel is the capacity to transcend the world's systems. Through faith and positive confession believers are able to reach a state of what I call *metaphysical physicality*. In other words, being properly in tune with the Word of God allows people to live a metaphysical existence in a physical world. This pseudo-Platonic understanding of reality mediated through the writings of the Apostle Paul transforms Plato's conception of the two realms (visible and intelligible) into two levels of existence, the lower and the higher life. Humanity is born into the carnal world, the lower level of existence. But whereas Plato's philosophical construction shows human beings as trapped in the allegorical cave of existence, Jesus extends a means of exiting the lower level of life and entering a higher life.[30] In this higher life people are no longer bound to the laws of the carnal realm. Laws of nature no longer apply to the believer.

Because through faith believers are able to reach a state of *metaphysical physicality*, Word of Faith congregations are not particularly concerned with social activism or community programs. Setting up community development corporations and health clinics and providing educational assistance and job training programs to church members are not priorities for most Faith congregations. Since Faith teachers interpret literally the biblical text that "as a man thinketh so is he," social programs and resources cannot help people who are not "walking in their anointing." For this reason the Word of Faith movement can be neatly classified in the thaumaturgic category. To overcome negative social conditions such as racism, sexism, and classism is to overcome the internal negative mind-set that thaumaturgics believe unleashes these "isms" in the world. Thus, rather than being community based or socially active, the majority of Word of Faith congregations are what sociologists of religion refer to as niche churches—congregations that have a metrowide or national focus while demonstrating little concern for nurturing their geographic locale.[31] These congregations attract a membership from a broad range but are not particularly concerned with investing financial or social resources back into community development.

As physical sites, the church campuses of most Faith congregations remind you of a secular business. The sanctuary is configured like an arena or convention center. The walls of the vestibule and sanctuary lack traditional Christian iconography. One will not find stained-glass images of Jesus, the symbols of the sacraments, or even so much as a cross in the building. The communion table is not needed, since the Lord's Supper is rarely, if ever, served. At best the church is decorated with flags from varying countries or a large globe to signify the global orientation of the movement.

Word of Faith teachers seldom if ever wear robes, opting for tailor-made three-piece suits. Rather than exotic colored zoot-suits or elaborate outfits, the apparel of these preachers seems to belong on the pages of a Brooks Brothers catalog. The men often wear pinstriped suits, crisp white French-cuff shirts, and conspicuous but conservative gold watches. This helps them to appear aesthetically as the business moguls they understand themselves to be. The women Faith teachers—usually the male Faith preachers' spouses—are similarly conservative. Business suits, pumps, and collared shirts replace the traditional "First Lady" attire of church hats and sequins. Faith teachers convey a sense of passion under control as opposed to uncontrolled zeal. They never sweat and rarely raise their voices. Their anointing is defined by erudition, temperance, and scriptural insight rather than extemporaneous inspiration and emotion. Without clerical collars or stoles, their head shots on the back of book covers often suggest the economic self-help acumen of Jack Welch, Donald Trump, or Suze Orman rather than the theological reflections of Bishop Eddie Long, Bishop Paul Morton, or Robert Schuller.

Since the Faith movement is an emerging, loosely organized fellowship of congregations without any classical Pentecostal or denominational ties, it is a part of the larger neo-Charismatic movement. This does not mean that the Word of Faith movement formed ex nihilo in the last quarter of the twentieth century. The movement can be traced back to the turn of the twentieth century in the writings of Essek William (E. W.) Kenyon. Though Kenyon's influence on the contemporary Charismatic community is profound, he remains an obscure figure in American religious history. In fact, were it not for Dan McConnell's *A Different Gospel*, which proves that the professed founder of the Word of Faith movement, Kenneth E. Hagin Sr., plagiarized entire sections of Kenyon's theological writings, Kenyon would have probably remained hidden in the shadow of the movement he helped to construct.[32]

Given that Kenyon was born in 1867 and raised during the rapidly expanding industrial revolution, his health-and-wealth orientation makes him a product of his time. The cultural atmosphere was one of anxiety, greed, optimism, and despair. With the rise of the city, America's shift from an agrarian-based to an industrially driven economy shook the secure ground on which many middle-class persons had believed themselves to stand. Industry became an invisible, omnipotent force frustrating the lives of everyday people. For this reason, the period has been referred to as the "Nervous Age." A plethora of nervous ailments arose that were categorized under the broad-based term *neurasthenia*.[33] In this context an abundance of metaphysical ideas concerning healing and cures were offered from both "cultic" and more traditionally orthodox faith communities. While studying at Emerson College of Oratory in Boston, Kenyon became immersed in the New England matrix of mind science, Transcendentalism, and the overarching philosophy of New Thought.[34]

Mind science philosophies provided power to those feeling powerless amid social upheaval and security to those who confronted uncertainty. Kenyon and others provided faith communities with the very thing the Good Witch Glenda afforded Dorothy in the Land of Oz, simplicity. According to his teachings, believers did not need to follow the yellow brick road of doctrinal rigor and ecclesiastical catechisms to a God of wonder; instead, they already possessed within themselves the power to heal and prosper, not by clicking their heels, but by verbally professing the truth of that power.

Kenyon's book *Two Kinds of Faith* contains a chapter entitled "Things That Belong to Us." Kenyon encourages readers to enjoy their rights in Christ, which include salvation, success, and healing. In discussing physical healing, Kenyon states:

The believer does not need to ask the Father to heal him when he is sick, because "Surely he hath borne our sickness and carried our diseases; yet we did esteem him stricken, smitten of God and afflicted."

God laid our diseases on Jesus.

Isaiah 53:10 states that it pleased Jehovah to make Him sick with our sicknesses so that by His stripes we are healed.

If we are healed then we do not need to pray for our healing.

All we need to do is rebuke the enemy in Jesus' Name, order him to leave our bodies, and thank the Father for perfect healing.

It is all so simple.[35]

The Growth of Word of Faith

In the contemporary moment, the late Kenneth E. Hagin Sr. is most credited with forming the Word of Faith movement. He is commonly referred to as "Dad" Hagin by leading Faith teachers and, in death, has gained sainthood in the Word of Faith subculture. Hagin's books and sound recordings are found everywhere Word of Faith literature is sold. Though it is confirmed that very little of Hagin's theological orientation was original, Hagin should be credited with diffusing this neo-Charismatic movement through the larger society. With the establishment of the Kenneth E. Hagin Evangelistic Association (later changed to the Kenneth E. Hagin Ministries) in Tulsa, Oklahoma, in the 1960s, his connections to Oral Roberts and Oral Roberts University, the broadcasting of his teachings on radio and television, and the establishment of Rhema Bible Training Center in the 1970s, Hagin nurtured countless Word of Faith pastors to prominence. Hagin's most notable disciples are Kenneth Copeland of Fort Worth, Texas; Frederick K. Price of Los Angeles, California; and the late John Osteen, father of Joel Osteen and founding pastor of the Lakewood Church in Houston, Texas. By the end of the 1970s, over twenty thousand people converged on Tulsa to attend the annual Hagin camp meeting at the Rhema Bible Training Center.[36] For our purposes here it is appropriate to give brief attention to Rev. Frederick K. Price. Price is of particular importance for two reasons: he is recognized in Charismatic circles as the first African American Word of Faith teacher, and he unwittingly played a pivotal role in Oral Roberts University's ultimate embrace of Word of Faith theology.

Rev. Price established the Ever Increasing Faith Ministries at the Crenshaw Christian Center in Los Angeles in 1973. He entered the ministry in 1955 and bounced around denominationally for the next twenty years, serving as an assistant pastor and pastor of Baptist, A.M.E., and nondenominational congregations. In 1975 he was ordained into the Kenneth Hagin Ministries. As the sole African American voice of the growing faith formula theology, Price soon became a hot commodity for Kenneth Hagin. Price was the African American franchise of the Tulsa-based movement. Much as Pearson had done for Oral Roberts, Fred Price gave Hagin's Word of Faith access into African American homes. Within a couple of years Price relocated his congregation to a thirty-two-acre campus that had formerly been the home of Pepperdine University and began a national television broadcast of his Ever Increasing Faith television ministry. Price and Copeland served as keynote preachers at Hagin's annual camp meeting, and this sort of exposure catapulted Price to national prominence.

As Hagin's movement grew, Charismatic powerhouse Oral Roberts found himself in a theological quandary. As the Word of Faith movement became increasingly popular, more traditional Charismatic preachers and theologians resisted the faith formula. Many of these theologians were professors at ORU who rejected the Word of Faith theology because of its failure to wrestle with the question of evil and the tragic dimensions of life. However, Roberts respected Hagin as a friend and ministerial colleague in Tulsa and admired the way Faith teachers were building entrepreneurial evangelistic empires outside denominational structures, much as Oral Roberts had done twenty years earlier. Also, both Oral Roberts and ORU received a large amount of financial support from churches and evangelists associated with Hagin.[37]

In 1980, Fred Price (whose congregation had contributed about $175,000 to Roberts's campus) was invited to preach at a chapel service at ORU. It is reported that while Price articulated the benefits of Word of Faith theology, a theology professor at ORU shouted "No" during Price's sermon. At the end of the message an infuriated Roberts chided the faculty and forced the heckling professor to publicly apologize to Price. Against the wishes of several faculty members, Roberts continued to invite Price and other Faith teachers to the campus. This event is catalogued in the university's cultural memory as the moment Oral cast his lot with the upstart neo-Charismatic preachers.[38]

To be sure, it is important to point out the possible racialized dynamics operating in this recorded narrative. Pastor Fred Price was hardly the first espouser of the Word of Faith doctrine to preach at ORU: both Kenneth Hagin and Kenneth Copeland had fostered close ties with Oral Roberts and the campus community. But Pastor Price was the first Faith teacher to be publicly shouted down during his sermon by faculty members and subsequently scapegoated by some Pentecostal theologians as the cause of ORU's theological decline. Further, it should be noted that opponents of the Word of Faith movement refer to this turn of events surrounding Pastor Price's sermon as "Black Friday" on the campus. Nevertheless, Pastor Price and the Word of Faith movement have greatly affected the larger evangelical and Charismatic movement across the color line in America.

Today the de facto leaders and ministry headquarters of the Word of Faith movement have shifted from Tulsa. Kenneth and Gloria Copeland are now the "godparents" of the Faith. The Believers Voice of Victory ministry, broadcast, and annual conference constitute the epicenter of the Faith world. And though the Rhema Bible Training Center is still the institution of choice for persons interested in Faith teachings, ORU has amended its curriculum by incorporating central tenets of the Faith philosophy. Up until 2007, when the Roberts family lost control of the university because of institutional scandals and lawsuits, major Word of Faith evangelists sat on the various boards of ORU and were often awarded honorary doctoral degrees during commencement exercises. Finally, African American preachers such as Leroy Thompson of the Ever Increasing Word Ministries in Darrow, Louisiana, I. V. and Bridget Hilliard of the New Light Christian Center in Houston, Texas, and Keith Butler of Word of the Faith International Christian Center in Southfield, Michigan, have arisen as influential black Word of Faith evangelists in the past decade.

The phenomenon of African American religious broadcasting in the contemporary moment is a result of the cultural, theological, ecclesial, and social shifts that have occurred since the civil rights movement. But rather than labeling the current phenomenon as "new," we might better regard it as a culmination of historical processes that have informed African American Christian practices. Broad descriptions like "new black church" do not accurately describe these processes, the multivalent traditions that inform black religious broadcasting, or the diversity of the phenomenon in its current state. I have identified the neo-Pentecostal, Charismatic mainline, and Word of Faith movements as the three distinct perspectives that constitute most of African American religious broadcasting. These categories are faithful to the histories and traditions that structure the ministries of leading televangelists, and they accurately reflect the recent ecclesial reconfigurations that a postdenominational climate has produced in America. From these three perspectives the leading producers of African American religious broadcasting, Bishop T. D. Jakes, Bishop Eddie Long, and Pastor Creflo Dollar, have emerged to inform the ministry of others. The next three chapters will turn to the individual ministries of each of these televangelists. Our aim is to accentuate their ministerial differences as well as to identify their common objectives in broadcasting themselves over the religious airwaves of America.

Bishop T. D. Jakes. Source: AP Images.

4

Come, Ye Disconsolate
The Ministry of Bishop T. D. Jakes

Come, ye disconsolate, wherever ye languish—
Come to the mercy seat, fervently kneel;
Here bring your wounded hearts, here tell your anguish;
Earth has no sorrow that heaven cannot heal.
— "Come Ye Disconsolate," in *African American Heritage Hymnal*

In 1994, gospel music legends Tramaine and Walter Hawkins recorded a song that was soon adopted by church choirs across the country. Entitled "The Potter's House," the song was inspired by the eighteenth chapter of the Old Testament book of Jeremiah, where God is presented as the potter and Israel as clay. The first verse begins:

In case you have fallen by the wayside of life,
Dreams and visions scattered, you're all broken inside,
You don't have to stay in the shape that you're in,
The Potter wants to put you back together again.
You who are broken, stop by the Potter's House!
You who need mending, stop by the Potter's House!
Give Him the fragments of your broken life, my friend.
The Potter wants to put you back together again.

So when Bishop T. D. Jakes opened the doors to his newly inaugurated ministry in Dallas, Texas, in the summer of 1996, it was no surprise for the over two thousand people who packed into the $3.2 million edifice that the marquee on the front of the building read, "The Potter's House." For those familiar with the public ministry of Bishop Jakes, the lyrics to this song metaphorically encapsulated the professed ministerial aims of the rising evangelical superstar. Whether those in attendance had previously watched him on TBN, listened to one of his cassette tapes in their car, or read a copy of his best-selling book *Woman, Thou Art Loosed!*, they understood Bishop Jakes as someone who could offer a message of spiritual forgiveness, healing, and hope.

Jakes, who had recently arrived from West Virginia, was far from your typical judgment and damnation Pentecostal preacher. In all the pulpits where he preached throughout the country, his most consistent message was God's ability to put hurting souls back together again. And this message has propelled Bishop Jakes to the forefront of American religious life. One might even argue that Jakes is one of the most recognized religious leaders in America today. As sociologist Shayne Lee asserts in the title of his comprehensive cultural biography of the famed televangelist, Bishop T. D. Jakes is indeed "America's New Preacher."

Biography

Thomas Dexter Jakes was born to Ernest and Odith Jakes in Charleston, West Virginia. Ernest Sr. was reportedly a local businessman and entrepreneur running his own janitorial service.[1] Odith, a graduate of Tuskegee College, was a grade school teacher who sold Avon products and fresh vegetables in her spare time. As a youngster, T. D. began attending a small Pentecostal church in Vadalia. The Greater Emmanuel Gospel became a sort of spiritual haven for this young man, who by then was dealing with his father's kidney failure, his parents' impending divorce, and then his father's death. Jakes candidly discusses what it was like to be deprived of a childhood— having to clean up after his father, run a dialysis machine, and assist his mother.

T. D. Jakes preached his first sermon at the age of nineteen at the Greater Emmanuel Gospel Tabernacle. This congregation was part of the Apostolic fellowship of congregations in Ohio and West Virginia under the leadership of Bishop Sherman Watkins, a prominent Apostolic pastor from Ohio. Bishop Watkins and other Apostolics affirm the "oneness of God" as revealed in Jesus Christ and thus do not baptize in the name of the Father, Son, and Holy Ghost. Referred to as "Jesus Only" or "Oneness Pentecostalism," Apostolic Pentecostalism nurtured the young T. D. Jakes in West Virginia. Through its ranks Jakes climbed within Pentecostal circles in the West Virginia and Ohio region. When Bishop Watkins formed a new Apostolic fellowship in 1988, the Higher Ground Always Abounding Assemblies, he appointed Jakes as a high-ranking bishop, an affiliation that Jakes still retains today.

Traveling throughout West Virginia and preaching at small storefront churches, Jakes earned his GED and attended West Virginia State College for a year, where he studied psychology. In 1979, he organized his first congregation in Montgomery, West Virginia, and shortly thereafter he met and married a local coal miner's daughter named Serita. Unfortunately the Union Carbide chemical plant where Jakes was employed would soon close down, leaving the young father and husband unemployed. Unashamed of his humble beginnings, Jakes emphasizes that his family suffered from extreme poverty even as he was deeply committed to the ministry.[2]

Over the next ten years Jakes's ministry experienced moderate growth. The social demographics of West Virginia and the insular world of Greater Emmanuel International Fellowship were not particularly conducive to a church's increase in numbers. With a local radio broadcast Jakes relocated his congregation from Montgomery to a dilapidated movie theater in Smithers. In another five years he relocated the congregation to South Charleston, where his interracial fellowship immediately doubled. Before long, Jakes again relocated the congregation to the affluent Charleston, West Virginia, suburbs of Cross Lanes.[3]

In Cross Lanes Bishop Jakes began a successful Women's Sunday school class entitled "Woman, Thou Art Loosed." Based on the Lukan narrative in which Jesus heals a woman of her infirmity, the aim of the class was to offer a message of hope and healing to women dealing with issues that the church often ignores. Jakes tackled taboo topics such as sexual, physical, and mental abuse of women, including child molestation and domestic violence.

In 1991, Bishop Jakes had the pleasure of meeting famed gospel singer Sarah Jordan Powell at a Pentecostal conference. As well as being the national fine arts director for the Church of God in Christ, Sarah Jordan Powell was in charge of hospitality for VIPs at Bishop Carlton Pearson's annual AZUSA conference in Tulsa. Bishop Jakes invited Sarah Jordan Powell to West Virginia to sing before his congregation. Being treated like royalty during her visit, however, was not the only thing that impressed the songstress from the Church of God in Christ. According to Powell, Bishop Jakes's preaching blew her away. At her continued urging, Bishop Carlton Pearson invited T. D. Jakes to Higher Dimension to preach at one of the regional meetings of the AZUSA Fellowship.[4] A small quarterly meeting of ministerial leaders that was dubbed mini-AZUSA, it was still a major opportunity to preach. Jakes closed out the three-night event on Friday night after two other noted evangelists spoke. Wearing a too-tight, copper-colored suit, the three-hundred-plus-pound evangelist preached a message entitled "Behind Closed Doors."[5] To advertise the videotape series of the mini-AZUSA conference, Bishop Pearson aired seven-minute clips of the three preachers on his Sunday evening TBN broadcast. By what Jakes considers now to be divine intervention, Paul Crouch, owner and president of Trinity Broadcast Network (TBN), was watching the Higher Dimension broadcast that same evening. Crouch was impressed by Jakes and contacted Pearson to inquire about the preacher with the booming voice. For the next eight weeks Crouch aired the hour-long sermon in its entirety.[6]

Undoubtedly Pearson was aware of Jakes's homiletic skill and star potential. He invited Jakes to keynote the 1993 AZUSA Conference.[7] Over twelve thousand people packed into the auditorium in Tulsa, Oklahoma, to hear the West Virginia evangelist preach a sermon based upon his popular women's Bible study class in West Virginia, "Woman, Thou Art Loosed." This sermon catalyzed a seismic shift in the world of black neo-Pentecostalism.

With the publication of the book *Woman, Thou Art Loosed!* and increased honoraria he was earning from his newfound prominence, Bishop Jakes began his own annual gender-specific conferences, "Woman Thou Art Loosed" and "ManPower." He attracted tens of thousands of participants from across the country, causing him to become a celebrity within Pentecostal circles. And within just two years of headlining AZUSA, Bishop Jakes was a bona fide millionaire. Luxury automobiles, a million-dollar mansion, and a variety of flamboyantly hued, custom-made zoot suits became a staple of Jakes's growing reputation.

Bishop Jakes's conspicuous consumption did not necessarily sit well with his working-class West Virginia community: several newspaper articles and editorials were published in West Virginia attacking his lavish lifestyle.[8] His hometown residents called him everything from a crook to a charlatan. Moreover, I am confident that Bishop Jakes was attuned to demographic shifts that were contributing to the megachurch phenomenon along the southern crest. The Sunbelt region of the United States, extending from the southeastern to the southwestern coast, was experiencing a notable population increase, particularly of African Americans.

Southern metropolises like Atlanta, Houston, and Dallas were attracting large numbers of African American professionals opting for a slower-paced and less expensive lifestyle than in northern cities like New York, Chicago, and Detroit. Thus, in the summer of 1996, Jakes departed West Virginia with his personal staff and fifty other families to begin the Potter's House Church in Dallas.

The Theological Thought of Bishop T. D. Jakes

In all of Bishop Jakes's sermons and writings the most pervasive themes are God's compassion and his desire for reconciliation with individuals so that they may become fulfilled. Jakes's theology is heavily influenced by what I have previously referred to as the neo-Pentecostal perspective. He has eschewed the God of hellfire, brimstone, and demands for purity that was historically associated with the traditional Sanctified church and has instead embraced a compassionate God of healing, deliverance, and forgiveness. In accordance with the African leitmotifs that inform black religion in general and classical Pentecostalism in particular, the bishop embraces an experiential religion that conflates the spiritual and the natural insofar as God is concerned with and actively involved in people's everyday lives. And in accordance with the black Spiritual movement and Oral Roberts's healing revivalism, Jakes believes in and promotes a "good God" who is not confined to the negativism and legality of traditional Apostolic faith but instead desires for each person that he or she "prosper and be in health, even as thy soul prospers."

From early on in his public ministry Bishop Jakes denounced classical Pentecostalism for its overemphasis on judgment and piety and its lack of preaching on forgiveness and healing. Jakes attributes this imbalance to a misconception of the nature of God. In his text *Naked and Not Ashamed: We've Been Afraid to Reveal What God Longs to Heal,* he argues that Pentecostalism has effectively promoted the rule-based standards of God but not the love and grace by which God operates in the world. "We have presented no solution to the tragedies of life that afflict our members. We have offered them no balm for the injuries that come from inner flaws and failure. Because we have offered no provision for the sons and daughters who fall, many of our Adams and Eves are hiding in the bushes. Our fallen brethren hear our message but cannot come out to a preacher or a crowd that merely points out their nakedness and has nothing in hand to cover them."[9] Shifting the focus toward the divine attribute of compassion enables Jakes to reconcile the love of God with what he understands to be the travails of life. The bishop regards life as a journey full of missteps and miscues. Some of the pitfalls of life are a result of bad decisions; others are a result of external forces beyond one's control. Yet the sources of hardship, according to Jakes, are irrelevant to God. God is not a cosmological traffic cop who finds pleasure in giving citations to people who have made mistakes on the road of life. On the contrary, according to Jakes, God, because of a compassionate nature, extends infinite grace to those who believe.

The infinite compassion of God leads to the second major theme of Bishop Jakes's theological thought, reconciliation. Reconciliation appears prevalent in his understanding of God and God's activity in the world. This includes the relations of human beings to God and to each other. The proverbial potter cannot put back together what remains alienated, whether this alienation entails isolation from God or estrangement from others in society. Therefore, reconciliation entails healing the wounds of one's past by restoring one's relationship to God and then to family members, friends, and others. This theme particularly rings true among Bishop Jakes's dominant audience, African American women. His books *Woman, Thou Art Loosed!* and *The Lady, Her Lover, and Her Lord* are both dedicated to the themes of overcoming the scars of abuse and ruptured relationships in order to foster healthy relationships and self-care.

Because of his compassion and concern for reconciliation, the God that Jakes advocates appears to be greatly concerned with progression toward individual fulfillment. This is the third and final aspect of Jakes's theological orientation. Again, Bishop Jakes often describes life as either a journey or a series of cycles. We must endure the ebb and flow of our existential circumstances as we do the changing climate of the seasons. But what separates persons of faith from those who have no faith, according to the bishop, is the capacity to continue to move forward, trusting and believing that God will supply provision and protection along the way.[10]

Yet one's ability to endure stress and strife is insufficient. Bishop Jakes is unapologetic about his faith-inspired optimism. *Faith* is an action verb. Accordingly, idleness and endurance in the sense of "just getting by" are not rewarded in the bishop's theological framework. His sermons and writings are full of illustrations, many personal, of the ways

God rewards those who are committed to personal advancement. Bishop Jakes exhausts this notion in books such as *Maximize the Moment: God's Action Plan for Your Life, The Great Investment: Faith, Family and Finance,* and *Reposition Yourself: Living without Limits.*

This unbridled theological optimism and constant call for persons to "live without limits" has caused many to align Bishop Jakes's theology with the Word of Faith movement. Shayne Lee's cultural biography, for instance, dedicates an entire chapter to linking Jakes to the prosperity gospel.[11] Lee connects the bishop's opulent lifestyle and creative fundraising techniques with the Word of Faith movement, though such practices are typical of a whole range of successful black ministers from Adam Clayton Powell Jr. to C. L. Franklin, none of whom could or should be called a prosperity preacher in any formal sense.

Throughout his ministry the bishop has taken pains—at least in print—to distinguish his theological perspective from that of the Faith movement. His writings on individual advancement and fulfillment situate themselves between a classical Pentecostal asceticism that shun worldly goods and a Word of Faith doctrine that considers health and wealth to be signs of godliness. Jakes regards both these attitudes as vices, the extremes of deficiency and excess. He rejects what he considers the vice of austerity insofar as he believes that people have often coped with their inability to advance in society by demonizing success and embracing poverty as a sign of spirituality.[12] The problem here, according to Bishop Jakes, is that poverty precludes viable possibilities for Christians to effect change in society. Speaking of his Pentecostal forebears, he raises the question, "How much more impact these good Christians could have had if they availed themselves of the riches the world offered?"[13] Jakes seems to suggest that Christians in general and Pentecostals in particular must overcome attitudes linking Christianity with poverty and pain if they are to develop a healthy faith.

But Jakes also denounces the other extreme. Just because poverty is not godliness does not mean that health and wealth are signs of one's faith. He has publicly referred to the prosperity gospel as "magic . . . a simple solution to a long term problem."[14] In an early book, he describes adherents to the Word of Faith as people who "believe their identity and acceptance by God is seen in the acquisition of things."[15] At another time he states, "Christianity's foundation is not built upon elite mansions, stocks and bonds, or sport cars and cruise-control living. . . . To make finances the symbol of faith is ridiculous."[16] And the bishop has even gone as far to say that the name-it-and-claim-it idea is "dangerous propaganda."[17]

In fact, unlike the Word of Faith teachings, T. D. Jakes's theological framework possesses an inherent blues sensibility. He can acknowledge tragedy and suffering in life as redemptive. As evidenced in his personal narrative, Jakes maintains a teleological view of suffering as a means of faith and character development.[18] He often and unashamedly recounts how poor his family was in the early days of his commitment to the ministry. And one would never hear a Word of Faith teacher say anything like "It is the agony that creates the ecstasy of life."[19] This is not to say that the bishop believes one has to suffer and experience pain as a mark of faith. But he does seem to assert that God can nurture one's faith amid the tragedies of life.[20]

The Church as a Culture Industry

The Potter's House is located in a developing section of southern Dallas. To enter the campus through the maze of orange cones and vast parking lots is to feel the electricity and attraction that is T. D. Jakes. The parking lot is full of Range Rovers, Cadillac Escalades, and Mercedes Benzes. Parishioners, largely buppies—or aspiring buppies doing their best to look the part—are stylishly dressed and heavily perfumed. On a typical warm Sunday it is common to see four- and five-button three-quarter-length suits on men and nicely fitted business pantsuits or sundresses on women. The tightly clutched Bibles in everyone's hand serve as one of the few, if not only, reminders that these people are at Sunday morning worship. The actual church building is more instrumental than architecturally inspiring. Like a sports complex or convention center, it seems built more to accommodate huge crowds than to impress. There is no question concerning the source of inspiration and entertainment at the Potter's House. The main captivating performer whom everyone has come to see is Bishop T. D. Jakes.

This is evident from how the sanctuary remains less than half full most Sundays even as the worship service begins. While associate ministers and "praise team" members lead the congregation in prayer, song, and praise, the lobby of the church is buzzing with persons making purchases at the Potter's House bookstore while other parishioners enter the expansive front entrance "socially late." The associate ministers and choir can be likened to an interchangeable opening act at a musical concert. The task seems less about quality entertainment (or in this case the effective leading of worship) than about giving everyone time to prepare for the headlining act. By the time Jakes enters the stage and assumes his seat, always to a rousing ovation, the sanctuary is near capacity and a spirit of exuberant expectation fills the air.

With Jakes in the pulpit the functionality of the sanctuary becomes clear. The eight-thousand-seat amphitheater is first and foremost a television studio. The television production cameras and soundboard are placed squarely in the middle of the congregation. Two large screens hang down on each side of the pulpit, displaying the service like a jumbotron in a sports arena.[21] People with cameras roam around the sanctuary to display crowd response on the large screens. Though there is a choir loft in the traditional sense, it appears to be reserved for special occasions. On most Sundays the praise team enters and exits the stage on demand so that during Jakes's sermon he is the only person visible on the stage.

There are no crosses or any other Christian symbols in the sanctuary. This is a growing trend among American megachurches, as conventional Christian icons are often interpreted as signs of traditionalism and denominationalism, two characteristics many megachurches reject.[22] In a similar vein, attendees are not expected to participate in the typical holy ordinances of the church or to abide by the ecclesial calendar at the Potter's House. On one occasion I asked my neighbor if we would participate in communion since it was first Sunday; he answered, "We only have communion a couple of times a year." The only religious images are the matching paintings on each side of the stage of praying hands over a broken water vessel. The message of this brand label is clear: *The Potter wants to put you back together again!*

Undoubtedly, Bishop Jakes's theology underlies his ecclesial commitments. The Potter's House is Jakes's theology incarnate. The notion of God's compassion and his desire that humanity be reconciled and fulfilled is revealed in the congregation's mission statement. It succinctly states, "We are the Voice and the Hand that encourages people to change their lives with hope, comfort and peace." What is more, the congregational vision statement reads: "We have established a reputation for reaching the lost and broken and to minister and serve them with the utmost level of dignity and respect. We are recognized for our dedication to academic and spiritual excellence and mentoring and supporting spiritual leaders. Our environment inspires maximum participation, promotes personal satisfaction, and supports and molds effective leadership."[23] In Jakes's thought, Jesus is the embodiment of ministerial outreach to the suffering and afflicted. The Gospel narrative presents a God of love that reveals Godself in a compassionate Christ figure. A ministry of compassion, then, should serve as the modus operandi for the church. Creating an environment where persons can be healed from their proverbial "issues of blood" (Mark 5.25) and restored to the larger society appears to be the supreme principle by which the work of the church should be measured.

One should not, however, look solely to the Potter's House to interpret Bishop Jakes's ecclesial orientation. The church is central but not exclusive. Though the bishop believes that it is Christ who offers redemption, the church is just one way to access Christ. Bishop Jakes is Christocentric, not ecclesiocentric. As he has written, "We must understand that Christ is the object of our pursuit, and His church is just one of the ways that we access Him. I realize that one does not need to attend church to encounter Christ. . . . Yes, congregational worship is important and essential, but the gathering of people without the presence of Christ is a futile exchange of human interests, religious rhetoric and jargon that does not bring life."[24] One might contend that this perspective has placed Bishop Jakes's ministry at the forefront of an American Christian consumer industry that offers believers sanctified alternatives while taking advantage of the varying culture industries of the larger society.

This is why one should not view the Potter's House as solely a local faith community. It is the institutional headquarters from which the many ministry-related products of either T. D. Jakes Ministries (Jakes's nonprofit entity) or T. D. Jakes Enterprises (the for-profit entity) are packaged, promoted, and distributed nationally and abroad. As in his youth, when he traveled from one congregation to another in West Virginia, the ministry Jakes offers today is larger than a geographic address or locale. Therefore, the Potter's House states that its "brand vision" is "to become a global voice, along a lifelong journey of spiritual and economic hope, encouragement and empowerment to people locally, nationally and around the world." And consistent with this brand vision, the Potter's House professes the following "commitments":

- Influencing generations by the power of our vision and by modeling the way.
- Being accountable for our every word and action.

- Treating each other with dignity and respect.
- Encouraging personal growth by developing and empowering our people.
- Improving the organization by improving ourselves.
- Capitalizing on our strength of ethnic diversity and teamwork.
- Leaving a legacy of hope and promise to future generations.

It also lists the following as "our focus":

- Be the industry leader in what we do.
- Operate the business professionally and efficiently.
- Have a competent, responsible people building a strong team.
- Support our partners and members to achieve their potential.
- Provide the best servant leadership programs.
- Increase communication and information.[25]

The mission statement supports my earlier characterization of neo-Pentecostalism as effectively integrating persons into all fields of human endeavor "in the name of Jesus," allowing the value systems of the culture industries to supplant traditional "holiness" mores, and fostering an emphasis on personal experience over communal concerns or even doctrinal authority.

These neo-Pentecostal characteristics can be specifically illustrated in the way every aspect of T. D. Jakes's ministry is affectively marketed and sold. In 1997, when Jakes shed almost one hundred pounds from his then obese frame, he immediately published *Lay Aside the Weight*. This book provides persons with practical steps for healthy weight loss. The same year when Jakes became famous for baptizing members of the Dallas Cowboys, he featured Deion Sanders, then the Cowboys' Pro Bowl defensive back, as a speaker at Jakes's "ManPower" conferences. Sanders's personal testimony of sexual addiction and attempted suicide was often aired on Jakes's television broadcast and widely distributed with the *ManPower* audio/video series.[26] Jakes also turned the *Woman, Thou Art Loosed!* book and conference series into a music CD, a gospel stage play, a women's study Bible and workbook, a cookbook, and eventually a full-length feature film starring Jakes alongside Hollywood stars Kimberly Elise and Loretta Devine. Continuing to cater to his target audience, African American women, the bishop has even published a romance novel and a musical CD entitled *Sacred Love Songs* with song titles such as "You Are My Ministry," "I Only Dance for You," and "Pillow Talk."

Between 2004 and 2006 Bishop Jakes combined his many annual conferences like "Woman, Thou Art Loosed," "ManPower," and "God's Leading Ladies" into one annual mass event known as MegaFest. This summer festival was held each year in Atlanta and was advertised as a fun family event for all generations. Like Jakes's traditional conferences, MegaFest incorporated the "You Are Not Forgotten" youth extravaganza, a celebrity basketball game, R&B soul concerts headlined by such artists as Chaka Khan and Gladys Knight, and even a comedy show that in 2005 featured famous *Kings of Comedy* host Steve Harvey. In 2004, over 250,000 persons from across the country descended upon the city of Atlanta for this event. To date Bishop T. D. Jakes and the Potter's House ministry hold the single event attendance record at the Georgia Dome. Clearly, the community of faith that T. D. Jakes serves reaches far beyond W. Kiest Boulevard.

The Political and Social Thought of Bishop T. D. Jakes

It is difficult to distinguish between Bishop Jakes's theological and ecclesial orientation and his political activity. Ironically, this can be attributed, in part, to the fact that Bishop Jakes has drawn a sharp line between the pastoral and political realms. When it comes to discussing politics, Bishop Jakes claims to be solely a pastor, someone concerned with the spiritual well-being of the individual on a micro level. Politics, on the other hand, involves social and structural arrangements on a macro level that affects the collective citizenry. The bishop's public professions on the topic reveal him as being principally concerned with the former rather than the latter. In a special editorial published on CNN.com just prior to the 2006 midterm elections, the bishop professed, "I do not believe that African-American ministers should allow their political views to dictate the subjects and tone of their sermons." In referring to the historical engagement of prominent African American clergy in political activity, Jakes said this role, so important in the past, was no longer necessary: "Though the black community was served well by ministers who doubled as political leaders in an era when the pulpit was often our only podium, today, the African-American community is no longer limited to the pulpit as our primary lecture post. We now have thousands of African-American politicians elected to serve our interests, nonprofit leaders funded to lead our communal efforts and academics educated to research our options, and convey their findings to the world."[27]

Recent mainstream commentators have placed Jakes at the helm of a new generation of black leaders. Eschewing the civil disobedience and clarion calls for justice that defined the 1950s and 1960s, Jakes rejects a politically oriented approach to ministry while embracing the social mobility afforded to African Americans by civil rights protesters. But even though the bishop rejects comparisons to historical figures, it is evident, even to the casual observer, that he sees his political activity as building on and moving beyond the work of politically active African American religious figures like Septima Clark, Adam Clayton Powell Jr., and Fannie Lou Hamer. Rather than being like Moses standing outside Pharoah's palace declaring, "Let my people go," Bishop Jakes understands himself to be more like Daniel, who was afforded access and influence to the Babylonian king Nebuchadnezzar as a result of his public piety and fidelity.

When asked during a public conversation between himself and Princeton University professor Cornel West, "What would be the conditions under which you would imagine your ministry to be in fundamental confrontation with the powers that be—the White House, Wall Street?" Bishop Jakes retorted, "I guess the question for me really is: Is all confrontation public?" He went on to add, "Because I find even in my own leadership style—for me, I respond better when you come to see me than if you just write a [public letter]. You can come and sit down with me and say, "You know, there might be a better way of doing that. Look at this and look at that. And bring about the right change in how I do things. Now you won't get the credit, because you don't do it in public."[28] Indeed, Bishop Jakes regards his stance of avoiding public conflict as consistent with his pastoral role. He understands his call as a pastor to be that of a priest, a spiritual mediator. But he takes on this role of mediation not just on behalf of the divine but also between those in political power. Therefore, he does not regard public acts of protest as in his best interest or in the interest of obtaining positive results. In responding to criticisms that he has remained conspicuously silent concerning the war in Iraq and the inept handling of Katrina by the federal government, the bishop defended his action by stating:

> As a man of God, I hate war. And I was horrified, and openly said so, about the handling of Katrina. However, as a man of God, I must do more

than protest—given a chance to do so, I must facilitate meaningful dialogue between opposing views for the betterment of all. To become totally identified with either side is not a luxury I believe we can afford when both major political parties will have long tenures of power when elected. In a crisis, actions outweigh anger, and often we must lay aside our frustrations and work to get our neighbors off the roof and out of the water rather than screaming at cameras for more to be done.[29]

Or, as the bishop rhetorically asked of Cornel West, "What is more effective? To scream in a mic or whisper in his [the president's] ear?" Evidently, then, the bishop understands his vocation as pastor as obligating him to do the latter while affirming what he regards as the biblical principle of working with those in positions of leadership.[30]

Bishop Jakes's conception of his pastoral role as precluding him from taking divisive political stances correlates with his economic prescriptions for the African American community. He emphasizes not outward protest but personal care. Such care includes an economic agenda for the church. In the same editorial from CNN.com where he encourages African American ministers to abstain from the political process, Bishop Jakes contends that the church should encourage "the spawning of entrepreneurial endeavors and business initiatives, including investments and a thoroughly considered community development initiative."[31]

So although Bishop Jakes draws a hard line between the ecclesial and political, he does not have a problem conflating the ecclesial and the economic realms. In fact, he embraces equally his roles as a Christian minister, business entrepreneur, author, recording artist, playwright, and movie producer. The bishop is multivocational when it comes to the respective spheres of the church and corporate America. This is one way he deflects inquiries into his sizable wealth and lavish lifestyle. As he told *Ebony* magazine:

As you know, T. D. Jakes Enterprises co-owns *Woman, Thou Art Loosed* the movie; no other movie producer or record label owner would be called upon to defend the quality of his clothes or the stature of his home. Additionally, the vast majority of the well-informed realized that any author who has 7 million books sold to his credit need not justify his enjoyment of some level of success as a reflection of his life's work. Unfortunately, people often limit preachers to one vocation while they themselves enjoy several. I chose not to allow my faith to restrict me from my for-profit entrepreneurial pursuits. I am proud to be one of Penguin Putnam's top three authors and to be the only African American so distinguished.[32]

This is part of the bishop's mass appeal. Financial success is not incompatible with righteous living. One can be saved, live a committed Christian life, and reap the benefits in all areas. This is the reward to the faithful steward of God's talents. In this sense, Jakes's neo-Pentecostalism is not very different from Max Weber's understanding of the Protestant work ethic and the spirit of modern capitalism. It is the believer's ethical duty to follow and fully exploit an opportunity to turn a profit—not toward the ends of leisure but toward the fulfillment of one's duty to glorify God with one's labor, whether as a successful CEO or a janitor.[33] According to Jakes, the aim is not material goods but "pride, dignity and fulfilling your true purpose."[34]

But even if material goods are not the aim, they have certainly been the reward for Bishop Jakes. His lifestyle embodies economic achievement. His personal aesthetic has become more conservative in recent years as he has traded in the purple and canary-yellow suits for navy blue, black, and gray. But what may have been considered West Virginia flashy has now become Dallas gentry. Bishop Jakes owns several high-end automobiles—including a Bentley he received as a fiftieth birthday present from fellow televangelist Paula White—and resides in a $5.2 million mansion in Fort Worth. And the bishop is not particularly coy concerning what he perceives as God's blessings on his life. He views himself and his many accomplishments as living proof of what faith coupled with the maximization of talents can do. This could be part of the reason why, despite his verbal protestations, some align him and his ministry with the Word of Faith movement. Even though Bishop Jakes disavows the prosperity gospel in theory, he unabashedly embraces and aesthetically performs a prosperous lifestyle in practice. Thus what some may perceive as crass hyperconsumerism, Bishop Jakes, as well as many of his followers, interprets as marks of economic empowerment as well as divine favor.

To be sure, Bishop Jakes places his economic prescription in the context of the peculiar position of African Americans. His emphasis on economic development is a result of America's racial hierarchy. This actually places the bishop along a continuum of several prominent African American leaders throughout the previous century—most notably Booker T. Washington, Rev. J. H. Jackson, and the Honorable Elijah Muhammad—who understood black economic development (over and against political protest) as an efficient way of dismantling racism in America. Bishop Jakes even attributes his own entrepreneurial efforts to the sting of white supremacy. When questioned about how racism has affected his ministry, he provided an account of witnessing his father being verbally berated by a white employer. The bishop went on to explain how that moment became the impetus behind his entrepreneurial pursuits because he was determined to never find himself in that situation.[35] Thus he understands entrepreneurialism as an effective course of action for all persons of color seeking to level America's racialized playing field.

But though Bishop Jakes openly acknowledges the particularities and prevalence of racism in America, he does not believe that the category of race itself should remain subsumed under one's Christian identity. Jakes opposes any conception of racial understanding that would foster or affirm racial separation. His ministry, dating back to the years in West Virginia, has always been concerned with attracting other racial groups,—which in Bishop Jakes's particular case tends to involve moving across the black/white binary. He thus believes that Afrocentric Christian congregations and nationalist faith movements such as the Nation of Islam promote unnecessary division. In his view, their religious faith is constructed upon and in reaction to the particularities of white racism, thereby placing African Americans in a defensive posture and encouraging blacks to paint all whites with the same racialized brush with which whites have painted blacks. The perpetuation of racial segregation in the church is the unhealthy result.

Finally, as it relates to the issue of gender, his ministerial success is built upon speaking to what he, as well as the hundreds of thousands of women who watch his broadcast, purchase his books, and attend his conferences, deems to be the critical issues affecting women's lives. Bishop Jakes's Gospel-inspired concern for extending God's compassion toward the ends of reconciliation and individual fulfillment particularly targets and seemingly resonates with those living under patriarchal abuse and authority, African American women.

Such compassion begins at the point of acknowledgment. According to Bishop Jakes, the *Woman, Thou Art Loosed!* franchise emerged from his concern that issues like sexual abuse and domestic violence were being ignored by the majority male leadership of the church. This acknowledgment was an undeniable and understandable source of attraction for women who were used to hearing the pervasive message of docile submission and self-denial in traditional Christian churches. Bishop Jakes neither sweeps the realities of physical and sexual abuse under the rug nor relegates women's concerns to a once-a-year Women's Day service. He is arguably one of the first male African American preachers of his stature to openly and consistently acknowledge women as the focal point of his ministry and God's concern.

An important correlate to Bishop Jakes's acknowledgment of women's issues is his affirmation of female involvement in all fields and on all levels of human endeavor. As a young man Jakes identified with and was informed by his own mother, Odith, as she sought to balance her professional pursuits with motherhood and a crumbling marriage. In fact, he credits both his grandmother and mother for setting a positive example of achievement in spite of the glass ceilings of gender injustice. Jakes often brags about his grandmother, who worked as a washerwoman yet at the age of fifty returned to college to fulfill her dream of becoming a schoolteacher. And in comparing his mother Odith to the "virtuous woman" described in Proverbs 31, he states, "Throughout my lifetime I watched my mother purchase many 'fields' and 'vineyards,' although in her case they were often rental houses or small business she could run from home. I learned to admire and appreciate the incredible combination of strength and creativity displayed by these [his mother and grandmother] resilient, resourceful women."[36]

Jakes strongly promotes the idea that women have the same capabilities as men because God is no respecter of persons across the gender line. "He [God] calls and uses women and men with equal pleasure and glorification to Himself," Jakes contends.[37] The bishop's book *God's Leading Lady*, from which the aforestated quotes are derived, is intended to move beyond his previous texts, like *Woman, Thou Art Loosed!* and *The Lady, Her Lover, and Her Lord*, that principally address overcoming past abuse and encourage personal care. *God's Leading Lady* engages gender-specific topics like the changing role of women in society and the balancing of domestic life with career aspirations. By acknowledging and addressing these concerns directly, the bishop understands himself as catering to those who most populate his pews on Sunday morning.

Bishop Jakes's perspective and promotion of gender equality are further manifested at the Potter's House and at any of his major conferences targeting women. Unlike the majority of traditional black Baptist and Methodist church leaders, Bishop Jakes has women on his ministerial staff. For a while his wife Serita ministered at the Potter's House, and she continues to sit alongside her husband in the pulpit each Sunday.

And Jakes regularly invites preachers like Paula White, Juanita Bynum, and Suzan Johnson Cook to minister at his sponsored events.

Yet even as Bishop Jakes actively affirms the equality of women in all respects, he makes concerted appeals to gender distinctiveness. His sermons and writings are permeated with allusions and assumptions that articulate his understanding of the essential differences between men and women. His gender specificity dates back to the creation of his gender-specific conferences in West Virginia. A cursory reading of his gender-specific writings reveals that for him "masculinity" and "femininity" are opposites. In other words, according to the bishop, men are from Mars and women are from Venus.

In *Loose That Man and Let Him Go*, for instance, Bishop Jakes calls for a "restoration of man to his God-given masculinity, strength and purpose." Throughout the book he employs hypermasculinist metaphors to illustrate the true nature of man. In a chapter entitled "When I Become a Man," the bishop uses David's slaying of Goliath to paint a picture of how a real man looks and lives. David, according to Jakes, was the embodiment of real manhood because he unashamedly worshiped God, freely expressed his emotions, and was extremely violent when necessary. Jakes writes, "David openly admired his body and enjoyed the deep male passions that God gave him." And after David became king, the bishop says, every male who came up under his influence became "more manly." This, according to Bishop Jakes, was because David was "a real man who knew how to protect his own. He was strong, deadly and tough, but his manhood went deeper than that. He was so secure in his masculinity that he was also sensitive, tender-hearted, and affectionate. He was both a poet and a warrior. David had a harp in one hand and a sword in the other. He lived a man's life in all its fullness."[38]

These sorts of masculine tropes are in stark contrast to Bishop Jakes's renderings of female identity. In *Woman, Thou Art Loosed!* the bishop traces the origins of femininity back to the Garden of Eden. Eve was derived from Adam to be a help-meet, a source of assistance and strength for Adam. Jakes goes on to delineate female uniqueness by saying, "Women were made like receptacles. They were made to be receivers." Men, on the other hand, are givers, "physically, sexually and emotionally." Therefore, women, like receptacles, are naturally open, while men are naturally closed. The bishop then extends this analogy by comparing a man to a power tool and a woman to the electrical source of power. Bishop Jakes uses this image to admonish women against being too open. He says women are naturally vulnerable because of their open feminine nature and therefore "must be careful what you [women] allow to plug into you and draw strength from you."[39]

In his follow-up book, *Daddy Loves His Girls*, the bishop goes further to accentuate gender difference. He protests against those who seek to take the term "Father" for God out of the Bible in favor of gender-inclusive language. "It is so pathetic to think," Jakes surmises, "that changing a word in a book would change a gender in reality." He argues that God as father is not averse to femininity but seeks to provide and protect. God blesses his sons who are made in his images but nurtures his daughters because they are the weaker vessels. To be sure, the bishop qualifies his choice of the otherwise pejorative adjective *weak* by stating, "Not weak in terms of substandard, but weak in terms of softer." He goes on to say, "A silk shirt is more delicate than a cotton one. But it is also more valuable. Weaker doesn't mean lesser, just softer, more satin like."[40]

Even in *Loose That Man and Let Him Go*, a publication that Bishop Jakes has advertised as "a book for men that every woman should read," the hypermasculine image of David the warrior is contrasted to an ultra-feminine image of women. Women, Jakes says, "surround themselves with beautiful things, flowers, and lacy, delicate things that help them to frame and enhance the beauty of their femininity."[41] And in a later text, *The Lady, Her Lover, and Her Lord*, Bishop Jakes even questions the aims of the women's liberation movement. According to him, women's liberation should not be a movement but a mentality that frees women from social oppression and a fear of being unequivocally feminine. For Bishop Jakes believes a woman's strength lies, not in her ability to be hard like men, but in her femininity, which is like "strength in silk wrappings."[42] He then presents what he perceives as positive images of this kind of femininity while simultaneously bemoaning its disappearance as women continue to advance in American society: "In her youth, she was covered with frills and bows. In her adulthood, she was silhouetted in class. In her maturity, she was demure and sedately assured. Have you seen her? Can you remember her? Or has she vanished in the night, unnoticed and unobserved? Has anyone noticed that we are losing a generation of women who have transformed before our eyes into some mutated synthetic replacement for what once was?"[43] Clearly, Bishop Jakes promotes equality and achievement while affirming heightened gender distinctions. In his own words, women should "fight not for equality but neutrality. Your distinctions are too valuable to forfeit."[44]

The ministry of Bishop Jakes illustrates a reordering of the priorities of the black Pentecostal tradition. Far from being "in the world but not of it," he wields a popularity and influence that derive, in part, from his ability to take advantage of America's culture industries. His best-selling books, national conferences, and feature-length Hollywood films have allowed him to transcend the sectarian commitments of classical Pentecostalism and become an iconic figure in the African American community. And by renouncing the asceticism of his Pentecostal roots, Bishop Jakes can openly embrace the luxurious fruits of his celebrity. Jakes has also modified his tradition as it relates to social issues affecting the lives of black people. Rather than assuming a stance of "take the world, but give me Jesus," he has attempted to adjust his ministry to the changing condition of African Americans in the post–civil rights era. This is seen most notably in his outlook on the role of women. His qualified endorsement of gender equality reveals a perspective that pushes the boundaries of African American Pentecostalism while adhering to traditional theological conceptions of what he believes God wants for humanity. As a prominent and influential figure in African American religious broadcasting, Bishop Jakes has provided an opportunity for evangelists of his ecclesiastical tradition to reconsider their views on the inherent capacity of women. On the other hand, he has also reinforced their beliefs about male authority and divine order. In short, Bishop Jakes remains as complicated as he is popular.

The ministry of Bishop Jakes shows how a tradition of commodifying black religious life that began with Pentecostal recording artists and radio figures in the 1920s has expanded into a distinct form of entrepreneurial evangelicalism. Aligning with a larger self-help market, this union between Christianity and the culture industries is not simply profit driven. The neo-Pentecostal perspective seeks to tear down the walls of the church in order to take the message of God's compassion, Christ's concern for reconciliation, and faith-inspired optimism to as large of an audience as possible. In the words of Bishop Carlton Pearson, neo-Pentecostals seek to "make Pentecostalism pretty" so that persons will no longer equate spiritual power with poverty and social apathy. Neo-Pentecostalism affirms spiritual power directed toward the ends of personal transformation and social advancement, which includes economic uplift, racial equality, and gender opportunity in all fields of human endeavor. The religious airwaves and consumer markets are simply a means to disseminate this message and inspire believers and nonbelievers alike.

Televangelists like Bishop Jakes are able to reap great economic profits as a result of their entrepreneurial efforts. But this, according to neo-Pentecostals, is not a bad thing. Rather, it testifies to the fact that they do indeed serve a "good God" who wants all believers to "have more, do more and be more."

Bishop Eddie Long, pictured here with Elder Bernice King at New Birth Missionary Baptist Church in Lithonia, Georgia. Elder King, the daughter of the late Rev. Martin Luther King Jr., is on the ministerial staff at New Birth and considers Bishop Long to be the spiritual successor to her father. Source: AP Images.

5

We Are Soldiers!
The Ministry of Bishop Eddie L. Long

Mine eyes have seen the glory of the coming of the Lord;
He is trampling out the vintage where the grapes of wrath are stored;
He hath loosed the fateful lightning of His terrible swift sword;
His truth is marching on.

> —"Battle Hymn of the Republic,"
> in *African American Heritage Hymnal*

On January 15, 2004, Bishop Eddie Long hosted Trinity Broadcasting Network's *Praise the Lord* broadcast. The audience that evening was primarily African American, and special guests included gospel recording artist Byron Cage and Elder Bernice King, the youngest daughter of the late Dr. Martin Luther King Jr. Though it was never stated explicitly, it was racially implied: this was the network's tacit acknowledgment of the Martin Luther King Jr. federal holiday.[1] But though host Bishop Long abstained from any overt recognition of the slain civil rights leader, the viewing audience did witness an interesting appropriation of Martin Luther King Jr. and the civil rights movement. Bishop Long used this broadcast to air a preproduced video of his congregation, New Birth Missionary Baptist Church, and a march that Bishop Long and Elder King had led the previous month under the title "Stop the Silence."

The video begins with recognizable images of King along with fellow civil rights protesters participating in the Selma march of 1965. Joining hands, they move through jeering, threatening crowds. Confederate flags are prominently displayed and hateful taunts are hurled. Then the video changes from black-and-white footage to colorful images African Americans gathered at the grave of Martin Luther King Jr. at the King Center for Nonviolent Social Change in downtown Atlanta, where Elder Bernice

King lights a torch from her father's eternal flame. As she passes through the crowd, repeatedly murmuring "Thank you, Jesus," she approaches Eddie Long and hands her bishop the torch, to rousing applause. Immediately a hip-hop track begins as we see images of thousands of New Birth members marching toward the state capitol.

Clearly Bishop Long is attempting to conflate his own movement and King's civil rights movement with this contemporarily produced footage. The video shows protesters mocking Bishop Long and his followers as they march through the city. But rather than ardent segregationists, those gathered along Auburn Avenue were actually members and allies of the GLBT (gay, lesbian, bisexual, and transgendered) community, protesting because on December 11, 2004, Bishop Long had called this "Stop the Silence" march to push for an amendment to the state constitution outlawing same-sex marriage. Long and many of his followers interpret "attacks on the American family" as one of the greatest civil rights issues of the contemporary moment. Over the hip-hop soundtrack on the video, Bishop Long's voice declares, "It's time for a revolution!"

Biography

Eddie L. Long was born to Rev. Floyd and Hattie Long in Charlotte, North Carolina. Rev. Floyd Long was a fiery Baptist minister who not only worked as a pastor but also owned a gas station and an auto repair shop. Reportedly, the elder Long had a gift for organizing churches but not necessarily for leading the congregation. Bishop Long now recounts that although he remembers his father organizing many churches, he never remembers him remaining the pastor for more than three years. As the bishop recalls, "He would go in and pioneer a church, build a nice building and then leave."[2] To another interviewer, Bishop Long stated more explicitly, "He [Floyd Long] built many brand new buildings. But shortly after he built them, he would get mad at the deacons and go somewhere else."[3]

Rev. Floyd Long's contentiousness apparently spilled over into his home life. In sermons, writings, and interviews, Bishop Long is candid about the less-than-ideal relationship he had with his father. He describes his father as emotionally distant at best and abusive at worst. Rev. Long never attended any of his son's high school sporting activities or his son's college or seminary graduation. He struggled with alcoholism and was prone to offensive behavior while under the influence. Like most children who were reared in such volatile conditions, the bishop admits to wrestling with the question of whether his father really loved him.[4]

But if Bishop Long describes his father as fiery and ill tempered, he describes his mother in sharp contrast. Hattie Long was a loving and nurturing mother who strove to transform the Long household into a safe place for her son as well as all for the children in the neighborhood. Long often presents his mother as a moral exemplar of a virtuous woman. The bishop credits Hattie with his own accomplishments and contends that it was his mother's faith in God and submission to her husband, in spite of his abusive tendencies, that led her husband to the church and subsequently to the ministry. As Bishop Long now recalls: "Mom would get up in the morning and cook breakfast from scratch— the old-fashioned way. If Daddy came home at eleven o'clock or midnight (even without a phone call, and sometimes with some very shaky reasons), she would get out of bed and fix him a plate of food. Then she would sit there until he was finished, wash the dishes, and have his clothes ready for the next day."[5]

At the completion of high school, Eddie Long headed to Durham to attend North Carolina Central University, where he majored in business administration. After graduation, he began a career as a factory sales representative for Ford Motor Company in Virginia. This career, however, was short-lived. He was fired from Ford for including personal phone calls on his expense accounts.[6] In retrospect, Bishop Long now believes that his firing was part of God's disciplining process. He says that he knew God was calling him to the ministry after college but he opted to pursue a career in the business world. Casting himself as a prodigal, Long describes dire financial circumstances that forced him to live in his car, do day labor, and on one occasion work as a temp shoveling pig slop.

Over the next few years, Eddie Long's fortunes changed for the better. He landed a job with Honeywell in Virginia and entered the ministry at the Springfield Baptist Church in Washington, D.C. He also married his first wife, Deborah, and relocated to Atlanta to attend seminary at the Interdenominational Theological Center (ITC). When Long graduated from ITC, he remained in the Atlanta area, assuming the pastorate of a small congregation in Jonesboro, Georgia. During this time, a budding congregation right on the outskirts of downtown Atlanta in Decatur, New Birth Missionary Baptist Church, was in the midst of a conflict of power and sexual innuendo that forced its organizing pastor, Rev. Kenneth L. Samuel, to resign. Like many African American congregations in major metropolises in the late 1980s, New Birth was experiencing dynamic growth. Persons who were there during the congregational transition remember the attendance as being around 1,500 in 1987. In July of that same year, the New Birth Baptist Church appointed Eddie L. Long as their new pastor.

Initially Rev. Long juggled his pastoral obligations with his newfound role as a single father. Having recently divorced his wife, Rev. Long spent his first four years at New Birth as a single man, a factor that some may argue contributed to his initial success. The charismatic, thirty-something minister's use of slang and hip parlance in the pulpit proved palatable to a growing crowd of young professionals who either had moved away from more traditional congregations or had never attended church at all. And over the years, Rev. Long began to embrace a more ecstatic and experiential form of worship at New Birth. In fact, the congregation would fit well into the category of "Bapticostalism." Long says he first experienced the baptism of the Holy Spirit, including glossolalia, while attending a conference held by televangelist Jimmy Swaggart. And in 1994 New Birth became a flagship congregation of the Full Gospel Baptist Church Fellowship as Bishop Paul Morton consecrated Eddie Long as the organization's third presiding bishop. Though Long severed his ties with the convention within a couple of years of his appointment over a power dispute with Morton, he retained the bishop appellation. That same year the congregation adopted the theme "Taking Authority," based on Jesus's admonition in Matthew 16:19, and began broadcasting on a local cable network.

Today the New Birth Missionary Baptist Church is considered a paragon of the African American megachurch. Having moved to a new 240-acre site in nearby Lithonia in 2001, New Birth constructed a $50 million facility complete with a bookstore, a television production studio, and a full-size recreation center. Bishop Long, an avid weightlifter, also constructed a fitness center, Sampson's Gym, on the property. It includes four full-sized basketball and racquetball courts, saunas, and a football field and has even hosted bodybuilding competitions. When the entire campus is complete (at a projected cost around $80 million) it will include a new building for the church's preschool through eighth-grade Faith Academy, a senior/assisted living community, and an entrepreneurship school. And Bishop Long's Emmy Award–winning television broadcast *Taking Authority* is now aired nationally and internationally on the Trinity Broadcast Network and Black Entertainment Television.

The Theological Thought of Bishop Eddie Long

No theme is more prevalent in theological thought of Bishop Eddie Long than the kingdom of God. His sermons and writings are full of what the bishop refers to as "kingdom business." God's kingdom, for Long, is not isolated to a particular realm but permeates the world. Divisions between heaven and earth, church and state, and sacred and secular are broken down. All things belong to God. This does not mean, however, that all persons have access to God's kingdom. In Long's view, "God has ordained a divine order for life, governments and the church—and this order is invisible to the natural eye. Only those who are saved and baptized into this invisible kingdom can see the order and the arrangement of God."[7] But his theology is not only about the saved and baptized seeing the order and arrangement of God. The church and society must be arranged in a manner consistent with this divine order. Hence, Bishop Long's theology appears to be grounded in a rule-based conception of the kingdom that interprets the role of God in the world as reestablishing God's kingdom according to divinely established precepts set forth during the Creation.

Bishop Long's candor concerning his own family structure, particularly the role of the father, makes sense when one understands that, according to Long's theological framework, God's kingdom begins with the ordering of what the bishop considers God's original institution. Long believes that the family should be the foremost witness to the world of a divine order originating in the Garden of Eden.[8] God instituted with Adam and Eve "a pattern of covering" (man covers and protects woman) that makes humanity complete. After the Fall this order was reconfigured to include a "chain of command" that would sustain healthy relationships. Often referencing the story of Creation, the bishop states, "Covering is related to completion. Chain of command is related to functional, operational working. This chain of command runs throughout God's creation."[9]

The divine order of the family begins with a Christian man who is under the covering of Jesus Christ. Long believes that a man is always under spiritual authority. Thus it is the man's responsibility to decide whether he will be "covered" by the kingdom of God through Christ. This is why Long believes that every major problem plaguing the world can be traced to those he considers to be the heads of families, men.[10] When men do not assume their God-ordained responsibilities, according to Bishop Long, "all hell breaks loose."[11] On the other hand, whenever men accept God's order and submit to Christ and take control of their families, the family, the church, and society are strengthened.

Three key concepts, then, describe the functional chain of divine command: respect, submission, and obedience.[12] First, men are to respect, submit to, and obey God. The functional chain of divine command then extends to women and children. Just as men submit to God, as set forth in the fifth chapter of Ephesians, women and then children must submit to the male headship. Long is clear that "the head of a woman is man— her father until she is married, her husband after her marriage, and if there is an interim period, her pastor. Children are under the authority of their parents."[13] Long says that when women begin to run households they are outside the order and will of God. To be fair, he does not believe that all single mothers are bad mothers. But he does believe that these women and children have been forced to live outside God's divine order, since "it takes a man to instill authority and maintain it."[14]

The requirement that women and children respect, submit to, and obey men does not depend on men's appropriate display of respect, submission, and obedience to God.[15] A man can be out of divine order in relation to his family (i.e., breaking divine commands, like the prohibition of adultery), but it remains the God-ordained call for women to submit to their husbands. In fact, the Bishop promotes his own brand of redemptive suffering when he argues that by obeying the divine command in relation to their husbands and children, women can serve as the redemptive force for the rest of the family. This, according to Long, is part of the power of a submissive woman. Hence the reason, Bishop Long holds up his mother, Hattie Long, as a quintessential example of the power of respect, submission, and obedience. He believes her submission to her alcoholic and abusive husband led not only to his entry into the ministry but to her son's as well. Bishop Long recounts: "I can remember the day that she almost left. She had just about had enough, and she started packing her things. I was crying my heart out in the bathroom, and finally I went to her because I knew my daddy was being a stubborn fool. I said, 'Mama, if you leave, I'll die.' And she said, 'I ain't going nowhere.' Because my godly mother was willing to cover me, I'm here fulfilling my divine call today."[16]

Long emphasizes that when a man takes authority over his family, when a woman submits to her husband (or another man in her life such as a father or pastor), and when children submit to their parents, they do so from a commitment to God. To fulfill one's role in the chain of God's divine command and submit oneself to the appropriate covering is to operate according to a sense of duty to accept God's order. From this sense of duty one can then reap the spiritual and natural benefits of familial relationships.

Bishop Long considers himself a spiritual leader, preacher, and pastor, not a systematic theologian. Though he is a seminary graduate and sits on the board of his alma mater, ITC, the bishop is known for disparaging learned theological scholarship. Further, his sermons and writings seem to be grounded more in practical insight than in established theoretical or philosophical categories. But his sentiments concerning the dominion of God, the salvific power of Jesus Christ, and the traditional interpretation of God's desire for the world are consistent with conservative evangelicalism in general and black Baptist theology in particular.

The Church and the Establishment of God's Order

New Birth Missionary Baptist Church is located approximately twenty miles east of downtown Atlanta in the heart of South Dekalb County. This predominantly African American suburb, composed of portions of Decatur, Lithonia, and Stone Mountain, is purportedly the second most affluent African American community in the nation. New Birth is situated among the gated neighborhoods and the sprawling mansions of Lithonia/Stone Mountain, where professional athletes and entertainers like Terrell Owens, Kelly Price, and Andre 3000 of Outkast reside. Aesthetically, at least, New Birth's 250-acre campus reflects this economic prosperity.

To enter inside New Birth's cathedral-style edifice is to partake of its splendor. One first encounters the frenzy of the lobby, where varying ministries and vendors attract participants and promote sales of B.E.L.L. (Bishop Eddie. L. Long) Ministries products.[17] As in many Charismatic black mainlines, it is easy for congregants to sign up for one of the many ministries of New Birth that participate in community service projects on a regular basis. New Birth's community outreach agenda offers ministries for all ages that include programs directed toward the elderly, the homeless, the imprisoned, and the addicted. Events such as the annual

Heart2Heart 5K Run/Walk for Cancer Research are able to advertise and solicit support from the ten to fifteen thousand congregants that enter the cathedral on any given Sunday. Most recently, New Birth developed Project Kingdom, which provides reliable transportation to single mothers and helps pay down the debt of qualifying parishioners. Moreover, both before and after the service, B.E.L.L. Ministries, and possibly any other televangelist that may be ministering for the morning, can set up tables to sell ministry-related products like audio and videotapes of sermons and books. The marketplace atmosphere seems to add to the sense of excitement as congregants prepare to enter the worship auditorium.[18]

The sanctuary is immaculate and meticulously decorated. Large gold crosses are positioned on each side as well as directly in front of the pulpit, banners that read "New Birth" hang from the rafters, and the church logo, an image of a sword, shines from the ceiling and is reflected on the carpet at the base of the pulpit.[19] Also inside New Birth's sanctuary are 6,100 amphitheater-style seats, four large video screens, a four-hundred-seat choir loft, and an orchestra pit for the church's complete band ensemble. On any given Sunday each of the two services extends into an overflow arena where congregants can view the services on additional full-size screens. To be sure, New Birth's sanctuary represents the changing face of today's churches that are being transformed by technologically innovative forms of worship and contemporary architectural structures. This is even evidenced in the language used to describe sanctuaries like that of New Birth. People are ushered in from the lobby rather than a narthex. Congregants are now seated in the worship auditorium as opposed to the nave. And the worship service is no longer led from the chancel but from the stage.

This sense of a theater is important, for the service at New Birth is dynamically orchestrated from start to finish. Though Bishop Long is a charismatic and captivating figure, the worship service at New Birth does not appear to depend on him as much as the Potter's House service does on T. D. Jakes. Whereas at the Potter's House a team of praise singers serve as an opening act to kill time until Bishop Long gets to the pulpit, the choir and musical ensemble at New Birth play an essential role in the service every Sunday. New Birth is known for its celebrity music ministers, gospel recording sensations who have ranged from Byron Cage to Darwin Hobbs. The sanctuary is packed from the beginning of the service because no one wants to miss the concert hall–style performance of New Birth's talented worship leaders. From the invocation to the benediction, the sense of spiritual expectancy and worship fills the sanctuary. In fact, many admit that they attend New Birth not so much for the bishop's homiletic ability as for the entire worship experience. Bishop Long is not necessarily celebrated for his preaching prowess like Bishop Jakes or his homiletic clarity like Pastor Dollar. And journalist investigations have even revealed that Bishop Long's sermon in response to the Virginia Tech shootings was purchased from www.esermons.com, a Web site where preachers can purchase a sermon for a fee.[20] But this seems to matter little to the thousands who pack into New Birth each Sunday. The electrifying and engaging entertainment orientation of New Birth Missionary Baptist Church has even earned it the nickname in the metro Atlanta area of "Club New Birth."[21]

New Birth's organizational structure is based on Long's God-ordained family order, since Long believes that the church should be modeled after the home. According to the bishop, the democratic systems in place at Baptist churches, featuring management by the traditional deacon or trustee boards, are "ungodly governmental structures" that are outside God's order.[22] Long believes that the church in the black community died around 1950 as a result of a failed order in the church.[23] He testifies that after he consulted God about God's order for the church, God told him, "I have nothing to do with most of the churches in America because they are run by constitutions that 'protect' them from the 'set ministry' I have placed in their midst to lead them. They have replaced My order with their own rules and regulations, and they have chosen to direct their own destiny by 'vote' instead of MY Spirit and My revealed Word."[24]

In Long's theological framework, the church in God's order, like the family in God's order, is run, not democratically, but according to divine authority and the concepts of respect, submission, and obedience. Like the family, the church must submit to one spiritual authority, and this authority is vested in the person of the pastor, who in turn answers to God. The ruling elders submit to the authority of the pastor, and the congregants submit to the elders. Therefore, in a move that surely his father, Floyd Long, would have approved of, Bishop Long dissolved the various boards at New Birth and wrested all decision-making power from the trustees and deacons. Bishop Long believes that on the day he changed New Birth from a traditional Baptist polity to his own church, no longer allowing a deacon board to "grip the purse strings" or accepting for himself the role of "the hired preacher," he became the "true pastor" of the congregation.[25]

For this reason, Long is regarded not just as a pastor but as the spiritual father of the New Birth family. Just as Long refers to God the Father as "Daddy," he often refers to himself and is referred to as "Daddy" in relationship to the congregation. Affirming the order of the church, he boldly asserts, "I tell the members of my congregation, you are the sons and daughters in the church, and I am the father. I don't do this because I'm an egomaniac; I do it because it is biblical."[26] Long derives this biblical mandate from the Apostle Paul and the ordering of the New Testament church.

In the epistle of Paul to Titus, the apostle leaves Titus instructions concerning the ordering of the faith community in Crete and the appropriate qualification of ministers: "I left you behind in Crete for this reason, so that you should put in order what remained to be done, and should appoint elders in every town, as I directed you: someone who is blameless, married only once, whose children are believers, not accused of debauchery and not rebellious. For a bishop, as God's steward, must be blameless; he must not be arrogant or quick tempered or addicted to wine or violent or greedy for gain; but he must be hospitable, a lover of goodness, prudent, upright, devout and self-controlled."[27] This is the order that Long has instituted at New Birth. Rather than following the traditional Baptist licensing and ordination practices of becoming a minister and reverend respectively, those in the ministry at New Birth assume the title of elder. In the episcopal hierarchy, an elder is ranked below the senior pastor. Eddie Long, in a sense, fills the roles of both Paul and Titus at New Birth in that he is both the presiding bishop and the senior pastor. Accordingly, everyone he ordains as an elder at New Birth becomes a "son" in the faith and ministry.

The Political and Social Thought of Bishop Eddie Long

Bishop Long is a devout patriot. He reveres America as the sovereign creation of God and interprets his ministerial role as getting America back to what he considers the sublime principles of her founding. For him, society must be divinely ordered by the same precepts that govern the family and the church if God's kingdom is to be reestablished. This is why Bishop Long traces all social maladies back to the failures of the church and family. When the home is in order, the church is in order. And when the church is in order, it can assume its rightful place as the governing force for the larger society.

But since the church has been "out of order" since around the 1950s, according to the bishop, the American government and larger society have gone awry.[28] Describing what he perceives as America's decline, Long states:

> God chose God-fearing men and women to establish this nation. By His sovereignty God established the United States of America; yet because of the failures of the Supreme Court and the executive branch over the last few decades, we have dared to push God away instead of pulling God close. We have rejected truth and refuse to inherit the hearts of our forefathers; therefore we have redrafted this nation into something other than what God ordained it to be. The United States today is a mockery before God and a shadow of what we are ordained to be because we have become a nation in rebellion.[29]

Long holds similar views concerning the leadership of civic and social organizations. Though he applauds volunteers and agencies that commit their time to helping others, they are still out of God's order. Thus he believes that all civic service organizations should submit themselves to the church under the banner of Christ.[30] Long avows that if American governmental and service organizations would do this then "all the nations of this earth would be blessed."[31]

It appears, then, that Bishop Long advocates a Christian theocracy, or, more literally, an ecclesiocracy for American society in which a religious body or leader rules in the name of God. Though Long's theology does entail a strong division between sacred and secular—practically more than theoretically, since all things belong to God but only the saints can identify and interpret God's kingdom and plan for the cosmos—Long does not believe in the separation of church and state. The church is the sacred and the state is the secular. But the state is the secular only insofar as it has not been rightly claimed by the church. Rather than believing that we should render unto Caesar what is Caesar's and to God what is God's, Long believes that all things belong to God. Therefore, it is the responsibility of Christians to seize all power and resources from the control of a secular Caesar.

Consistent with having such an orientation to society, Bishop Long has never been shy about his social and political involvement. In 1997, when a student was stabbed to death at a local high school, Bishop Long transformed a schoolwide assembly into an old-fashioned revival service. In 1999 Long invited former Republican presidential candidate Steve Forbes to speak at a Saturday morning service.[32] Sharing the pulpit with Forbes and then-Republican congressional candidate Sunny Warren, who was in a bitterly contested race against then-incumbent Cynthia McKinney, Long told his congregation, "Somewhere, maybe in the 67th book of the Bible, I guess, it says, 'Black people, thou shalt not vote for Republicans—but that is not true. Vote for change. Change gets results." And in 2004, Bishop Long organized what can be considered his most public and controversial event to date: the previously described "Stop the Silence" march in support of the constitutional amendment to ban gay marriage. Though critics have accused megachurch ministries of being apolitical, Long's actions exemplify his megachurch's aggressive involvement in politics.[33]

If Bishop Jakes portrays himself as being in conversation with the ruling elite, Bishop Long has attempted to portray his ministry as one in conflict with the powers that be—a lone truculent voice attempting to establish God's true order. Bishop Long refers to Bishop Jakes as his spiritual father and mentor, but Bishop Long's adherence to a Father God of justice and divine order contrasts with Jakes's emphasis on love and reconciliation extending from a compassionate Christ. When Long makes the charge that Christian ministers have "watered down the gospel to make it seeker-friendly" and "in doing so . . . have come into agreement with homosexuality, abortion and countless other vital issues about which God's word is clear," he would seem to be criticizing Bishop Jakes.[34] This criticism is consistent with ultraconservative bloggers' and ministries' attacks against ministries like that of Jakes. Whether Bishop Long is actually in contention with the establishment is a debate we will return to in a later chapter.

But though Jakes and Long present themselves very differently in the public square, both men believe that economic empowerment is the key social issue affecting African Americans today. Long contends that the church can change the larger society only by becoming financially independent. His sermons are often directed toward parishioners' becoming financially empowered and debt free. On a recent broadcast he encouraged New Birth members to come and lay their credit cards at the altar and volunteered to pay the remaining balance on selected cards.[35]

To be sure, Long has taken advantage of the many economic opportunities available to him as pastor of New Birth. In 1996, Bishop Long and the New Birth Missionary Baptist Church purchased 170 acres of real estate property near Atlanta's Hartsfield-Jackson Airport for a mere three million dollars. In less than two years the congregation was able to sell the property for fourteen million. With this enormous profit New Birth was able to clear all congregational debts, purchase the 240 acres in Lithonia out of pocket, and erect New Birth's current state-of-the-art facility.

Bishop Long also boldly and overtly models a personal aesthetic of economic empowerment. His style is more that of a hip-hop mogul than that of a traditional Baptist preacher: three-quarter-length custom-made suits, alligator shoes, and gold chains. His conspicuously placed ring with the New Birth sword logo is as much of a Bishop Long fixture as the microphone it wraps around. A large-faced, diamond-bezel watch that was reportedly designed by hip-hop icon "Jacob the Jeweler" is often prominent on the bishop's wrist. Skin-tight muscle shirts, worn either under his suits or alone, as well as sleeveless cassocks and tightly fitted robes, are staples of the bishop's wardrobe. And Bishop Long's private garage at New Birth holds a fleet of luxury cars, including two Bentleys, a Rolls-Royce, and a Maybach.

Bishop Long's opulent lifestyle has attracted both criticism and admiration. Alongside Senator Grassley's investigation into Bishop Long's ministry spending patterns, the bishop has come under increased media scrutiny for what some believe to be violations of IRS regulations concerning tax exemption. In 2005 an Atlanta Journal and Constitution article entitled "Bishop's Charity Generous to Bishop" revealed that Bishop Long had accepted over three million dollars in compensation from a nonprofit, tax-exempt charity that he had established a decade earlier to assist the needy and spread the Gospel. Over a four-year period Long received a $1.4 million, six-bedroom, twenty-acre home; a $350,000 automobile; and more than a million dollars in salary from the charity. The bishop's attorney defended Long's use of charitable funds by claiming that the decisions had been approved by an oversight committee, a four-member board on which Bishop Long and his wife Vanessa occupy two of the seats. And Bishop Long defended his compensation from the tax-exempt fund by stating: "We're not just a church, we're an international corporation. We're not just a bumbling bunch of preachers who can't talk and all we're doing is baptizing babies. I deal with the White House. I deal with Tony Blair. I deal with presidents around this world. I pastor a multimillion dollar congregation. You've got to put me on a different scale than the little black preacher sitting over there that's supposed to be just getting by because the people are suffering."[36]

But regardless of the Atlanta newspaper's report, IRS regulations, or Senate inquiries, many celebrate the bishop as an example of African American economic empowerment and business success. Along with Bishop T. D. Jakes, he has even made the cover of *Black Enterprise* magazine. The bishop's parishioners believe that his lifestyle is commensurate with that of other CEOs in corporate America. And since the bishop's business involves "kingdom business," many feel that Bishop Long deserves to earn more than those operating in the secular realm.

Bishop Long's emphasis on economic empowerment goes along with a downplaying of issues of racial injustice and inequality. According to Long, racism is no longer an issue affecting African Americans. Money is the key. In a 2002 sermon delivered in Martin Luther King's former pulpit at the annual Martin Luther King Jr. holiday celebration at Ebenezer Baptist Church, Long admonished African Americans for refusing to "forgive and forget" racism in America. According to Long, Martin Luther King successfully led blacks out of the wilderness of racial discrimination, and as "children of the Promise" black people have the responsibility to seize and conquer the economic opportunities that God has made available to them:[37]

> The paralysis of analysis has held us for forty years. We are sitting up here remembering slavery, remembering this, remember that, rehashing this, rehashing that. Getting caught up in every meeting because we keep remembering stuff that happened. Please understand there are bumper stickers that say "stuff happens." The Bible says that in this world you will have tribulations, but God is saying "get over it because I have already overcome the world." . . . In order to reach for some things we have to let go of some things and quit trying to figure out who did it, why they did it, how they did it and all that sort of stuff because there is a greater goal, greater mission and greater purpose and God has called us to walk in all of that.[38]

After rearticulating King's final speech in which he declared that God had shown him the Promised Land, Long, despite the visibly tepid response that he received from those assembled in Ebenezer, continued:

> I want to make an announcement to this second generation, the generation that we are living in right now. Not only have we seen the Promised Land but if you open up your eyes we are walking in it. We can't no longer stand on the other side of the mountain and not go over to the other side. I have

an announcement for you: we are already in the Promised Land and if you open up your eyes you will see that a lot of the things that we are fighting have gone away and are therefore memories.[39]

Here Long takes the exodus theme—a staple of African American religious practice and political thought since the antebellum South—to its logical conclusion, that of conquest. This theme of conquest is consistent with the aggressive, militaristic tone that typifies Long's ministry. Long's television broadcast is called *Taking Authority*, and four of his books are entitled *Taking Over, Called to Conquer, Gladiator*, and *It's Your Time: Reclaim Your Territory for the Kingdom*. The bishop even runs a bookstore at a local mall named "Conquest," and sermon titles such as "Conquer and Subdue," "Obedience," and "Rein or Maintain" are common.

If Martin Luther King Jr. is considered the Moses of the black church for leading African Americans out of the dark night of Jim Crow, Bishop Long views himself as God's Joshua. The "Stop the Silence" video attempts to convey that Bishop Long has assumed the spiritual mantle of Martin Luther King. Many of his followers feel that he is leading African Americans out of a the wilderness, where they have wandered for forty years since the civil rights movement, and into the Promised Land, where they will achieve a divinely promised economic prosperity.[40]

To be fair, this reputation for taking over King's leadership is not solely based on Bishop Long's own delusions of grandeur. Elder Bernice King has publicly promoted Bishop Long within televangelist circles as the spiritual successor to her father. She ceremonially passed him the torch in 2004 at the King Center, and in 2006, at the death of Coretta Scott King, she stirred up controversy among her siblings and the larger community when she elected to hold her mother's funeral at New Birth with Bishop Long presiding rather than at the historic Ebenezer Baptist Church. In promoting her bishop as the heir apparent to her father, Elder King has even adopted the militaristic imagery that characterizes Bishop Long's ministry at New Birth. In the foreword to Long's text Taking Over, Elder Bernice King writes,

Bishop Long's voice and message will propel the body of Christ to the forefront of every segment of our American society. We will listen and take heed, not merely because his message is biblically accurate and precise, but because he has successfully developed a ministry that is a force with which to be reckoned. . . . I believe that more and more of us, church leaders in particular, will be referring and deferring to the leadership of Bishop Eddie Long and his ministry at New Birth for our marching orders. I say "marching orders" because we are at war with Satan and his imps, and we will lose if we don't know how to prepare and how to position ourselves for this war.[41]

But more than a metaphor, this rhetoric of conquest, domination, and submission tied to the establishment of God's kingdom and divine order informs the bishop's geopolitical outlook in relation to the U.S. military-industrial complex and American foreign policy across the globe. On September 12, 2001, the day after the horrific attacks of September 11, Bishop Long argued for retaliation on the basis of his view that "every major move of God happened after a great tragedy." After claiming that both World War I and World War II had ushered in great Charismatic movements, Long suggested, "Do you realize what is about to happen, the borders are about to explode. . . . It's about God's Kingdom, it's about His rulership, it's about God Almighty, it's about subduing nations, it's about snatching folk out of darkness into the marvelous light."[42]

Also, in March of 2003, the night President George W. Bush declared war against Iraq, Long cited Genesis 3 to argue that modern-day Iraq is the original Garden of Eden. The Bishop went on to make his case by saying,

> Ya'll missing it. Ya'll been watching too much CNN, this is what happened, it is the Kingdom of God. Watch This. . . . Watch This. . . . It might look small at first but we are establishing God's kingdom. We are coming together and what God is doing with the Body of Christ in America is developing a world view because we have been so narrow-minded and short sighted because we have been so spoiled and ain't been touched that everything about *our religion has been confined to the borders of the U.S.A. But God is saying I am bigger than the borders of the U.S.A.* So I have to bring you into a worldview. *You cannot talk Kingdom and stay in America. . . . You better get ready to fight because it really ain't about Iraq, it is about the Kingdom of God.* [Emphasis mine][43]

One can surmise, then, that according to Bishop Long support for the extension of American imperialism is an effective means of establishing God's kingdom on earth. A jingoistic patriotism pervades his sermons and writings. In the "Stop the Silence" march video, Bishop Long's voice can be heard saying, "I am not against anyone, I love everybody. But what people must understand that when they come into my house, there are rules in my house. The problem with America is that we have opened our doors to a whole lot of different people. But if you don't like the rules of the house, you can go on back to where you came from."[44] Like John Winthrop's historic address to the Massachusetts Bay Colony, Long interprets America as a "city on a hill," a moral beacon to the rest of the world. This orientation of American exceptionalism, once again, places the bishop squarely in the tradition of conservative Protestant politics dating back to the Puritans and evidenced in subsequent American religious patriots ranging from Billy Sunday to Prophet James F. Jones and from Rev. J. H. Jackson to Rev. Jerry Falwell.

In terms of the issue of gender, it is apparent that Bishop Long's theological orientation is constructed on a sharp gender divide and hierarchy. Men are called to a place of domination and authority, and women, like children, are called to submission and obedience. Men cover, and women and children submit to being covered. One would think that as a result of these strict gender norms and his adherence to the biblical text of Titus Bishop Long would disavow women in the ministry. This is not the case. Like the Full Gospel Baptist Church Fellowship of which Long was once a part, he affirms the ministerial role of women. Women are appointed as elders at New Birth; some of the most notable are Elder Bernice King and Elder Vanessa Long, the bishop's wife. Also, prominent women evangelists like Pastor Darlene Bishop, Pastor Paula White, and Dr. Cynthia Hale, pastor of the Ray of Hope megachurch in the greater metropolitan area of Atlanta, often minister at New Birth. Though this may appear to be a contradiction, a closer look reveals that Long is consistent in his thought. These women, while affirmed in their ministry, have all submitted to a male ministerial covering.

For example, aside from the female clergy who submit to Bishop Long's spiritual authority as senior pastor of New Birth, Pastors Darlene Bishop, Paula White, and Cynthia Hale typify leading female evangelists' relationship to male authority figures in this mass-mediated evangelical subculture. Until recently, for instance, both Darlene Bishop and Paula White submitted to the authority of their co-pastor husbands at their local congregations. This remains true for Darlene Bishop, and although Paula White and her husband Randy White announced their divorce in 2007, White continues to call Bishop T. D. Jakes "Daddy" in public and has also partnered with the Family Praise Center in San Antonio, Texas, which is led by her current romantic interest, Bishop Rick Hawkins. In addition, Bishop Long refers to Dr. Cynthia Hale as "daughter." Dr. Hale, who is not married and is well respected as an accomplished and erudite pulpiteer from the Disciples of Christ denomination, is one of the many pastors from across the country who has submitted her ministry to Bishop Long. Long founded a loosely organized network of partner churches that he refers to as "The Father's House." Their relationship with him, not unlike the relationship between Oral Roberts and his organized team of local partners in every major city, can prove beneficial for local pastors. With the bishop's assistance, in 2001 Dr. Hale was able to relocate her growing congregation, Ray of Hope Christian Church, into the 3,500-seat facility in Decatur that New Birth had owned before its relocation to Lithonia. So despite being powerful and influential women in their own right, these women whom Bishop Long affirms in ministry still model outwardly the divine chain of command and order of God in their own homes and churches.

Further, Bishop Long's ministry is principally masculine centered and directed. Restoring men to their rightful place of kingship and what he commonly refers to as "rulership" is his primary objective. According to his conception of divine order, women cannot be "loosed" or "delivered" until men are restored. Hence, men play a messianic role: neither women nor children can be what they are called to be unless they are nurtured under male authority. Men were placed on earth to protect and provide. Anything less, for Long, is outside God's will. Bishop Long believes that the devil is out to destroy black men. As he sees it, "The devil knows that if he gets the man, he also gets the woman and child."[45]

The bishop's understanding of man's essential nature is still primarily homosocial. A man's role in the kingdom depends, first, on his fulfilling and performing a particular masculinist role. According to the bishop, man has the God-given nature of a fighter. Men are called to join forces with other men since "warriors gravitate to warriors." Long continues: "Every man I know is looking for someone to cry, 'Charge!' Men will move locations, switch jobs, and even change religions because they see a leader of men crying, 'Charge! Let's take this territory. Let's move in and rule!' Men all over this world are looking for someone to say, 'Let's go, brother. Lock your arms with mine and let's conquer this thing.'"[46] While it is not exactly clear to what Long is referring in his metaphorical call to conquer, I do not think identifying the object of conquest is the bishop's main point. The intention here is to express the essence of

manhood. Men are warriors who need to perform their masculine proficiency publicly. It appears, therefore, that in Bishop Long's worldview it
is incumbent on men to join with other men in homosocial space, away
from women, in the name of physical authority and violent conquest so
that they may bring "things" into submission. This, for Bishop Long, is
the essence of true manhood.

The ministry of Bishop Long both extends and reconceptualizes the
theological, ecclesial, and sociopolitical orientations of the black mainline tradition. Consistent with the respectability discourse and activity that have historically defined mainline congregations of the middle
class, Bishop Long affirms a conservative orientation toward economic,
racial, and gender issues with the aim of effectively integrating parishioners into the dominant society. Yet New Birth and Bishop Long would
fit well into the category of "Bapticostalism" since the congregation
encourages experiential encounters with the divine. Further, as pastor of
the New Birth Missionary Baptist Church, Bishop Long oversees wide-
ranging community-minded ministries and is known for his civic and
political involvement. Bishop Long understands himself to be a political
power broker with access to the powerful, in the tradition of Rev. Joseph
H. Jackson. And Long interprets his role in the public realm as that of
sounding a moral alarm in the tradition of Dr. Martin Luther King Jr.
From Trinity Broadcast Network and Black Entertainment Television in
the United States to television networks in the Philippines, Amsterdam,
New Zealand, and Holland, Bishop Long has a global presence across
the religious airwaves. And through his *Taking Authority* broadcast and
video distribution, he seeks to spread his message of moral conservatism
and Christian values in order to foster change on a societal level, bringing into submission all forces that he perceives to be in conflict with the
establishing of God's kingdom order.

As a prominent figure among black mainline congregations that are
embracing religious broadcasting, Bishop Long has set an example for
evangelists of the mainline tradition. He publicly performs the righteous indignation of previous generation of black preachers who engaged
social issues while at the same time adapting to a Charismatic, postdenominational climate that has turned from an emphasis on the church to
an emphasis on individual spiritual encounters. Charismatic mainlines
affirm conservative values and the goals of mainstream integration and
social advancement. Thus they largely encourage full participation in the

capitalist economy, embrace the cultural mores of the dominant society, and advocate a Victorian ordering of the family as a viable means of social stability. The religious airwaves are used, then, not only to disseminate the message of a particular televangelist but to confer authority on individuals who understand themselves to be extending the traditional role of African American religious leaders as the principal moral voices of American society.

6

Fill My Cup, Lord

The Ministry of Pastors Creflo and Taffi Dollar

What shall I render unto God for all His blessings?
What shall I render, Tell me what shall I give?
God has everything; Everything belongs to Him.
What shall I render, Tell me what shall I give?
——"What Shall I Render?" in *African American Heritage Hymnal*

The World Changers Church International is located just southwest of downtown Atlanta in the city of College Park. If New Birth Missionary Baptist Church reflects the prosperity of its South Dekalb zip code, then the World Changers Church stands out as a spiritual oasis in a vast desert of urban decay and blight. Situated off Old National Highway—a major thoroughfare that runs through College Park and is known for its abundance of pawnshops, auto repair stores, and a number of after-hour establishments—the gilded dome of the World Changers sanctuary is as conspicuous in the community as Pastor Dollar's Rolls-Royce in the parking lot.

As one of the principal voices of the growing prosperity gospel movement, Creflo Dollar is by no means reticent about his emphasis on financial gifts. Inside the sanctuary, large white plastic buckets are attached to the end of each row for the offering. And a typical Sunday service begins with recorded testimonies, broadcast on the theater screens in the front of the sanctuary, in which people tell how they have been blessed by Dollar's teachings and how God has allowed them to reap financial harvests according to their obedience in giving. Televangelism, then, even permeates the worship service. Behind the choir stand, the rear of the pulpit is adorned with a large revolving gold globe to signify the ministry's global orientation and aim—World Changers Church International is "Changing Your World."

Biography

Creflo A. Dollar Jr. was born to Creflo Sr. and Emma Dollar in College Park, Georgia. Creflo Sr. was one of the first African American police officers in this southwest Atlanta community. College Park, Georgia, was then, like many southern towns in the 1970s, undergoing a racial demographic shift from predominantly white to almost exclusively African American. Young Creflo Dollar experienced firsthand the pressures that came along with formal and informal desegregation efforts. In fact, when he entered elementary school he was the first, and for a while the only, African American to attend College Park Elementary School, where his mother, Emma, worked in the school cafeteria.

As a youngster, Creflo Jr. was not particularly religious; he was more interested in athletics. His father coached youth football and baseball, both sports at which Creflo excelled. After graduating from Lakeshore High, where he was a star student athlete and student government president, Creflo Jr. went on to play football at West Georgia College. In college Creflo Dollar became active in the church and accepted, though reluctantly, his call to ministry. In 1983 he was ordained at the Shiloh Missionary Baptist Church and organized a Bible study group on campus.[1] The next year Dollar graduated with a bachelor's degree in education and began teaching in the Atlanta public school system while working part time as an occupational therapist at Brawner Psychiatric Institute. The young Baptist minister and schoolteacher married Taffi Bolton, a former classmate at West Georgia who had accepted Christ at one of Dollar's Bible study meetings. The couple then moved back to the College Park community of Creflo's youth. And in the cafeteria of the same elementary school where his mother had once worked and where he had attended, Creflo Dollar organized the World Changers Church.

In three years World Changers was up to a membership of about five hundred. Many early members recall and credit Pastor Dollar's lucid yet laconic preaching style with attracting new members each Sunday. Once they outgrew the elementary school cafeteria, the congregation moved into an abandoned Baptist church in College Park. Though ordained Baptist, Pastor Dollar consciously claimed no denominational affiliation

Pastor Creflo Dollar seen here promoting one of his several self-help books entitled *Eight Steps to Create the Life You Want*. Source: Raymond Boyd, photographer, Getty Images Entertainment.

for himself or his church. At some point, he came under the tutelage and ecclesial auspices of the prominent Word of Faith evangelist Kenneth Copeland. Creflo Dollar partnered with Copeland's ministry and became one of Copeland's largest financial supporters. Never having attended seminary or undertaken any kind of formal theological preparation, Dollar received his ministerial training from attending Believers' Voice of Victory conferences and listening to his mentor's audiotapes for hours at a time. Before long, Creflo Dollar began preaching Copeland's Word-Faith theology in College Park.

The impact of Kenneth Copeland's ministry on the young Atlanta preacher remains unmistakable and undeniable. To close one's eyes and listen to a Creflo Dollar sermon is to hear his mentor Kenneth Copeland. The latter's southwestern sermonic cadence, voice intonation, and punctuated "Glory be to God" are all Dollar staples today. And as Creflo Dollar testifies, their spiritual bond is so strong that he refers to Copeland as "Dad" and to himself as Copeland's black son.[2] Further, Creflo Dollar's interracial ecclesial realignment has clearly been materially beneficial to him. Within five years of partnering with Copeland, World Changers was building a state-of-the-art eight-thousand-seat worship center, referred to as the World Dome, and the Dollars were whisking across the country in a private Lear jet, reportedly a gift from Copeland.

Throughout the 1990s World Changers Church became one of the fastest-growing congregations in the country, and Creflo Dollar became a major player within the national Word of Faith community. The latter is due, in part, to a racial rift within the movement. In 1996, Rev. Frederick Price, who was arguably then the leading African American within the Word of Faith subculture, became embroiled in a conflict with his previous mentor, Kenneth Hagin Sr. The dispute involved overtly racist remarks made by Kenneth Hagin Jr. on a tape-recorded sermon from 1993. According to the Hagin heir, miscegenation was against God's will and Hagin had made it clear to his children that they could have African Americans as friends but never be involved with them romantically. In outrage, Rev. Price protested to Hagin Sr., who took the side of his son.

Over the next few years, Price began decrying racism in the Christian church in general and the Word of Faith community in particular. He preached a yearlong sermon series on racism at Crenshaw Christian Center and self-published a three-volume book entitled *Race, Religion and Racism*. Rev. Price's protests, however, did little to dismantle the expanding Word of Faith movement, particularly in relation to its hegemonic influence in the world of Christian broadcasting. Thus Rev. Price, despite his previous status in the Faith community, received less television time for a while on major networks like TBN and was harshly criticized by many of his former white allies and benefactors.

Rev. Price's racial awakening could not have happened at a more felicitous time for Pastor Dollar. Distancing himself from Price and the controversy, Pastor Dollar remained connected to the Tulsa-based movement. While Rev. Price was increasingly marginalized, Creflo Dollar and the World Changers Ministry came to the fore. A review of the preaching rosters of the prominent Word of Faith national conferences sponsored by Kenneth Copeland that were held in the ensuing decade shows that Creflo Dollar is the one constant African American representative along-side prominent white evangelists like Kenneth Copeland, Jerry Savelle, and Jessie Duplantis.[3] With an international television broadcast reaching millions and a host of books being published by the Tulsa-based Harrison House, Creflo Dollar became the de facto African American spokesman of the Word of Faith message.[4] In 1998, Oral Roberts University awarded Creflo Dollar an honorary doctorate degree and appointed him to the university's Board of Regents.

By the new millennium, Dollar had further diversified the outreach of World Changers Church International. His wife, Taffi Dollar, entered the ministry and was named co-pastor of World Changers. Pastor Creflo Dollar developed International Covenant Ministries, a service to provide leadership and instruction to like-minded ministries across the globe. And the Dollars founded Arrow Records, which they describe as a Word-based record company that packages and promotes a variety of gospel music styles. In 2004, the Dollars established World Changers New York in response to his growing national appeal. The congregation meets every Saturday evening in the auditorium at Madison Square Garden, boasting a weekly attendance report of around five thousand. The Dollars purchased a $2.5 million apartment in the Manhattan Time Warner Center and commute back and forth between Atlanta and New York in his private jet each week.[5]

Pastor Creflo Dollar's visibility on the national stage has increased both the attention and the controversy around his ministry. As in the case of Bishop Jakes in Charleston, West Virginia, and Bishop Long at New Birth, much of the intensive media scrutiny centers upon the Dollars' financial accountability and high-profile associates. In 2000, Creflo Dollar became embroiled in the very public and unpleasant divorce proceedings of then–heavyweight boxing champion and World Changers member Evander Holyfield. Janice Holyfield accused her estranged husband of concealing finances when she discovered that Evander had made a three-million-dollar ministry donation to Creflo Dollar just five days before filing for divorce. When the court ordered Pastor Dollar to provide a deposition in the divorce hearing, Dollar refused to comply. He cited pastor-parishioner privilege and contended that participating in a divorce trial would violate his faith as someone who affirmed the sanctity of marriage. The court therefore found Pastor Dollar in contempt, and the county sheriff's department issued a warrant for his arrest. Fortunately for Pastor Dollar, Evander and Janice Holyfield reached an out-of-court financial settlement that kept their pastor out of jail. But despite what many would consider negative public attention, such controversies made Creflo Dollar's supporters rally around him and further enriched the church. Rather than turning persons away from World Changers Church, intense media scrutiny and even a Senate investigation into ministry spending seem to have had the opposite effect of rallying the faithful and heightening Creflo and Taffi Dollar's allure and mystique.

The Theological Thought of Pastor Creflo Dollar

As we saw in chapter 3, the Word of Faith theological orientation is based upon a pseudo-Platonic understanding of reality. Mediated through the writings of the Apostle Paul, Word of Faith theology transforms Plato's conception of the two realms, visible and intelligible, into two levels of existence, the lower and the higher life. According to Pastor Dollar, the lower level is the earthly realm. This is a realm of carnality or flesh where Satan has dominion. Humanity is born into the carnal world because of the sin of Adam, but belief in Jesus and proper appropriation of scripture affords a way for persons to ascend to a higher level of existence. Here they are no longer bound to the laws of the carnal world, since the laws of nature no longer apply to the believer. Pastor Dollar cites the example of Jesus's disciple Peter defying the law of gravity and walking on water in Matthew 14.[6] This is what I have previously referred to as a state of *metaphysical physicality*. Being in sync with the Word of God affords persons a metaphysical existence in the physical realm.

Pastor Dollar's belief in the human capacity to eclipse the physical world is indicative of one of the more conspicuous and controversial aspects of Word of Faith theology. There appears to be a doctrine of human deification operative in Word of Faith that classifies human beings as gods or at least as having the potential to be gods. Being made in the image of God, according to Pastor Dollar, means being of the same class and constitution as God. Humanity is of the same "kind" and thus is endowed with a supernatural capacity. In Dollar's words, "We are superhuman beings, possessing supernatural, creative power. We were supernaturally created and are God-natured in spirit, soul and body."[7] While citing the creation account from Genesis 1:26, Pastor Dollar's sermon

"Made after His Kind" clearly expresses his conception of the human-divine correlation and constitution. Pastor Dollar argues:

> If everything produces after its own kind, we now see God producing man. And if God now produces man and everything produces after its own kind . . . [pause] If horses get together they produce what? [Congregation: "Horses!"] If dogs get together they produce what? [Congregation: "Dogs!"] If cats get together they produce what? [Congregation: "Cats!"] [Long pause] . . . [Congregation applauds] And if the godhead gets together and says, "Let us make man," then what are they producing? (Congregation: "Gods!"] They are producing gods! . . . I am going to say to you right now you are gods, little g. You came from God and you are gods. You are not just human, the only human part about you is this physical body that you live in.[8]

Much as the early Christian church fathers used the term *homoousios* at the First Council of Nicea in 325 CE to affirm the Trinitarian equality of the Father, Son, and Holy Spirit, Pastor Dollar extends this idea to human creation. Human beings are of the same substance as God. But rather than building upon the consubstantial position of Alexander of Alexandria, which affirms that the individual members of the Godhead are "of one Being," Pastor Dollar is informed more by his theological mentor Kenneth Copeland.

Robert Bowman's *The Word-Faith Controversy: Understanding the Health and Wealth Gospel* argues that the doctrine of humanity as little gods came to full expression within Faith circles through Copeland's teachings. He was the first within the Word of Faith lineage to use Genesis 1:26 to describe Adam as the result of God's desire to reproduce Godself. And, according to Copeland, "He [Adam] was not almost like God. He was not subordinate to God. . . . Adam is as much like God as you could get."[9] Copeland then uses the Genesis account to make the following ultimate claim about the nature of humanity: "Man was created to function on God's level. . . . Your spirit is just as big as God's because you are born of Him. My son has the same capacity for strength that I have. He has just as many muscles in his body as I have in mine; but at his present age he is not as strong as I am. Why? Because his muscles are not fully developed. He is still growing."[10]

This notion that humanity has the same substance and capacity as God reveals the pantheistic dimensions of Creflo Dollar's theological thought. According to pantheistic beliefs, the universe, nature, and God are equivalent. God is in all, and all is in God. While Pastor Dollar may not believe that all of creation possesses the same God-stuff as human beings, it is difficult to deny the ways both New Thought and New Age tenets inform his theology—most notably, the belief that all humanity is endowed with the divine because human beings were made in the image of God.[11]

But just because all humanity is endowed with the substance of God does not mean that all persons are able to unleash the benefits of being little gods. Like most New Thought adherents, Pastor Dollar contends that people are divine to differing, relative degrees. The level of one's divinity is directly proportional to one's faith in Jesus Christ and adherence to the scriptures. Thus, for Pastor Dollar, living the higher life in Christ correlates with what New Thought and New Age thinkers refer to as having an increased God consciousness. The more people are aware of the God in them, the more they are able to take advantage of their divine power to change or transcend their physical world.

Pastor Dollar offers Jesus as a consummate example. He teaches that Jesus was born no different from any other human being but that through the study of scripture he came to the realization of who he was in God.[12] Jesus, according to Dollar, was not born as God but was born a mortal being with a God consciousness. Jesus was neither divine or perfect. Instead, he meditated on the Word of God so diligently that "he became what He meditated."[13] In a two-part sermon broadcast entitled "Jesus Growth into Sonship," Dollar argues:

> Somebody said, well, Jesus came as God. Well, how many of you know the Bible says, "God never sleeps nor slumbers." And yet in the book of Mark we see Jesus asleep in the back of the boat. Please listen to me. This ain't no heresy. I'm not some false prophet. I'm just reading this thing to you out of the Bible. I'm just telling you, all of these fantasy preachers have been preaching all of this stuff for all of these years and we bought the package. . . .

> Somebody said, "Well, Jesus knew all things." Well, what happened to that fig tree situation? Seeing a fig tree far off, He saw leaves on the fig tree and thought if haply He might come to that fig tree and eat of that fig tree. But when He got there He saw that there were no figs on that tree. Well, wait a minute. We better hope God knows when figs are on a tree. [Congregation

laughs] But Jesus didn't come as God. He came as a man. Because if Jesus came as God He would have known figs were on a fig tree without having to see the leaves on the fig tree.[14]

Despite the New Thought texture of Pastor Dollar's understanding of God, particularly as it relates to the human-divine consubstantiation and the realized divinity of Jesus, his theology hinges on a substitutionary soteriology. Original sin caused a defect in God's perfect replication of the divine self, and through Christ believers can be restored to their equality with God. Jesus Christ is the Word incarnate and confers righteousness on an otherwise fallen humanity. For Dollar, "When you accepted Him as the sacrificial Lamb Who [sic] died on the cross for your sins, that means the Word elevated you out of this realm where Satan operates and put you above the law of sin and death."[15] Therefore, Pastor Dollar appears to hold in tension beliefs in both substitutionary and moral exemplary theories of atonement. Jesus Christ is the sacrificial lamb that must be slain for the sins of humanity as well as a moral example of one who achieved ultimate God consciousness. Jesus's ability to overcome the world, then, reveals the power and potentiality of those who live in Christ. Salvation is dependent not only on what Christ did on the cross but on what humans have the capacity to do as believers in the cross, since, according to Pastor Dollar, believers have the ability to transcend any realm of sin as well as literally speak into existence a cornucopia of tangible blessings that include physical health and material wealth. This latter part leads to the second key aspect of Dollar's theological system, positive confession.

Drawing on Proverbs 18:20-21, which states, "A man's belly shall be satisfied with the fruit of his mouth and with the increase of his lips shall he be filled. Death and life are in the tongue: and they that love it shall eat the fruit thereof," Pastor Dollar teaches that positive confession is a demonstrative act of one's inner faith.[16] He links the practice of positive confession with one's confidence in the scriptures. It is imperative that believers articulate their trust in God, and tangentially themselves, through verbal expression. By doing so, they can manipulate their physical conditions. Once again, we see the syncretic fusion of various thaumaturgic faith perspectives such as mind science, New Thought, and the black Spiritual tradition. The principle of positive confession is the audible expression of one's faith in mind over matter.

This act of positive confession is a paramount theological principle and infuses every aspect of the worship at World Changers. The service is always upbeat and optimistic, and the blues sensibility that has been a staple of traditional African American Christian practice is noticeably absent. The guttural cries of gospel songs such as "How I Got Over" or "I'm Coming up the Rough Side of the Mountain" are antithetical to the positive environment Creflo Dollar seeks to create. There is no concept of "joy in sorrow" or pedagogical appropriation of pain and suffering. The liturgical themes of suffering, sacrifice, and hope are replaced with themes of prosperity, increase, and overflow. Too much pain is associated with suffering and sacrifice. And the concept of hope conveys mystery and uncertainty. But according to the Dollars' theological framework, those who are in covenantal agreement with God based on the scriptures can manifest good things for their lives through speaking their faith with confidence and certainty.

This is why Pastor Dollar uses the theological principle of positive confession to critique sorrow songs of black Christian tradition. Speaking at one of Kenneth Copeland's Believer's Voice of Victory conferences, he stated:

> I look back at some of the songs that we used to sing in church when I was assistant pastor at the Shiloh Missionary Baptist Church in College Park, Georgia. Singing in the male choir. And we used to sing this song: "Trouble in my way, I've got to cry sometime. . . . So much trouble, I got to cry sometime. I lay awake at night, but that's all right."
>
> No, it's not all right. [laughter] You sleepy, you not gonna be able to function the next day because you stayed awake all night when you ought to been sleepin *[sic]*. But watch this: "But that's all right, because Jesus will fix it after while *[sic]*." The whole attitude of the whole thing is that serving the Lord is a burden.
>
> Or, we used to sing this song: "It's so hard to get along, It's so hard to get along, It's so hard to get along, I just can't hardly get along." [laughter] If it's that bad, spare me.[17]

Pastor Dollar is not alone in his ill-regard for this dimension of the African American musical tradition. In fact, his sentiments are historically and culturally embedded. Many black mainline congregations dating back to Reconstruction rejected the Negro spiritual and sorrow songs. Though Creflo Dollar cloaks his disdain for this form of spiritual expression in the language of positive confession, one can identify resemblances between the bourgeois sensibilities of late nineteenth-century black Christians and those of African American Word of Faith adherents in the contemporary moment. According to both groups, these songs act as an oppressive force that downgrades rather than uplifts the spiritual consciousness of black people in America.

The final principal aspect of Creflo Dollar's theological thought involves the concepts of seedtime and harvest. According to Dollar, living the higher life in Christ and positively confessing one's faith are insufficient. Believers must begin the process of financial seedtime and harvest to unlock divine health and material wealth, which includes the practice of donating 10 percent of one's gross income to the church. In traditional ecclesial communities, this practice is referred to as tithing. The tithing principle is based on a passage in Malachi 3:10 that reads, "Bring all the tithes and offerings to the storehouse so that there may be meat in my house. Put me to the test. I will open up a window of heaven and pour out a blessing that you will not have room enough to receive." The Word of Faith principle of seedtime and harvest, however, transforms the practice of tithing, which faith communities across the world understand as a form of spiritual obligation and discipline, into a guaranteed means of receiving divine provision. As noted in chapter 2, Oral Roberts instituted this notion of seed-faith as a means of fundraising. According to Roberts, the natural order of God's law is for believers to reap materially in tenfold proportion what they sow by faith. Financial offerings are considered sown seed: like any seeds that are planted, they will produce a recurring harvest. Pastor Dollar thus understands and encourages tithing as not only a spiritual but a financial investment that produces a tenfold financial return.

There is an important caveat here, however. According to Pastor Dollar, the financial seed cannot be separated from the proverbial ground in which it is planted. This entails where the seed originates (the heart of the believer) and where it is sown (the faith community). In terms of the place of origin, believers should not sow *as faith requires* but *because faith requires*. Pastor Dollar promotes a Charismatic categorical imperative concerning seed-faith by avowing that God knows a person's heart and level of faith commitment. One can reap God's reward only if the motivating principle behind one's sowing is pure. "The right action with the wrong motive won't get you very far," according to Dollar.[18] Also crucial is the motivating principle behind desiring a financial harvest. Dollar teaches that wealth attainment is not an end in itself. Rather, it is a means to a greater end, that of spreading the gospel message. Therefore, it is incumbent on the believer to sow generously to the ministry so that the Gospel may go forth and to make charitable contributions. Only in this way are greed and selfishness kept at bay. Finally, persons must sow in fertile ground. The principle of seedtime and harvest only works in a Word of Faith congregation.[19] Why? Because one can only reap tenfold blessings after living the higher life in Christ through contractual agreement with the scriptures and positively confessing the desires of one's heart. In other words, seedtime and harvest are inextricably tied to the theological commitments of the Word of Faith doctrine.[20]

The Church as Corporation

The buzz of excitement that one feels entering the lobby of the Potter's House or New Birth is muted on the World Changers campus. A surfeit of uniformed police officers and identifiable security teams blanket the parking lot and church entrance. Both Bishop Jakes and Bishop Long employ armed guards that act as a personal secret service "jump team" as well as monitor the sanctuary. But the sense of surveillance seems more conspicuous at World Changers. From the moment persons walk in the building they are greeted and quietly ushered through the doors into the auditorium under an omnipresent gaze. Opportunities to extend pleasantries or pass business cards, acts I regularly witnessed at both the Potter's House and New Birth, are limited. This level of heightened security extends throughout the building, contributing to the monitored feeling of the service.

The inside of the sanctuary is like an entertainment arena or convention center. The walls of the vestibule and sanctuary bear no Christian iconography. One will not find stained-glass images of Jesus, the symbols of the sacraments, or even so much as a cross in the building. The sanctuary provides amphitheater-style cushioned seats for up to eight thousand parishioners. A large choir loft behind the pulpit holds the full-band ensemble and the large choir. And the pulpit resembles an orchestra stage with a portable glass lectern in the middle from which Dollar preaches.

The worship service at World Changers, like the television broadcast, is defined by erudition and scriptural insight rather than ecstatic frenzy and emotional exuberance. The muscularity of New Birth's worship service and Bishop Long's *Taking Authority* broadcast, often in the forms of bass thumping music and homiletic bravado, is absent. And the cathartic healing release that listeners obtain from Jakes's introspective and emotional sermons is unlikely to be inspired by Creflo Dollar's technical and litigious appeals to the scriptural text. Dollar never visibly sweats and seldom raises his voice. His sermons appear quite calculated, and his passion always seems to be under control. Even when Creflo Dollar speaks in tongues, as he does quite often, it comes across as reserved and methodical. Such a reserved pedagogical approach to preaching causes his followers to refer to Pastors Creflo and Taffi Dollar as teachers rather than preachers. Creflo Dollar appears to appreciate and promote such a faux distinction between teaching and preaching, since he often mocks the homiletic art form of whooping during his sermons. One might gather that this is his way of discrediting what he considers to be the unbridled emotionalism of African American worship.

The organizational structure of World Changers and the overall aesthetic of the ministry convey a corporate rather than an ecclesial identity. Along with the World Dome, the World Changers headquarters is located in a renovated strip mall adjacent to the church. The church campus is configured like a corporate facility. The eighty-one-acre campus houses a children's academy, publishing firm, and record label. World Changers employs around 350 employees, has an annual budget of about eighty million dollars, and has five offices abroad. And rather than a ministerial staff, World Changers has a leadership team. Titles such as *executive administrator, director of business and international affairs,* and *director of operations* make up the operational chain of command. And each week Pastor Dollar holds "cabinet meetings" at the College Park campus.[21]

The corporate as opposed to ecclesial identity is further conveyed by World Changers' own self-descriptions. On the World Changers New York Web page, the Dollars offer the following description of their ministry: "WCCNY is part of the World Changers Ministries (WCM) family. WCM is the "parent" company of World Changers Church International (WCCI), World Changers Church New York (WCCNY), Creflo Dollar Ministries (CDM), and International Covenant Ministries (ICM). Arrow Records is an affiliate member of the WCM family of companies. Dr. Creflo A. Dollar is the CEO of WCM and President of ICM. Taffi L. Dollar is the CEO of Arrow Records. WCM is responsible for all the administrative support and corporate oversight of the various entities."

Finally, the personal aesthetic of Pastors Creflo and Taffi Dollar typifies the ministry's corporate orientation. Like most Word of Faith pastors, the Dollars have traded in traditional ecclesial vestments for a style more representative of Wall Street. Dollar's regular attire is a solid dark or pinstriped suit, a French-cuff shirt, and a Rolex watch. Three-quarter-length suit jackets, baggy pants, and any other forms of "hip" zoot suit tailoring appear to be out of the question for Dollar. Moreover, the varying levels of "conked" or "processed" hair preferred by famous black television preachers such as Rev. Ike, Bishops Carlton Pearson, and Bishop Long seem to be anathema to Creflo Dollar, who instead has a conservatively cropped haircut.

Taffi Dollar is similarly conservative. Aesthetically she strays away from the role of the traditional "First Lady." You will never find Pastor Taffi Dollar in an oversized church hat and ornate outfit. Instead, she tends to wear business pantsuits, pumps, and collared shirts. Many could note that, her face appears younger and tighter today than it did a decade ago before she began preaching in the late 1990s and was elevated to co-pastor. Taffi Dollar's immaculate make-up and well-coiffed hair has become her signature of sorts. She has even entered the woman's image consultation industry with her recently published book *21 Days to Your Spiritual Makeover.*

In recent years, Creflo Dollar has projected his name over the broadcast and in many of his published books as Creflo Dollar, PhD.[22] Perhaps he feels that by saying he holds a doctorate as opposed to an ecclesiastical designation such as "bishop" he can further portray himself as a polished professional rather than a traditional southern black preacher. But regardless of his intent, the *Changing Your World* broadcasts, as well as the ministry they represent, are more like a corporate seminar or professional conference than a Charismatic worship service.

The Political and Social Thought of Pastor Creflo Dollar

Pastor Creflo Dollar refrains from tackling any particular political or social issue directly. Unlike Bishop T. D. Jakes, he does not present himself as a counselor or confidant to national political figures. Nor does he does actively align himself in any tradition of African American social uplift like Bishop Eddie Long. And he rarely expresses a public stance concerning subjects of national or international concern.

Pastor Dollar is, however, clear and consistent concerning the core beliefs of Word of Faith theology. It seems that he believes that adherence to Faith principles offers a panacea for all social ills and problems. Matters of class, race, and gender can be resolved according to the major tenets of his theology. Living the higher life in Christ, engaging in positive confession, and sowing financial seeds to reap the harvest of financial health and wealth trump all other worldly systems, structures, and ideologies, which in fact preclude self-actualization. A true-to-form thaumaturgic, Pastor Dollar appears to have no conception of or belief in systems of capitalist exploitation, white supremacy, or patriarchal domination. Humanity's capacity to ascend to a state of metaphysical physicality renders systems of injustice and evil nonexistent or at least ineffective. Consequently, according to Pastor Dollar, the only glass ceilings are in the minds of individuals. To gain control of oneself is to develop the freedom one needs to operate unencumbered in society. This is what Creflo Dollar means when he claims to preach a social gospel.[23] As journalist Kalefah Sanneh appropriately points out, the theme of Dollar's ministry is changing *your* world, not changing *the* world.[24]

But just because Pastor Dollar is reluctant to take public stances on political issues does not mean he is apolitical. In fact, a nonposition in the realm of politics can be interpreted as a position in itself. Refusing to oppose a particular stance is essentially accommodating to the status quo. And, as we have seen, accommodating to macro systems in order to carve out a space of micro achievement is a long-standing tradition of African American religious response to social injustice.

To be fair, Pastor Dollar may not perceive this to be the case. He may interpret his unwillingness to raise his voice in opposition to the powers that be as following the Apostle Paul's admonition to submit and pray for those in power. This is how he presented his opinion while offering latent support for President George W. Bush in an article published during the 2004 presidential campaign season. The article, originally published on his ministry Web site and entitled "United We Stand, Divided We Fall," expressed Pastor Dollar's concern about the increasing number of Americans protesting the president's War on Terror. Dollar then offered three lines of positive confessions for people to profess in support of the president as well as members of the armed forces. He concluded the article by calling all protesters to prayer and repentance:

If you have taken part in any protests or have allowed any corrupt communication to flow out of your mouth concerning the president, repent
and begin to show your support for him by calling his name out before
God. Pray for wisdom and wise counsel regarding the decisions he must
make for this nation. Obey what the Word says in 1 Timothy 1–2 and 1
Peter 2:13 and: 1) continue to pray for those in authority over you; and
2) submit to that established authority. In doing so, you honor God, our
president and thousands of service members. When the temptation comes
to murmur or complain, rejoice that there is a man in the White House
who walks and talks with God daily. Remember, united we stand, divided
we fall (Matthew 12:25)![25]

Pastor Dollar, then, professes a position neither of political correction
nor of mediation with governmental authority but of submission. Insofar as this is the case, though Dollar may contend that his stance is not
inspired by political belief but is merely following biblical mandates, it
leads him to the same accommodating stance previously discussed. Submission and accommodation to power structures are yet different names
for the same mode of political response.

From this posture of political accommodation, Pastor Dollar assumes
consistently conservative stances on matters of class, race and gender.
Again, these are not social issues per se in the life of Faith adherents. A
life committed to Creflo Dollar's theological prescriptions nullifies social
injustice. Though Dollar does acknowledge that issues of class, race, and
gender function on a personal level. Hence, persons must be equipped
with positive and practical strategies to short-circuit the ways poverty,
racism, and sexism foster a negative conception of the self. Persons battle
the forces of poverty, racism, and sexism not externally but internally.
They are for Dollar states of mind that are not grounded in the material
conditions of existence.

For instance, a recurring theme throughout Dollar's broadcasts and
books is that of possessing a poverty spirit. People have a poverty spirit
when they fail to see themselves as God does. A poverty spirit encourages low self-esteem and deceives people into believing that they do not
deserve infinite health and wealth. Poverty is viewed as a spiritual curse
that attacks the mind, not as a structural reality that must be called into
question or analyzed from a socioeconomic perspective. Poverty is an
internal disposition and negative self-conception that must be overcome.
People are poor, according to Pastor Dollar, because they do not have

enough faith that God wants them to be rich. Poverty is essentially all in one's mind. This is how Pastor Dollar can deliver the same message of health and wealth to a crowd in Madison Square Garden and at an evangelistic crusade in Uganda. In the Dollars' world, the theological principles of overcoming poverty apply regardless of context, economy, or continent.

The same holds true for issues of race. It seems that for Dollar racism consists of the discriminatory actions of individuals. Accordingly, Pastor Dollar considers racism a sin that individuals must come to terms with in their pursuit of holiness. This is why he has stated that racial reconciliation is one of the most important activities for the Christian church to encourage.[26] His concept of reconciliation, however, has nothing to do with power relations. It is instead based on individuals' interpersonal exchanges across racial lines. African Americans must reconcile to whites and whites must reconcile to African Americans in order to foster healthy Christian relationships. Pastor Dollar appears to believe that racism is a sin of which all persons are guilty. Therefore, it is the responsibility of all Christians to efface racial difference in order to negate racial bigotry. Any minority group that emphasizes its distinctiveness is guilty of sin and contributes to racial discord.

To be sure, the Dollars unashamedly model themselves as moral paragons of racial cooperation. This is true not only of their involvement in the predominantly white Word of Faith movement but also of their personal lives. Before giving birth to three daughters, during the early years of World Changers Church, Creflo and Taffi Dollar expanded their family by adopting a white teenage son. Pastor Dollar testifies today about how sharing his personal challenges with racial reconciliation helped to deliver many persons in his congregation—99 percent of whom are African American—from their own sins of racism.[27] Also, a recent *Essence* magazine article published several photographs of the Dollar family in their Atlanta home. Besides the luxurious décor of the Dollars' palatial mansion, what stands out in these photographs are the prominently placed paintings depicting an Anglo Jesus on the cross and Anglo disciples gathered around a white Jesus at the Last Supper.[28] Yet despite the polyvalent racial messages that those pictures transmit, the Dollars say they are color-blind. There is no color for those who live the higher life in Christ Jesus.

With regard to gender, the World Changers ministry attempts to present itself as radically egalitarian. Creflo and Taffi Dollar are co-pastors and ministry partners in every capacity. Photographs of the couple, often in a loving embrace, are strategically placed in abundance on their litera-ture to signify a marital ministry team. And the *Changing Your World* broadcast often involves Creflo and Taffi sitting together while fielding questions from the studio audience. In recent years, rarely does one see Creflo ministering without Taffi or vice versa. If there was ever an exam-ple of partners in romance, life, and career, Creflo and Taffi Dollar work hard to make certain that they typify the image.

Gender equality does not mean parity, however. For the Dollars, being equal in capacity is not the same as being equal in purpose. The Dollars affirm equality in intellectual, spiritual, and emotional capacity, yet they teach that God has divinely ordained and established a set of rules and roles for men and women. Though they profess that women can do any-thing men can, they also affirm that it is not in women's best interest to do so and indeed that it is against the will of God.[29] God, according to the Dollars, has a purpose and plan for the sexes.

The Dollars' teachings on gender roles are most explicitly articulated in their coauthored text *The Successful Family*. A treatise on Victorian morality and patriarchal ordering, it expresses the Dollars' adherence to specific gender roles that are constructed on a biblical chain of authority. But unlike Bishop Long, as we saw in the previous chapter, the Dollars include the laws of government and governing officials (as opposed to the church) in their chain of authority just below God. From there, the divine chain of command extends to the family: men submit to God, hus-bands to wives, wives to husbands, and then children to their parents.

Consistent with Victorian mores that establish the domestic sphere as the gendered terrain of women, teachings on gender roles and respon-sibility are most often expressed by Taffi Dollar. Again, she is an active participant in the ministry in every way. This includes affirming the rules of gender engagement. It appears that she, more often than Cre-flo, preaches and writes about gender roles even as he performs his role in every broadcast. Further, though the Dollars' interpretation of sub-mission includes the submission of husbands to wives, *submission* takes on a different meaning across the gender line. For women, submission means obeying one's husband and encouraging him in his decisions. For men, submission translates into the willingness to lead one's family while submitting to the will of God.[30]

For example, in the chapter entitled "Follow the Leader," Taffi writes about being delivered from her past problems by the concept of submission, especially where it involved the notion of obedience. She says, "I didn't see how he [Creflo] could make me to do something that I didn't want to do. I wanted to be an independent and career focused woman. I didn't want to be accountable to him for every little thing I wanted to do." Taffi Dollar admits that she did not at first understand God's design for submission or its benefits. But she says that after she aligned her thinking with the Word of God she became "a mighty woman of God" and "saw miracle after miracle take place in our [her and Creflo] lives and marriage."[31]

Consistent with the larger evangelical Christian tradition, Taffi Dollar promotes the belief that women were made to be a help-meet. It is a God-given responsibility for a woman to support and encourage her husband to be all God has called him to be. Prescribing the virtues of female adaptability and docility, she writes that men always have something on their minds and as a result can become "moody and withdrawn." She thus recommends "giving [a man] some space to think and unwind when he comes home instead of attacking him with bills, questions or other issues."[32] A virtuous woman offers support and encouragement rather than confrontation and challenge. She does distinguish submission from being a slave or a doormat. Submission implies function, not worth. Hence, Taffi Dollar believes that women can be dehumanized only when they shirk their God-given responsibility to be a help-meet in the form of humble submission.

Conversely, Taffi Dollar contends that submission for a husband involves his ability to submit to God and "communicate God's plan for their lives clearly." God has called men to a position of leadership, what the Dollars often refer to as headship. Yet the man cannot lead autocratically or independently of God, according to Taffi Dollar. Why? Because men must submit to God. But through submitting to God, they are directed on how they should lead their family. A man must lay aside his personal will for God's will. Taffi Dollar contends that submission for a man involves providing "the necessary leadership and direction she [the woman] needs and desires."[33] This includes, but is not limited to, keeping his anger in check, "valuing his wife just as he would a precious possession," spending time with his children, and ensuring the family's "well being, protection and financial security."[34]

According to the Dollars, when men and women fail to adhere to these roles, they are not living a life in Christ. In her book *A Woman after God's Own Heart*, Taffi Dollar refers to a woman's failure to submit and a man's failure to lead as a Jezebel and an Ahab spirit, respectively—terms drawn from the narrative of the wicked king and queen in I Kings. A Jezebel spirit engages in "acts that promote self-will, which include manipulation, deception, seduction, rebellion and craftiness."[35] The Jezebel spirit is antithetical to the principles of "submission, humility, reverence and holiness—everything that produces a powerful Christian."

But a Jezebel spirit in a woman is a by-product of an Ahab spirit in her man. When men demonstrate irresponsibility in their affairs and fail to assume their God-ordained role of headship, women are forced to function as Jezebels. Taffi describes the Ahab spirit as a man who has "surrendered his authority to his wife. Men who lack the courage and diligence to see matters through to the end."[36] Thus the Dollars conclude that the "weak-willed Spirit of Ahab and the controlling, rebellious spirit of Jezebel will cause trouble in your relationship with your spouse, eventually destroying or killing the marriage altogether."[37]

Pastors Creflo and Taffi Dollar are representative of a new generation of African American ministers that have left both the classical Pentecostal and black mainline traditions to align with what is essentially a new religious movement in America. Emerging out of the postdenominational and neo-Charismatic context of postwar America, the Tulsa-based Word of Faith movement has always viewed advanced media technology as central to its ecclesiology. Therefore, not only are its theological tenets grounded in the New Thought milieu of late nineteenth- and early twentieth-century America, but other prominent principles of the faith, such as "seedtime and harvest," are directly linked to the fundraising practices of Oral Roberts and his televangelist protégés. The Word of Faith movement seeks neither to tear down the walls of the church and spread its message to the larger society like neo-Pentecostals nor to transform the social and political landscape of this society like the Charismatic mainlines. Rather, by prescribing the three theological principles of the higher life in Christ, positive confession, and seedtime and harvest, Word of Faith pastors like the Dollars encourage individuals to bypass the constraints of the material world by living a life of *metaphysical physicality*. As the theme of their ministry avows, the Faith teachings can "change your world."

By modeling a life of health and wealth, erasing the divisions of race, and encouraging the Victorian order of the family, Word of Faith televangelists promote the belief that persons can live their lives unaffected by economic lack, racism, or gender discrimination. The belief in such magico-religious practices as a way of taking control of oneself and one's world did not enter the African American community simply through the Word of Faith movement. We have seen in preceding chapters that this message is consistent with the thaumaturgic tradition of African American religious life in general and the black Spiritual tradition in particular. Using the tools of positive confession and ritual behavior to transcend the evils of this world is long-standing for black people who have sought to keep the temptation of nihilism at bay. I would argue that this is one of the reasons why the Word of Faith movement may resonate with African Americans in the contemporary moment. From Voodoo/Hoodoo workers in the South, to Prophet James F. Jones in the 1950s, to Rev. Ike in the 1970s, there have always been those who sought both to reject and to embrace the dominant society through their attempts to manipulate the spirit realm on behalf of their own personal needs. For those involved, such magico-religious manipulation is a form of liberation in itself.

7

The Reasons Why We Sing

The Competing Rituals of Self-Affirmation and Social Accommodation

Someone asked the question: why do we sing?
When we lift our hands to Jesus, what do we really mean?
Someone may be wond'ring; when we sing our song
At times we may be crying and nothing's even wrong.
I sing because I'm happy. I sing because I'm free.
His eye is on the sparrow, that's the reason why I sing.
— "The Reason Why I Sing,"
in *African American Heritage Hymnal*

The world of black religious broadcasting represents a subculture about which mainstream society is ambivalent. Bring up the name of any leading televangelist in any barber or beauty shop in the African American community and you will hear passionate sentiments of both appreciation and apprehension, sometimes from the same person. There are good reasons for this. On the one hand, many televangelists are respected for their apparent business savvy and seeming concern for the community. Even if people do not watch a particular preacher on television or attend their megachurch, they most likely have a mother, brother, cousin, or aunt who does. Thus they often force themselves to search for the positive aspects of a particular televangelist even when they are personally indifferent. On the other hand, many tend to be suspicious of what many think to be the crass materialism and fraudulent fundraising efforts of these charismatic personalities. Often the luxurious lifestyles that televangelists live irritate those who are living from paycheck to paycheck. As one woman recently told me, "I'll be damn if I sow another seed just to lace some greedy preacher's pocket."

This latter sentiment seems to be the most pervasive. The stereotype of televangelists and their viewers that is circulated within black popular culture shows a bumbling yet conniving male preacher preying upon overzealous, generally female congregants who are demonstrably "full of the spirit." Indeed, a review of African American sitcoms, movies, or standup comedic routines that engage almost any form of the black church reveals that African American religious expression is tried-and-true comedic fodder. The late Richard Pryor began his 1970s sketch comedy show by introducing America to His Holiness the Reverend James L. White. The preacher was dressed in a skin-tight, white jump-suit and adorned with jewelry, and his faux telethon theme song was the O'Jays "For the Love of Money." A recurring character on the classic *Flip Wilson Show* was Reverend Leroy, pastor of the "Church of What's Happening Now." And whenever Martin, Gina, and Pam would attend church on the 1990s hit *Martin,* they would encounter the Right Reverend Leon Lonny Love, a skirt-chasing, money-hungry scam artist. These memorable characters are only a few of the many satirical and salacious representations of black preachers that circulate throughout black popular culture.

But the more I witness such representations of black preachers in general and televangelism in particular, the greater my concern about these puerile tropes. To be sure, I do not want to downplay the manipulative aspects of the phenomenon. The huckster image is not unfounded. Deceit and subterfuge are part of the game. However, chicanery and stratagem cannot account for the enduring success of African American broadcasting. Viewers are not passive spectators trapped in Marxian false consciousness. To reduce participants to "suckers" diminishes the active engagement of black religious folk who are already committed to many of the beliefs, values, concerns, and ideals that televangelists promote. We should not obscure the viewers' religious interest or deny their moral agency by portraying them as manipulated by what we may consider to be the dubious practices of preachers. Viewers and producers obviously have similar belief systems and moral outlooks. And when participants turn on television, purchase a DVD, or attend a megaconference, they bring with them their own aims, interests, and concerns.

Ritual of Self-Affirmation and Spiritual Longing

Much of the literature that focuses on the viewers of televangelism deals with the social drama of marginalization. Stewart Hoover and Bobby Alexander, for instance, have identified televangelism's audience as principally conservative white Christians living along the boundaries of the white mainstream. For the most part, they adhere to a rigid religiosity, a truncated theology, and a myopic morality. Persons watch religious broadcasting as a means of fulfilling certain individual needs. Often these needs involve healing for one's body, the resolution of a financial crisis, or the management of disturbances on the domestic front. Moreover, viewers watch out of a religious obligation or spiritual affinity. They feel compelled to hear the answers to life's quandaries wrapped in a religious language that they are familiar with and that confirms already held beliefs.

To be clear, viewers of televangelism do not participate in this phenomenon because they are psychologically cognizant of their own social marginality. This, according to Alexander, is largely hidden from viewers, just as many religious persons misrecognize what is animating their religious choices. But once they tune in, televangelists corroborate their rigid views of the world, since the vast majority of white televangelists emerge from the social margins of their community as well. Thus viewers are able to identify with these seemingly authoritative figures who justify their social insecurities and anxieties.

Yet there is another side. Though televangelism's viewers, along with televangelists, reside on the margins of mainstream white society, the social drama of marginalization is emboldened by a longing to become a part of the mainstream. Both the producers and viewers of televangelism appear to be struggling with anxiety concerning their social alienation and desire for social inclusion. To avoid being viewed as backwater hicks or country yahoos, leading white religious broadcasters offer their viewers representations of social respectability by engaging political issues in journalistic fashion (Pat Robertson), erecting imposing church edifices and institutions of learning (Rod Parsley), and becoming politically engaged on the local and national levels (James Dobson and Jerry Falwell).

Now, if this is true for white conservatives, how might such a social drama of marginalization play out for a community that has historically been deemed always and already outside the mainstream? For a race of people who suffered 244 years of chattel slavery, another century of legalized racial apartheid, and the continued vestiges of white supremacy on this nation's soil, joining the mainstream has proven to be an elusive and illusory goal. Nevertheless, each generation has made concerted efforts to achieve equality and inclusion. This profound desire for acceptance can be identified in Maria Stewart's "cause of God and cause of freedom," in Du Bois's clarion call to "lift the Veil," in Langston Hughes's "I, too, sing America," and in Prathea Hall and Martin Luther King's eloquent articulation of a "Dream." Most African Americans desire nothing more than to be fully regarded and respected as participatory citizens in America's democratic project. Such respect includes the affirmation of human dignity and personality as well as equal access to viable educational, political, and economic opportunities that are principally the domain of whites and the wealthy.

Theologian Stephanie Mitchem describes this collective desire in terms of a spirituality of longing. Based on a shared marginalized existence in America's political economy, it emerges from the black community that longs to overcome the cognitive dissonance between America's promises to her citizens and the lived reality of most black people. Mitchem's use of the term *spirituality* is not limited to the metaphysical or the ecclesiastical. She defines spirituality as expressing a holistic cosmology that does not divide the body from the spirit or the individual from his or her community. Thus her notion of a spirituality of longing articulates the strivings of black people who seek to re-envision their world. This may or may not be informed by eschatological hopes or utopian visions, but it definitely seeks to transform African Americans' material conditions.[1]

I believe Mitchem's concept to be helpful even as I keep at bay any essentialist or exceptionalist underpinnings concerning the shared spiritual connection of African Americans. But because of the common reality of white supremacy, in each given epoch of African American history black people have longed for something beyond their given reality. During the era of slavery, they longed for physical freedom. The Reconstruction and the racial nadir that followed stirred African Americans' longing for social mobility and protection from a terroristic and unwelcoming nation. One can identify a longing for increased economic, educational, and occupational opportunities as black people have migrated across the nation during the first half of the twentieth century. And the civil rights era revealed a longing for equal rights that had marinated within the hearts of many black communities for generations. As Mitchem contends, "Black Americans have experienced longing in some form throughout time in the United States."[2] But common to all eras is the desire to be accepted as full citizens, as co-laborers in a multiracial democracy, or as human beings who deserve the same respect as anyone.

Here lies one of the primary tasks of African American religion. Black communities of faith have typically created a space where black people can be passionately human and express their innermost wants and desires. Experiential encounters with the divine that suspend the material world allow people to transcend the negative cultural identifications that are associated with their class, race, or gender while having their own inner desires and spiritual longings affirmed. This is why I consider televangelism to be a ritual of self-affirmation. It creates an experience where participants can become actors on the stages of ritual drama. Televangelists authenticate and make authoritative already held assumptions and spiritual longings of their adherents that allow and encourage them to experience and envision themselves being created anew according to their personal aspirations.

For instance, despite the diversity of theological thought, ecclesial outlook, and political and social orientations among leading black televangelists, three common themes in African American religious broadcasting unite neo-Pentecostals, Charismatic mainliners, and Word of Faith adherents. Bishop Jakes, Bishop Long, and Pastor Dollar, regardless of their contrasting views, all seem to promote similar aims, objectives, and desires for the African American community—economic advancement, the minimizing of race, and Victorian ideals of family. This is neither surprising nor limited to the world of contemporary religious broadcasting. Each of these can be traced back to the Reconstruction era and reflects ruling ideals of bourgeois, racial uplift politics that remain very much intact. Economic enterprise has typically been heralded as the most viable means of overcoming racial discrimination and gaining full acceptance in American society. And the same is true of patriarchy. The vast majority of black churches have always extolled the virtues of adhering to rigid gender roles within the family as an effective strategy of gaining social acceptance. So it should be no surprise that large numbers of African Americans gravitate toward the dominant themes of televangelism. The messages that televangelists declare in their sermons and writings and that they visually model project the lifestyle many African Americans have been culturally conditioned to desire. These messages may resonate, not because viewers strictly adhere to any particular belief about issues relating to class, race, or gender, but rather because they have a spiritual longing to overcome the ways issues of class, race, and gender preclude possibilities in their lives. Hence what attracts viewers to African American religious broadcasting may not be the means that televangelists prescribe as much as the ends that they appear to model. The ritual of self-affirmation makes viewers feel that their hopes and aspirations are validated and encouraged. More importantly, they can participate in the ritual activity with a televangelist who appears to be and have what they so greatly desire. Through the life of the televangelist viewers are able to further experience "what God can do."

Methodologically, I realize that I am skating on thin ice here by trying to express something as subjective as religious experience. Since very few studies have examined the viewers of African American broadcasting, there is little information on which to base any definitive claim. But enough work has been done on the interrelations of religious thought and ritual activity to indicate that we cannot fully understand the phenomenon of televangelism unless we engage with its viewers' experiential world. The experience, what people feel in their soul that corroborates the belief in their mind and heart, extends beyond the frames of aesthetics and ideology. That is, the allure of televangelism cannot be reduced to how well televangelists perform, the strategies they employ, or the systems of cultural and political power that their message may reinforce.

There is no linear communicative process between producer and participants engaged in ritual activity. All ritual action has levels of indeterminacy where persons have the potential to *misrecognize* the intended aim of an activity as well as produce their own meanings. Viewers of televangelism reflect on the ideas expressed by televangelists and confirm or call into question their own beliefs. Further, viewers filter the intended messages of televangelists to adjust and apply them personally as they see fit. As Stuart Hall's classic essay taught us, viewers of television engage in an active decoding process.[3] Or, in proverbial terms, you can eat the fish and still spit out the bones.

For instance, just because Rev. Ike wanted listeners to pick up the phone and donate money when he sang "Call Him Up" at the end of each broadcast does not mean that all viewers would. Some did, but many did not. This could become a moment for some viewers to direct their attention away from the broadcast toward God in prayer. And in the process some of Rev. Ike's viewers, if only for a moment, might transcend their material world and cast all cares and concerns upon the divine. This act in itself might change how these viewers would think of themselves and their situation when the broadcast was over. Or, to use a different example, Pastor Dollar may understand his theology as a means of transcending racial injustice in America, since the principal tenets of positive confession ignore race as a social reality. But as Milmon Harrison's in-depth analysis of African American Word of Faith adherents reveals, many African Americans interpret, adopt, and appropriate Word of Faith teachings as a way of directly responding to their particular conditions as African Americans. Some of them interpret the Word of Faith movement as a way to confront and resist what they understand to be a racially unjust society rather than as a way to ignore racial injustice.[4]

It is quite possible, then, that as a ritual of self-affirmation, televangelism offers participants a way to feel empowered. Though I am using the term *empowered* here on a micro level to describe a feeling of freedom to take control of one's life, in some cases it can lead to the enlargement of social opportunities. Victor Turner and his notion of liminality offers instructive insight into this aspect of ritual as it relates to personal empowerment and the possibility of social transformation.

According to Turner, liminality is the moment in the ritualization process "when the past is momentarily negated, suspended or abrogated, and the future has not yet begun, an instant of pure potentiality when everything, as it were, tumbles in the balance."[5] The term *liminal* is used metaphorically to describe the phase of subjective transition from the physical to the metaphysical world. In a nutshell, a liminal space is "betwixt and between" those two worlds. Examples of the liminal space of religious ritual from more traditional black Christian practices can be found in W. E. B. Du Bois's previously mentioned description of the frenzy or James Baldwin's description of "the threshing floor" at the close of *Go Tell It on the Mountain*. In this suspended realm that some describe as "catching the Spirit" or "being filled with the Holy Ghost," participants are democratized into a new *communitas* where issues of class, race, and gender inequality are temporarily suspended. This does not have to take the form of demonstrative physical expression such as holy dancing or audible wails, though it often does. The liminal moment may also happen during quiet and contemplative moments of prayer or engagement with "the Word of God." Regardless of the form it takes, it is a moment within the ritual where people are able to imagine themselves and their world differently, what Turner refers to as a "subversive flicker" of potentiality as it relates to personal or social change.

I understand this to be a positive aspect of this religious phenomenon that should not be quickly dismissed. Persons victimized by classism, racism, and sexism can enter into this dramaturgical ritual of self-affirmation, beautification, and legitimization over and against a society that makes participants believe that they are less than human. Such a *communitas*, for example, counters the dehumanizing of black bodies that is a characteristic of white supremacy. Those who feel alienated and isolated from mainstream society because of their lack of capital can ritually align with perceived multimillionaires and financial geniuses through the ritual of televangelism. And those who are rendered invisible by the acute visibility of their skin complexion and gender can find within this religious phenomenon a place where their humanity is affirmed and on full display.

Thus when Bishop Jakes appeals to the Lukan narrative to illustrate God's ability to release women from the bondage of abuse and the scarring effects of shame, the story, for some, does not stay at the level of metaphor. Rather, these women become, if only for a moment, the woman in the biblical narrative who can rise up and be loosed from her infirmity. When Bishop Long evokes images of authority, either through his overt displays of masculinity or his identification with government officials, some viewers, through him, are able to envision themselves and their world as socially independent rather than bound by their current situation. And when Pastor Dollar discusses the benefits of debt relief, some congregants may actually enter a creative cognitive space where they can imagine an existence that is not framed by bill collectors and bad credit. This imaginative space, we must admit, has the potential to inform and animate lived reality.

Cultural anthropologist Marla Frederick observes that programs like Creflo Dollar's *Changing Your World* broadcast have helped to encourage and transform the financial consciousness of viewers. In her *Between Sundays: Black Women and Everyday Struggles of Faith*, Frederick records the faith practices and testimonies of African American women in Halifax County, North Carolina. One such woman, Gloria, provides Frederick with an account of her attraction to particular televangelists. Engrossed with the straightforward teaching style of Creflo Dollar and his emphasis on economic empowerment, Gloria states that she was able to overcome her financial anxieties by incorporating Dollar's teachings into her daily practice. As Frederick recounts Gloria's experience,

During one message Dollar challenged the congregation to believe that "you will never be broke again in your life." She [Gloria] said that she received his prophetic word, and "from that day to this, whether it's five dollars or ten dollars, or one dollar, I always have money in my pocket." This testimony in itself keeps her from worrying constantly about bills and the possibility of ever being broke. She simply trusts God to provide when funds are insufficient. Although she and her husband are now financially stable and paying for her youngest to complete college, Gloria has long had a tendency to worry about money, especially after she left her first husband and began raising their children on her own. Dollar's teachings about financial prosperity in the believer's life has at the very least encouraged her not to worry about financial matters. This sense of peace and security, she explains, is leaps and bounds above where she used to be.[6]

Even those who adopt a Ricoeurian hermeneutic of suspicion must concede the identifiable results that Gloria experienced in her life. Perhaps the "prophetic word" that Gloria received was nothing more than the reassurance that she needed to take greater control of her finances by becoming a better steward. Not that Gloria received a greater income—this I do not know—but she may have felt more empowered to be responsible with and for what she did have.

Similarly, Milmon Harrison records the testimony of a thirty-something-year-old African American woman who is a member of a prominent Word of Faith megacongregation in Sacramento, California. Cassandra credits her membership at the church with helping her transcend her inner-city Oakland roots. After leaving the black mainline tradition in 1985 to join the Word of Faith movement, Cassandra, earned a master's degree and began working in a corporation; Harrison also noted that she was in visibly better physical shape than he remembered from the previous decade. And Cassandra had since taken up the sport of golf. She distinguished between Methodism and the Word of Faith movement by stating, "I think the difference was what I felt. I felt personally more empowered to bring about the changes I wanted in my life. I wasn't just someone standing by waiting for God to bestow some sort of blessing, or privilege, on me. That's what the difference was. I feel like I'm more in control. I have more of an active part in what happens to me in terms of my Christianity, that's it."[7] Cassandra went on to describe the message of the Word of Faith movement as both liberating and empowering. She contended that as an African American woman she no longer felt put in a box. Cassandra testified to what she considered self-imposed limitations prior to joining the Word of Faith movement. The Word of Faith teachings allowed her to subsume her racial identity under her spiritual identity as a "child of God." From that point on, she said, "I didn't feel limited anymore; I didn't feel limited by the color of my skin."[8] By citing testimonies such as Cassandra's, Harrison reveals the many ways that African Americans are able to appropriate the Word of Faith message in order to confront rather than efface the color line in America.

What is more, televangelists resonate with and affirm those who already possess upwardly mobile aspirations, like the aspiration of Walter Lee Younger to "have a big desk and drive a big car" in Lorraine Hansberry's classic play *Raisin in the Sun*. The economic themes and aesthetic representations of televangelism affirm that it is socially acceptable and God-ordained to "have more, do more and be more." In assessing the followers of Rev. Ike in the 1970s, journalist Clayton Riley said they were

> recognizable as members of a special tribe, bloods whose families work two, three, perhaps four jobs to maintain homes in suburban New Jersey or those portions of the Bronx and Brooklyn where Negroes could not live as recently as 15 years ago.
>
> They are the responsible black people white Americans adore but seldom know. . . . A few are doctors, a small number fix teeth for a living, some have income-producing property. They have always been proud, and clean and neat. Many have waited nearly all their lives for a Reverend Ike to come along and say that their hard and decent work deserves commendation while they are still on earth.[9]

This journalistic description offered over three decades ago is consistent with an explanation recently offered by cultural critic Michael Eric Dyson for the exponential success of the prosperity gospel. According to Dyson, "The prosperity gospel is a way to justify black upward mobility and middle class existence without feeling guilty."[10] Though Dyson was judging the theology negatively, the exoneration of guilt concerning wealth attainment is morally neutral. It could lead to selfishness, social irresponsibility, and greed, as Dyson argues, or possibly to greater social concern and involvement. But what we do know is that participants are able to satiate their anxieties as an oppressed class with the seemingly satisfying symbols of American success—fancy home, luxury cars, expensive clothes. And for a historically victimized group that merely desires equal opportunity, such behavior is understandable, even if, as we will see in the next chapter, it can be intellectually myopic and politically shortsighted.

The same seems to hold true for issues of gender. The success of Bishop T. D. Jakes's ministry among women shows how many women feel "empowered" by his message. This is why Frederick argues that observers of this phenomenon should not make the mistake of dismissing Jakes as someone who is just trying to cash in on black women's pain. Women who watch Bishop Jakes on television, attend his conferences, and purchase his books, says Frederick, "are obviously experiencing something that they are not getting from their traditional black churches."[11] As Shayne Lee notes, when we compare Jakes to the context from which his ministry emerges, the evangelical black church, the bishop comes across like a male feminist. The fact that Bishop Jakes seems to acknowledge and affirm the concerns of African American women like no other black male preacher of his status speaks volumes. And his constant calls for women to "take center stage" coupled with his vocal criticisms of gender injustice in the church are a radical departure from traditional black church culture, which has historically viewed women as objects to be seen but not heard.[12]

Moreover, Bishop Jakes's affirmation of black women as "God's Leading Ladies" counters the dominant cultural images that insult black female identity at every turn. Corporate media outlets such as Viacom (the owner of Black Entertainment Television) and major record labels have helped to exacerbate cultural assaults on black women with the weapons of stereotypical depictions and negative representations. Whether in the forms of movies like *Big Momma's House* and *Norbit* or hypersexualized music videos, such images in contemporary popular culture extend a legacy of social constructions dating back to slavery that portray black women as socially deviant, devoid of feminine virtue, and oversexed. Black women are forced to live in a media-dominated culture where talking heads like Rush Limbaugh and Don Imus feel they can call an African American congresswoman a "crack whore" and successful African American female student athletes "nappy-headed hos." But through participating in the ritual of televangelism, African American women are no longer "Mammies," "Jezebels," "welfare queens," or "video whores." Bishop Jakes affirms their sense of self by referring to them as worthy and deserving of love and compassion. In this context, many women find that being called "Daddy's Little Girl," "God's Leading Lady," or "God's Special Elect" is a welcome and affirming alternative.

These examples underscore my claim that televangelism is a ritual of self-affirmation that nurtures the dignity of its participants. They demonstrate that the liminal space offered by aspects of black religious broadcasting provides a form of empowerment—though microsocial—to participants.[13] It gives people a vision and language for thinking and acting differently in their material world. Such a liminal space allows them to imagine themselves in ways that are resistant to their everyday realities. For this reason it is understandable that large numbers of African Americans gravitate to the message of individuals like Bishop Jakes, Bishop Long, and Pastor Dollar. Simply put, the phenomenon of African American religious broadcasting cultivates a sense of recognition and promotes self-respect in a society that debases black bodies.

There is another side to Turner's concept of liminality, however—a side that belies its potential for positive change. Liminal space is inextricably wrapped up with the social conditions of the material world from which it emerges. Thus the creation of a new *communitas* created within the liminal space will always seek to institutionalize itself. Turner describes it as the moment the *experience of communitas* becomes the *memory of communitas*.[14] Here a community will institutionalize its liminal experience in another normative structure that is built according to the perceived archetype of the very material conditions that persons originally attempted to transcend or resist. The subversive flicker of spontaneity and revolutionary potentiality, then, will quickly solidify itself into another structure of dominance. Hence Turner argues that liminality is both more creative and more destructive than the structural norm.[15]

This is the paradox of African American religious broadcasting. Once we acknowledge the phenomenon as a microsocial ritual of self-affirmation and resistance, we must come to grips with the fact that it is counterbalanced by what I would like to call a ritual of social accommodation. That is, to commodify the ritualized dimensions of the phenomenon, producers of religious broadcasting must embrace the cultural myth systems that resonate with the larger culture. Like entertainers or politicians who seek to transcend a particular genre or demographic, they have to employ all of the tools, trades, and tricks of the mass media in search of wide appeal. And they have to become as pliable as possible to a cross section of the population. In the process, the ministry of televangelists both adapts and reinforces the cultural ethos and social mores of the dominant society.

Ritual of Social Accommodation and Cultural Myths

African American religious broadcasting is a ritual of social accommodation insofar as televangelists embrace the cultural myths of the dominant society. By *cultural myths* I am referring to widely accepted narratives of a given society that both guide that society and glue it together. Cultural myths bind people together through a collective way of thinking that encourages cultural cohesion and stability. And cultural myths are guides insofar as the stories a society tells about itself are fundamentally moral in scope and romantic in outlook. These narratives often divert people's attention from disturbing experiences of the past and the harsh realities of the present by offering a nostalgic tale and an embellished conception of what our society is and what persons can expect from a future that offers infinite possibilities.

Here I am, in part, borrowing from the insightful examination of American culture provided by sociologist Robert Wuthnow in his book *American Mythos*. Wuthnow describes American cultural myths as the content of public rhetoric that explicitly and implicitly reflects our private collective understanding of the nation. These are common narratives, according to Wuthnow, that "tell us what it means to be American, how America is good, and why some people are more successful than others."[16] One might think of American society as the "land of opportunity," where all persons are created equal. These stories are often the stock of immigrant narratives and involve "bootstrap" motifs of finding prosperity in the "land of the free, home of the brave." And it is quite common to hear tales of persons transcending the barriers of class, race and even gender purely by hard work and good morals. Cultural myths, then, animate our religious choices, determine how we define ourselves according to race and ethnicity, inform our opinions on poverty and wealth, and codify our roles along gender lines.

Such narratives may have a kernel of truth even when they largely based on the anecdotal or totally fictitious accounts. But this does not matter. The important question when evaluating the function of cultural myths is not whether particular stories are true or false. This is irrelevant, for clearly the narrative resonates with a critical mass of people or it would not rise to the level of cultural myth. A better question to ask concerns the work these myths perform in the public discourse as well as private space. The answer is simply this: cultural myths provide us with an epistemological framework to make sense of our worlds. They help to establish a cosmos in the midst of what appears to be social chaos. They provide a or map for navigating the rough terrain of life. And myths posit diachronic values and character traits—those that extend across space and time—to encourage good (read: socially adaptive) behavior and an optimistic orientation. Again, cultural myths are less about what is than what can be. For through these stories, society affirms one of the mantras of the black church tradition: "It is no secret what God can do. What He has done for others, He can do for you."

The dominant themes and messages of the leading ministries of African American religious broadcasting are based on persistent cultural myths concerning American society. I say this because for the ecclesiastical aims of Jakes's, Long's, and Dollar's ministries to be fulfilled particular mythic understandings of American society must be true.[17] And by interrogating the theological, ecclesial, and social orientations of the leading ministries described in the preceding chapters, we can show that the principal themes and objectives of their respective ministries, to varying degrees, presuppose and reinforce three pervading cultural myths: the myth of American success, the myth of black victimology, and the myth of the "Strong Black Man" as savior of the race.

The Myth of American Success

The first cultural myth is *the myth of American success*. Commonly referred to as the "American Success Syndrome," this most enduring national ideal promulgates the belief that every person born in America is afforded a clean slate of equal opportunity.[18] While this cultural myth has adjusted itself to each generation, two central themes have remained consistent. First, neither family lineage nor class can supplant individual ability to control one's destiny. Second, success is deemed the reward for moral virtue and good personal character.

The narratives of self-made men and women in America are a central part of American culture. They carry as much meaning as the stars and stripes and are as influential as the Gospel narrative if not more so. The story of the heroic man or woman, though usually a man, who carves out his own path and rises to prominence by his own efforts is well known.

Though in actuality such people are rare, they have come to signify the dreams and ambitions of the common person. Like the Gospel depiction of Jesus's miracles of healing the sick or raising the dead, myths about persons overcoming bleak situations and being rewarded for their hard work, moral character, and faith inspire hope among those who feel as if their back is against the wall.

Inspired by the Enlightenment era's emphasis on the individual and faith in rationality, the myth of American success obscures the social and tragic dimensions of life. The self-made man or woman is essentially an ahistorical, decontextualized character who can guide his or her own destiny over and through the complex web of social relations. Hence, this myth encourages people to think of themselves as autonomous moral agents who can declare, like the British poet William Ernest Henley, "I am the master of my fate: I am the captain of my soul."

One of the cardinal progenitors of this cultural myth is Horatio Alger Jr. The late nineteenth-century author penned over 130 dime novels that glorified and fetishized "rags to riches" accounts of once-underprivileged young men.[19] Alger's novels all followed a similar format. The protagonists, often orphaned boys, were pitted against evil mill owners or other exploiters. By demonstrating the appropriate character traits of hard work, thrift, honesty, and altruism, these courageous young men were able to overcome adversity and drink from the fountains of American success. It is ironic that although Alger's dime novels were written amid the smoldering ashes of the industrial revolution, his heroes opposed the spirit of the Gilded Age. The author seemed more concerned with affirming rugged individuality and the frontier spirit that he felt was disappearing with a dying agrarian order. But by virtue of their character, the young men in Alger's texts were rewarded, not with exorbitant riches per se, but with quality middle-class lives and fulfilling personal relationships.[20]

Since Alger was a former Christian minister, his relationship to the church should not be overlooked. American religion has always served as one of the greatest conduits for diffusing cultural myths throughout American society.[21] Beginning in the nineteenth century, prominent ministers such as Henry Ward Beecher and Russell Herman Conwell directly and indirectly sanctioned the capitalist mode of production by equating capital returns with God-ordained blessings. Though progressive on many social issues, Beecher still affirmed that all social problems could be dealt with by an emphasis on personal responsibility and puritanical morality. A common Beecher homiletic refrain was "No man in this land suffers from poverty unless it be more than his fault—unless it be his sin. . . . There is enough and to spare thrice over; and if men have not enough, it is owing to the want of provident care, and foresight, and industry, and frugality, and wise saving."[22]

Beecher's sentiments were far from anomalous and hardly restricted to the church. By the late nineteenth and early twentieth centuries, leaders of business, government, and religion formed alliances to impress the value of free-market capitalism and the rapidly expanding corporate structure on the hearts and minds of the American people. American cultural heroes such as J. P. Morgan, Andrew Carnegie, Harold Bell Wright, and even Booker T. Washington became noted "saints in a cult of success" with their rags-to-riches tales.[23] Through popular publications, the belief that everyone in American society could share in the American dream of progress and plenty through hard work and untrammeled competition was indelibly inscribed upon the popular consciousness.[24]

We have seen this myth adjust itself to the economic, social, and psychological changes of the twentieth century. From Norman Vincent Peale's 1952 release of *The Power of Positive Thinking* to contemporary texts like Bruce Wilkinson's *New York Times* bestseller *The Prayer of Jabez* and Rhonda Byrne's *The Secret*, Christian booksellers continue to draw on and profit from the cathartic function of this cultural myth. Insofar as African Americans are concerned, one can even see the myth's expression in the popular television shows that succeeded the civil rights movement. Shows like *The Jeffersons, Different Strokes,* and *The Cosby Show*—positive representations that were sorely needed to make up for the earlier representations of African Americans on television as primarily butlers, maids, and ghetto dwellers—helped African Americans of the post–civil rights era to numb painful memories of the past and cultivate an optimistic outlook toward the future. It is understandable that a historically oppressed group would attempt to transcend, at least psychologically, their existential circumstances by latching on to this particular version of America's myth-driven morality.

Even a casual viewer can discern that African American religious broadcasting is informed by and promotes the American myth of success. The dominant themes of personal and economic empowerment that are pervasive in the social orientations of leading televangelists presuppose that the larger society is conducive to social mobility on a large scale. For example, in describing the aims of his ministry, Bishop T. D. Jakes recently stated,

From my pulpit I not only sought to win souls to Christ but to also challenge them that they be freed from poverty, narrow-mindedness and the lack of information that can keep you still enslaved even in our contemporary society because you can't control your destiny. . . . And for my current generation some of the challenges that we face are not just racism but they are economic empowerment, moving beyond self-hatred; It's giving ourselves permission to be successful, it's rather than yelling at the door of someone else's business, I choose to rather open up my own and to build it the way I think it ought to be built and let you come and yell at my door. This is about switching the tables today.[25]

Bishop Jakes's rhetoric of self-choice, controlling one's own destiny, and moving beyond self-hatred in the service of promoting entrepreneurship and economic empowerment operates from the assumption, as in the myth of American success, anyone with a frontier spirit can claim possession of the golden apples of prosperity. Certainly Jakes's own spiritual genius combined with an adroit business sense and unbridled ambition propelled him toward the front of the economic line in black America. This is why Shayne Lee compares Bishop Jakes to other mythic "self-made American characters like Jay Gatsby and Benjamin Franklin."[26] But should we believe that Jakes's own success within America's capitalist economy is an option readily available to all? Or, as some have accused, did Jakes control his destiny and obtain economic prosperity by actually taking advantage of the pain and optimism of the majority of Americans for whom economic empowerment will always be elusive? Jakes may give his viewers a positive sense of self. And some viewers may already have a positive sense of self even as they confront harsh economic conditions and forms of discrimination. But the question then becomes: What effect does Jakes's message have on the economic conditions that structure their daily existence? This is a question we take up directly in the next chapter.

Similar questions can be raised about the prevailing messages of the ministry of World Changers Church International. It is true that for Pastor Creflo Dollar and other Word of Faith preachers America's social systems are inconsequential. The magico-religious rituals of forming a covenant with God through the Word, positive confession, and seed sowing allow persons to reach a state of *metaphysical physicality* that surmounts the restrictions of America's capitalist economy. However, this theological orientation has not prevented the Dollars from embracing a "captain of industry" lifestyle and promoting the moral virtues of wealth attainment. The more corporate than ecclesiastical identity of the ministry affirms and advocates commercial enterprise as a means of African American social uplift. Pastor Dollar's assertions that self-discipline and mastery of the principles of the Word of Faith theology can take persons up the economic and/or corporate ladder reveals his assumption that America's capitalist economy is just. I understand that Dollar may counter this with a theological claim arguing that economic prosperity for Christians is independent of the world's systems. But if Dollar really believes, as I am convinced that he does, that faith without works is dead, then Christians must exercise their faith in the material world. So fatuous theological declarations aside, the recurrent and predominating themes of economic advancement in Dollar's ministry presuppose equal opportunity for wealth attainment in any society where he ministers.

Further, the autobiographical statements of leading African American televangelists all hold in tension contradictory self-conceptions. On the one hand, televangelists, dating back to Rev. Ike, describe coming from families that have a history of entrepreneurial success. Yet each of the televangelists under consideration offers a narrative of financial hardships and strife to situate himself in this myth of the "self-made man" with a spiritual twist.

Rev. Ike's father was preacher and businessman in Ridgeland, South Carolina. He owned properties that he rented to whites because his business acumen was, according to Rev. Ike, "respected by whites and blacks alike." Yet Reverend Ike was also a shoeless and shirtless boy who lived off his mother's meager salary of sixty-five dollars a moth. Bishop Jakes claims to have grown up in a home where his father started a cleaning business that grew to over fifty employees (a well-sized corporation) and where his mother Odith owned several small businesses including rental property. But he also describes experiencing financial hardship as a child and being a young struggling husband unable to pay the electric bill. Bishop Eddie Long's father owned a gas station and auto repair shop, and Eddie majored in business management and worked in corporate America. But he also recounts a story of being homeless and living out of his car while working at a day labor pool. And while Pastors Creflo and Taffi Dollar present themselves less as rags-to-riches entrepreneurs than as well-connected and corporate-groomed executives, there is no shortage of homiletic anecdotes in Pastor Dollar's sermons and writings concerning what life was like when "Taffi and I struggled to make ends meet."[27] Though inspirational, these hyperbolic narratives about "the way of the bootstrapper" or the rise from "rags to riches" or from "GED to PhD" may also be interpreted as the recirculation of melodramatic mantras and cultural myths that obscure the real economic and social conditions that parishioners face.[28]

To be certain, if the American myth of success with its valorous image of the plucky individual is culturally accepted as what is good about America, there is also a preconceived understanding of what is morally base. This is how myths operate and resonate within particular cultures. It is safe to conclude, then, that anything perceived as a failure to take individual responsibility for one's actions is problematic. Not viewing oneself as a self-directed, autonomous moral agent is considered blame-worthy. And the inability of an individual or group to pull themselves up by their own bootstraps and transcend their current situation is un-American. While this charge applies to all Americans, it is particularly laid upon those in American society who have been perennially and pejo-ratively described as a "problem people."[29] This leads us to the second cultural myth to which African American religious broadcasting appeals, *the myth of black victimology.*

The Myth of Black Victimology

Over the past forty years neoconservative academics, public intellectual policy makers, and everyday neighborhood race theorists have made a concerted effort to affirm the declining significance of race in America. In their opinion, with the victories of the civil rights movement over legalized segregation, racism has been reduced to the behavior of fringe groups, white and black separatist organizations such as Aryan skinheads and the Nation of Islam. They believe that white supremacy, rather than being embedded in American society, has vanished since the passage of the 1964 and 1968 Civil Rights Acts and 1965 Voting Rights Act.

Therefore, in the post–civil rights era, the same conservative forces that have sought to keep African Americans trapped in second-class citizenship have begun to accuse African Americans of playing the victim. This is true, in part, because the end-of-racism discourse assumes that racism can be defined only in terms of the personal interactions of individuals rather than the in terms of systemic, ideological, or institutional-ized effects of four hundred years of white supremacy. Moreover, anyone who seeks to call attention to the ill effects of racism in any form is

186 The Reasons Why We Sing

raising false alarms of a white supremacist threat "playing the race card" for his or her own selfish interests. Thus with a deceptive sleight of hand worthy of Harry Houdini, those who once ardently fought against civil rights in America have appealed to civil rights victories and racial progress to silence any viable and sustained discourse about racial justice in America.

Numerous pseudo–social scientific publications have attempted to argue that either biologically or culturally the problems plaguing African American communities are internal rather than external. Less than a generation removed from racial and economic apartheid in America, the Reagan years ushered in a new age that began trafficking two dominant notions about black people: that African Americans were not intellectually or culturally prepared for full and equal participation in American society and that African Americans, on the whole, would rather wallow in victimhood and accuse others of racism than accept personal responsibility that could lead to success.

What is worse, this era also produced a new generation of African Americans who became representative spokespersons for this white supremacist viewpoint. Though the strategy of using blacks to regulate their own people and reinforce the mores of the dominant society is as old as the slave ship *Good Jesus,* this was the first time that African Americans had been afforded access and entrée to the highest positions of power, whether in media, academe, or government. President George H. W. Bush's choice to replace Supreme Court Justice Thurgood Marshall with Clarence Thomas stands as a tragicomic metaphor for the systematic silencing of African American voices committed to racial justice in the public square. Hence political, business, and academic professionals like Thomas Sowell, Ward Connerly, and Shelby Steele rose to a new level of public prominence through conservative think tank funding. Conversely, oppositional voices that sought to extend the legacy of civil rights activism and social justice came to be viewed by the dominant society with skepticism and suspicion. This is how the myth of black victimology has come to define the public discourse on race over the past few decades.

The phrase *black victimology* was coined by African American academic Shelby Steele in his book *The Content of Our Character* and subsequently peddled by John McWhorter in his 1995 *New York Times* bestseller *Losing the Race: Self Sabotage in Black America.* The myth of black victimology says that African Americans have pathologically embraced victimhood as an identity in America in the post–civil rights era. McWhorter and others aver that African Americans do not actually experience racial discrimination; instead, they concoct exaggerated narratives of racial discrimination to psychologically compensate for their insecurity about open competition in America. Since racism is on the wane in America, African Americans have the capacity to overcome any lasting vestiges with the right attitude and commitment to hard work. Yet proponents of the black victimology thesis contend that African Americans have internalized the derogatory messages of past white racism in a crippling way that only leads to delinquency in the educational and professional realms. Hence, according to McWhorter and others who promote this myth, the terms *black* and *victim* have become synonymous.[30]

Though McWhorter's understanding of black victimology begins with a particular moment in the late 1960s, the myth of black victimology antedates the civil rights movement. One can identify dimensions of Steele's and McWhorter's reasoning in the economic optimism of Booker T. Washington, the nationalist orientation of Marcus Garvey, the psychological message of mental liberation promoted by Elijah Muhammad, and the scathing critique of the black bourgeoisie levied by E. Franklin Frazier. Not that any of these legendary figures considered racism to be on the wane in America; but they did describe how the stigma of racial inferiority could handicap black humanity in destructive ways. Therefore, embracing the social posture of a victim should be eschewed at all costs. But what makes this myth distinctive today is the way arguments about black victimology assume a color-blind society. The myth perpetuates the belief that race is reduced to insignificance for African Americans who work hard and play by the rules to achieve success.

We have already noted in previous chapters how accommodationist responses to white supremacy by black preachers informed Rev. Ike's own theological orientation. It is no surprise, then, that Rev. Ike's entire philosophy is based on the myth of black victimology. For example, Rev. Ike's *Science of Living* asserts that the eradication of racism begins and ends with the individual. According to Ike, blackness is a state of mind that connotes negativity. As he stated to one interviewer, "Poverty has become, for blacks in this country, not as much a condition as a badge of self-identification. Black means poor. Black means help me, Boss, because I can't do anything for myself." And when obviously asked about the protest activities of civil rights organizations, he replied, "All these poor people's crawl-ins, and poverty council beg-ins, are used as part of the

negative self-image psychology that is the real oppressor of black people in this country, because it keeps black people turned against themselves, hating themselves for needing help so much."[31] Rev. Ike seemingly
believes that the only way for blacks to overcome racism is to overcome
the negative mind-set and sense of stigma that perpetuate racism. A positive mind-set will enable the fulfillment of human needs that Rev. Ike
believes have nothing to do with the color of one's skin; for on the material level human beings need money, and on the total level of living they
need health, happiness, success, and prosperity.[32]

Pastor Dollar conveys a similar sentiment. His acrimonious characterizations of African American preachers are just one example. Dollar
begins his text *The Color of Love: Understanding God's Answer to Racism, Separation and Division* with a letter he allegedly received from a
"sixty-five-year-old black woman" challenging his teachings on overcoming racism. The letter states, "I was upset and angry at you concerning the
reconciling between blacks and whites. You are just saying these things
to please those white folks. You don't understand how it has really been.
They wouldn't let me eat in their restaurants or drink out of their water
fountains. . . . Yes, I am a bitter, black woman, but I can't help it—or I
don't want to help it. I will never *forgive!*"[33] If it is not ironic enough
that Dollar constructs a text about overcoming racism in America on the
basis of a letter from a fictitious elderly "bitter" black woman, he spends
the rest of the book arguing that racism is essentially an evil spirit in the
mind that individuals must overcome in order to prosper.

The myth of black victimology, overtly advocated by preachers in the
thaumaturgic category of African American religious broadcasting, is
also tacitly accepted even by those in the Charismatic mainline category.
The dominant theme of Bishop Long's ministry, which refers to the contemporary black church as the "Joshua Generation," is a quintessential
example. The call for the contemporary black church to seize and conquer the economic opportunities made available by Martin Luther King
and other civil rights leaders and activists is based on the premise that
the dismantling of legalized segregation opened up a floodgate of opportunities for all African Americans. Why else would Bishop Long suggest
that African Americans forgive and forget racism, as he did during the
King Day Celebration in 2002?

Here Bishop Long's theological sampling becomes somewhat contradictory, if not outright confused. Though Long claims that the church
has been "out of order" since the 1950s, he consciously seeks to graft

his own ministry onto the legacy of Dr. Martin Luther King and the civil rights movement of the 1950s and l960s. He embraces Martin Luther King through the conservative appropriation and co-optation of King's legacy by Christian neofundamentalists such as Pat Robertson, James Dobson, and the late Jerry Falwell. And while the latter movement is unapologetic concerning its disdain for the civil rights era and protests of the 1960s, it has no problem decontextualizing and referencing King in order to disrupt and dismantle King's agenda for society, namely social and racial justice in America.

For certain, Christian conservatives display a form of revisionist, if not recalcitrant, amnesia by sugarcoating at best and outright denying at worst their willful opposition to Dr. Martin Luther King and the civil rights movement.[34] Today they quote ad nauseam King's dream for his children to "live in a nation where they will not be judged by the color of their skin but by the content of their character." And they regularly invoke the tropes of racial equality, equal opportunity, and a color-blind society to make it appear that they embrace rather than reject King's vision for American society. But in doing so they deceptively deploy the rhetoric of color-blindness to suggest that those who actively promote racial justice or race-based policies such as affirmative action are actually in opposition to Martin Luther King and the civil rights era. In fact, Christian conservatives often use King's words to argue that today white males are the victims of racial discrimination because of race- and gender-specific college admissions programs and hiring practices. Among Christian conservatives, King's vision for racial equality and equal opportunity has already been realized with the passing of civil rights legislation that prohibits racial discrimination on paper. Any subsequent corrective efforts, they argue, contradict the spirit and intent of Dr. King and reveal the victim mentality embraced by too many minorities in America. I argue that this sentiment is central to Bishop Long's political and social thought as set forth in chapter 5. Therefore, rather than extending the legacy of Dr. King and the civil rights movement, Bishop Long is more representative of the Christian conservatism of Pat Robertson and his ilk.

To be fair, the Charismatic mainlines' affirmation of the myth of black victimology, as well as the myth of American success, is consistent with the social orientations of many of their ecclesiastical progenitors. The vast majority of the black bourgeois leaders of the civil rights movement who offered a formidable challenge to racial injustice failed to critique the liberal capitalist economic system that exacerbates gross inequality.

Their aim was the dismantling of structural barriers such as Jim Crow so that African Americans could have greater access to America's economic opportunities. Apart from Martin Luther King in his later years, few of these leaders were concerned with how economic goods and opportunities were being distributed. They just assumed that with the repeal of segregationist policies such as *Brown v. Board of Education* African Americans would be able to fully integrate into American society. The color line would be erased. This is why one need not necessarily agree with the hypercapitalist economic views of leading African American clergy such as Bishop Long or his emphasis on mass participation in the capitalist economy as an effective means of liberating black people to acknowledge that these beliefs are to some extent consistent with those of earlier black leaders.

The Myth of the "Strong Black Man" as Savior of the Race

The final and most prominent cultural myth expressed in African American religious broadcasting is that of the "Strong Black Man" as savior of the race. According to cultural critic Mark Anthony Neal, the Strong Black Man is an imaginary hypermasculinist hero who figures in black cultural discourse as far back as the eighteenth century. Essentially a constructed archetype of black male perfection and refinement, the Strong Black Man holds the future of African Americans in his powerful hands. He is a model of racial respectability, familial stability, and economic prosperity. He is respected by old men, emulated by young men, and desired by all women—as either father, son, or lover. The Strong Black Man motif took shape from in the writings and actions of original "race men" such as Prince Hall, Martin Delaney, and Paul Robeson, and this figure is reinvented and identified in the African American cultural imagination by each succeeding generation. Whether he has taken the form of a member of the "Talented Tenth" elite, a soberly attired civil rights protester, a fervent black nationalist, or a hustling hip-hop mogul, the image of the Strong Black Man has been, according to Neal, the "functional myth on which the black nation could be built.[35]

According to Steve Estes's *I Am A Man: Race, Manhood and the Civil Rights Movement,* the myth of the Strong Black Man—which he calls the continued black masculinist movement in American society—originated as a counteroffensive against white masculinist terror during slavery. The struggle for black emancipation was conceptually bound up with a struggle to assert black manhood. Many early race men interpreted the social and civic death experienced by slaves as a symbolic castration of black masculinity, since chattel slavery made it impossible for African American men to conform to the masculine standards of American patriarchal values. Naturally black men were frustrated by their inability to protect women and children from the physical and emotional abuse of white male domination. At the same time black men still viewed white male patriarchal domination as the authoritative ideal of manhood. Therefore, ever since emancipation black men have wrestled with this paradoxical relationship to white masculine power that is grounded in both disdain and emulation. The schizophrenic result is that African American men attempt to fight fire with fire, countering white masculinity with black masculinity.[36]

Patricia Hill Collins refers to this culturally dominant and enduring demarcation of gender roles as hegemonic masculinity and femininity. Hegemonic masculinity becomes the standard by which all "real" men are judged. Its benchmarks include being the opposite of feminine (hard, strong, and forceful), having control over the women in one's life (girlfriend, wife, daughter), not being like a boy (boys are quasi-women in that they are less muscular than grown men and have not yet matured into responsibility), and being heterosexual ("real" men are not sissies, faggots, or queens). Being a "real" man in American society means conforming one's identity to these socially constructed categories.[37]

Collins also notes that ironically, although dependency is considered a female attribute, masculine identity is the dependent one in the sense that it depends on women's fulfillment of particular roles in society. Hegemonic masculinity is a parasitic identity: being masculine depends on one's capacity not to be whatever is culturally deemed as feminine, boyish, or gay. Therefore, hegemonic masculine identity must be supported by a culturally correlate feminine identity to which women must adhere; "real" men cannot fulfill their role unless women meet certain gender identity standards. According to Collins, the benchmarks of hegemonic femininity are maintaining the appropriate bodily and behavioral demeanor (soft, deferential, and demure), being domesticated (married and managing a family), not being taken for a man (accentuation of bodily parts, straight or long hair, soft and/or light skin) and being heterosexual and sexually pure (a woman's body is meant to be given to one man). These are the appropriate feminine gender markers that must be demonstrated to affirm the Strong Black Man as a means of integrating African Americans into mainstream American culture.

Mark Anthony Neal is fair in his assessment of the myth of the Strong Black Man insofar as he acknowledges both the positive and negative attributes of embracing this masculinist subjectivity. Positively speaking, the majority of men who aspire to this status have a genuine love for the black race. These men tend to be civically and socially minded and therefore easily counter demeaning representations of black men as lazy, shiftless, and indifferent. Strong Black Men care for, protect, and provide for their children and afford black women the same sort of chivalrous love and respect that they assume is afforded to women of other races. These men are celebrated as cultural knights in shining armor that "know how to handle their business." Famed gospel playwright and recent Hollywood film sensation Tyler Perry has constructed his own neo-blaxploitation genre—largely directed at black women—around his Strong Black Man protagonists who are able to redeem the black woman, black family, and larger community by virtue of their strong character and testicular fortitude.[38]

On the other hand, the Strong Black Man myth has inspired many black men to embrace extreme views about patriarchal domination that sanction exploitation and abuse. Eldridge Cleaver in his (in)famous autobiography *Soul on Ice* describes rape as an act of insurrection against white supremacy. But though white women were Cleaver's alleged ultimate target, he used the bodies of poor black girls in the ghetto as his training ground. And Stokely Carmichael's embarrassingly misogynistic assertion that "the only position for women in the SNCC is prone" shows the damaging implications of the Strong Black Man myth. Thus whether the myth takes an idealized romantic form, as in the movies and plays of Tyler Perry, or more brutal manifestations, as in the actions of Eldridge Cleaver, "the figure of the 'Strong Black Man' can be faulted for championing a stunted, conservative, one-dimensional, and stridently heterosexual vision of black masculinity."[39]

The dominant themes in African American religious broadcasting that are based on the myth of the Strong Black Man are legion. We can begin with the ministry of Bishop Jakes, though the explicit and implicit messages of his ministry are contradictory in this regard. As Shayne Lee describes in his chapter "Woman Art Thou Really Loosed?" Jakes's affirmation of women and willingness to address women's concerns make it difficult to dismiss him as a raving patriarch. Lee argues that in comparison to other leading ecclesiastical figures such as Bishop Long, Jakes is a black male feminist. Holding the image of his mother Odith near his heart, Bishop Jakes champions the cause of women in every sector of society. For this reason alone, Bishop Jakes contributes to the dismantling of the Strong Black Man myth.

Yet a closer look at Jakes's writings and public reflections, particularly his early work, reveals essentialist themes of manhood that rely upon and promote the myth of a salvific black masculinity.[40] In his book *Loose That Man and Let Him Go!* Jakes constantly appeals to the myth by calling for men to be restored to a place of authority and purpose. And as noted in chapter 4, Bishop Jakes often employs hypermasculinist metaphors to explain the essence of manhood. Comments like "There is a hunter in you whether you are stalking a contract, a deer or a woman" reinforce themes of male domination and female subjugation.[41] In a later section of the same book, entitled "Celebrate Masculinity," Jakes asserts that men need to take pride in being men and contrasts what he regards as men's lack of interest in cultivating and displaying their masculine identity to women's considerable interest in cultivating and displaying their feminine identity: "Women, for the most part, enjoy being women. They surround themselves with beautiful things—flowers and lacy, delicate things that help to frame and enhance the beauty of their femininity."[42] To be sure, these gendered contrasts simultaneously affirm and obscure the very real power dynamics that subordinate African American women to Strong Black Men.

Jakes's romanticization of hyperfemininity in women, rather than his call for a renewal of hypermasculinity among men, is what many would consider most problematic about his ministry. To be fair, Bishop Jakes's book on manhood *He-Motions* aims to disparage a hypermasculine identity among men. But when Jakes falls into romance novel mode in his attempts to affirm the beauty and sanctity of women, he promotes, not relations of mutual respect between the sexes, but a naturalized gendered understanding of the female body as something that should be paternalistically protected. In describing the creation of Eve, for example, Bishop Jakes writes: "When Eve was created, she was heralded onto the face of the planet like a bride who is carried across the threshold of a new home. She was not created until all of her needs were provided. She was the climax of the creation. . . . Her backdrop was the earth. The only thing that covered her soft satiny skin was the bright yellow rays of the sun. In the night, the moonlight cradled her breast with tender hands and a radiant glow. She may have showered in the cascading current of a rapid water-fall. As she ran, her strong thighs whipped through the tall grain with a synergy that cannot be adequately described."[43]

Shayne Lee states that while Bishop Jakes's emphasis on the softer and sensual side of women may seem harmless at first glance, it can actu-ally delimit a woman's capacity to define her own physicality, personal style, and life options. Moreover, often implicit in Bishop Jakes's descrip-tions of women, as in the case of Eve, is the symbiotic relationship to and dependence upon a masculine presence. Thus Lee questions whether athletic, headstrong, single, and extremely competitive women such as Venus and Serena Williams or WNBA basketball stars would fit within the bishop's category of the "demure and sedately assured" women that Jakes longingly remembers.[44]

The bishop's fetishization of the hyperfeminine female body and acceptance of the benchmarks of hegemonic femininity could even explain some of his choices in and relationships to certain female evangelists. The bishop's public spat with Prophetess Juanita Bynum in the late 1990s over royalties from her "No More Sheets" series delivered at the "Woman, Thou Art Loosed" conferences is well docu-mented. Bynum, who was then known for her fiery and physical ora-tory, short kinky hair, and disinclination to wear makeup, endured a sort of ecclesiastical blacklisting from Bishop Jakes that limited her speaking engagements at megachurch conferences across the coun-try. Not long afterward, Bishop Jakes began to introduce and present evangelist Paula White at his mass events as well as on his television broadcasts. Though lacking Bynum's oratorical gifts and singing abil-ity, Paula White is seemingly valued for her thin frame, golden hair, and stylish manner of dress. She has become a consultant and "life coach" on the Tyra Banks show and has been referred to on Trinity Broadcasting Network as the "Princess Di" of the Pentecostal world. In choosing Paula White to appear with him, Bishop Jakes probably realized her marketability, but one can also surmise that her promi-nent blonde hair, blue eyes, and breast lift were more consistent with his idealization of the "soft" and "dainty" virtuous woman. It is both ironic and tragic that since Paula White emerged on the scene, she has often become the lone female evangelist invited to many of the African American megachurch conferences across the country. Thus, without even saying a word, leading male pastors like Bishop Jakes are unwit-tingly reinforcing white supremacist and narrow notions of femininity among thousands of African American women by presenting Paula White to them as the archetype of a "godly" woman.

Further, though Jakes's catchy book, sermon, and conference titles may prove effective at garnering mass appeal, they implicitly reinscribe the submission of women under a Strong Black Man. The passive acceptance of liberation signified in the title "Woman, Thou Art Loosed" is in sharp contrast to the virile exercise of agency suggested by his popular conference title "ManPower." Similarly, the challenge offered to men in the title *So You Call Yourself a Man?* is very different from the message in titles like *The Lady, Her Lover, and Her Lord* or *Daddy Loves His Girls.* The former offers a call to responsibility; the latter imply a parasitic female dependence on a loving God at best and on an earthly male figure at worst. So even as Bishop Jakes claims to move African American women toward positive self-actualization, the messages of his ministry suggest an obsession with having power over women. It is perhaps telling that Bishop Jakes allows men to preach at conferences for women only but has yet to allow a woman to preach at a conference for men only. As Marla Frederick concludes, "Evidently a man can liberate a woman but a woman cannot liberate a man."[45]

Certainly Bishop Long and his ministry are emblematic of the myth of the Strong Black Man. His commitment to the reordering of society based on his patriarchal understanding of the family is informed by his desire to see men literally take control. Men, in his worldview, take on a messianic role, since neither women nor children can be what they are called to be unless they are supported and guided by a Strong Black Man.

An example of this in Bishop Long's thought is the Strong Black Man as warrior. This hypermasculine figure, for Long, epitomizes the true God-given nature of man as a fighter. As we saw in chapter 5, Long believes that "warriors gravitate to warriors."[46] Conversely, for a man not to join forces with other men of the same kind is to be reduced to the opposite of manhood, emasculation. Men are warriors who need to perform their masculine proficiency in public space so as not to be perceived as "wimps." To be sure, they can perform this role in a myriad of ways. At New Birth Baptist Church these may include being involved in the Nation of Jesus men's ministry; standing proud and tall when Bishop Long makes one of his common calls for the "real" men to stand up during worship; or proudly displaying one's physical masculinity, as one might argue Long is doing when he wears stretch-fitted shirts over his muscular frame, a choice that aesthetically typifies the hypermasculinity and warrior-like nature of his theological, ecclesiastical, and social orientations. Bishop Long appears comfortable presenting himself as a masculine archetype or ideal male like the Greek god Adonis or Michelangelo's David for male congregants to admire. And in the performance ritual, the "thing" that these men are conquering can be interpreted as their manhood, in a campaign to gain control over themselves that can be then extended to others, namely women and children.

According to Long, when a rhinoceros is locked up in a zoo and has its horn removed it becomes "wimpified" because it is "no longer in a position to be a warrior or to engage in a fight." Long believes that the same is true for men. When women attempt to capture men and keep them from operating fully within the homosocial space of warrior performance, they put men "in a zoo of sorts. . . . What they [women] don't realize is that they are putting their rhinoceros-spirited men in a position where they will become wimps."[47] It is obvious that Long is contrasting the Strong Black Man to the cultural stereotype of the henpecked male. Men who are culturally prevented from enacting their natural and God-given gender role are reduced from being warriors to being emasculated punks. But clearly Long is not concerned by the misogynistic, homophobic, and homoerotic implications of this line of masculine performance and thought. In his view he is proclaiming God's order.

Finally, though in a more sophisticated way than Bishop Long, Pastors Creflo and Taffi Dollar adhere to the same conceptions of masculinity and femininity. In fact, a critical examination of their teachings on gender reveals their reactionary participation in what the womanist ethicist Emilie Townes has called "the cultural production of evil," or the circulation of a set of images that define black women as morally depraved.[48] Taffi Dollar's reflections on women's role all draw on and seemingly respond to pervasive stereotypes in American culture about African American female identity: the mammy (Aunt Jemima), the emasculating bitch (Sapphire), and the castrating matriarch (Jezebel).

Let us look back at the Dollars' coauthored book *The Successful Family*. In the chapter "Always a Lady," Taffi Dollar provides four principles that she says all women must understand to establish a successful relationship with a man: (1) You have value, (2) You are a helper, (3) You carry yourself well, and (4) You are not a gossip. Surely it is difficult to disagree with Dollar's first affirmation. Encouraging a woman to understand and appreciate her own self-worth is laudable. But what I find telling is the common strand that runs through her discussions of all four principles. In each case, she portrays a virtuous woman as docile, demure, and diligently committed to elevating and empowering a man. For example, in discussing a woman's worth, Taffi Dollar immediately turns to a woman's redemptive role in male-female relationships. She contends, "As a woman, you are so valuable to the plan of God that creation couldn't continue to exist without you! Through these God-given abilities and the words you and I speak, we have the power to make kings and leaders of men. If that power is abused, however, these same men can be made into weak-willed and complacent individuals, unwilling to stand in their God-given place within the family. Think about your words. They can either make or break a man!"[49] The same theme appears in the next principle as she discusses the "anointing" that women have been given as a help-meet to men. A woman's primary role, it seems, is to assist men to fulfill their purpose in life. And the principles concerning how a woman should carry herself and the prohibitions against gossip are both predicated on Pastor Taffi Dollar's a priori understanding of women as "being arrogant, prideful, loud, or gaudy in appearance."[50]

By no means do I believe it to be an accident that Dollar contrasts her ideal "virtuous woman" over and against such negative and stereotypical characterizations of the "ungodly woman." The popular conception of black women as "arrogant, prideful, loud, or gaudy in appearance" is a staple of the American imagination. In the early twentieth century, the image of an overweight, asexual, and long-suffering Mammy was supplanted by the image of Sapphire. Emerging from the minstrel show era, Sapphire has been described by Emilie Townes as "smaller than Mammy and Aunt Jemima, but stout. She had medium to dark brown complexion, and she was headstrong and opinionated. She was loud-mouthed, strong-willed, sassy and practical. The Sapphire stereotype made her husband look inferior, and in doing so, her image set detrimental standards for the Black family."[51]

Sapphire's strength, independence, and employment outside the home to help support the family are all antithetical to the hegemonic femininity of white women, who are often culturally depicted as docile and domesticated. And it is this image of Sapphire as "bitchy, loud, bawdy, domineering and emasculating" that Taffi Dollar appears to have in mind as she offers such advice to women as "Don't yell, shout, scream or speak in a loud voice when carrying on a normal conversation."[52] When we couple this with Taffi Dollar's constant warnings against women possessing a Jezebel spirit, a spirit that she describes as "fiercely independent and intensely ambitious," it is clear that she is concerned with exorcising not only Sapphire but also the image of the black woman as a castrating matriarch—perhaps as alter egos within herself from which she seeks deliverance. As described earlier, Taffi Dollar believes that a Jezebel spirit fosters an Ahab spirit, a weak-willed man. Her statement that "if a man will step up and take his rightful position as the leader, then order can be established" suggests that Taffi Dollar is evoking the myth of the Strong Black Man not only to save the community but to deliver it specifically from Sapphire and Jezebel.[53] Like the other figures previously discussed, she is thus trying to fight oppression by buying into oppression.

If the popularity of religious broadcasting in the African American community teaches us anything, I would argue it is simply this: black people are American too. African Americans long for this nation to live up to its noble ideals and sublime principles of opportunity, equality, and justice for all. In this regard, black people are American patriots and radical democrats in the most prophetic and best sense of the terms. Through televangelists, viewers are able to ritually participate in and affirm their own longings and desires. Televangelists are ingeniously able to create a liminal space where the unjust realities of race, class, and gender are suspended long enough for viewers to imagine themselves living and thriving in such a world.

Yet just as in the dominant society, many African Americans adhere to values of individual achievement defined by careerism, mass consumerism, and a parochial, leisure-driven existence, not to mention stridently romantic and conservative views about the functioning of class, race, and gender in society. Thus televangelists are able to sing the recognizable songs of American cultural myths. The myths of American success, black victimology, and the Strong Black Man as savior of the race have been remixed and looped to a beat that is familiar to a cross section of the population. In the process, viewers wittingly and unwittingly participate in and adapt to the unjust class, racial, and gendered ordering of the larger society.

8

Lift Every Voice

Authority, Ideology, and the Implications of Religious Broadcasting for the Black Church

> Lest our feet stray from the places, our God, where we met Thee
> Lest, our hearts drunk with the wine of the world, we forget Thee
> — "Lift Every Voice and Sing,"
> in the *African American Heritage Hymnal*

Taking or Making Authority?

Throughout this book, I have attempted to situate African American religious broadcasting in a multitraditioned framework of black cultural practices in order to account for differences as well as similarities within the contemporary phenomenon. I have also sought to demonstrate that African American religious broadcasting is a skilled art form and strategic practice. Religious broadcasting is neither a natural occurrence nor simply the transmission of worship over the radio, television, and Internet. Since the days of recording on wax, the artistic skills of prominent African American evangelists have been exploited and varying media strategies have been employed. As noted in the previous chapter, the attraction of televangelism should never be reduced to how well a televangelist may perform or how convincing a preacher may be, since viewers bring their own sets of assumptions, interests, and spiritual concerns to the table. Nevertheless, the tactics that televangelists use to transmit their messages and garner spiritual authority remain a critical aspect of the phenomenon. And though the approach varies according to the preacher and the media format, from our analysis thus far we can identify three primary strategies that African American religious broadcasters utilize in the contemporary moment to authenticate and substantiate their authority.

First, there is the primacy of the "Word." Religious broadcasters emphasize the Bible as an authoritative source. Most televised sermons begin with the reading of scripture, and biblical texts are generally projected on the screen throughout the remaining broadcast. By constant appeals to scripture, televangelists' views of God, the church, and society are made compatible with the divine order. What could be considered merely a broadcaster's or cultural worldview becomes reified as the "Word of God." As Bishop Long constantly reminds New Birth parishioners and *Taking Authority* viewers, "I didn't write the Bible. If you got a problem with it, take it up with God."

Second, the preacher's aesthetic symbols of prosperity serve as an authoritative source. As the living embodiment of faith in action, these dynamic personalities are able to authenticate the worldview that they promote. An aesthetic of prosperity is intended to impress participants in such a way that they might embrace the dominant themes of televangelists as an effective strategy for living. This includes but is not limited to the modeling of luxury goods. Bishop T. D. Jakes's perceived connections with cultural power brokers such as popular entertainers, athletes, and business moguls are often played up as evidence of his faith in action. Throughout his sermons and writings, the bishop often uses illustrations and anecdotes pulled from his interactions with the rich and famous. Bishop Eddie Long similarly emphasizes his relationships to elected officials, including those in the White House, and other respected citizens like the late Coretta Scott King to portray himself as a prophet who has the ear of the powerful. His *Taking Authority* broadcast often opens with plugs from celebrities like Yolanda Adams and Angela Bassett and even displays an image of Bishop Long posing with R&B superstar Usher. And Pastor Creflo and Taffi Dollar's private airplanes, Manhattan penthouse, and CEO designation would make it appear that by adhering to the Word of Faith principles anyone can become the next Ken Chenault or Richard Parsons. The Dollars thus become the prosperity message incarnate. As Bishop T. D. Jakes told his interviewer from *Time* magazine, "Persons need an example of success."[1]

Finally, such an aesthetic of prosperity is reinforced by the very media televangelists employ. Because of television's reality-making capacity, the medium can create the sense that what is seen and heard is an objective reality. When one couples this "objective reality" as seen on television with cultural myth systems that have demonstrable resonance among a cross section of the population, it is hard to deny televangelism's ability to codify social norms and relations. Televangelism articulates views and values that are already held by viewers or that, if not personally held, are quite recognizable. And by giving viewers repeated exposure to particular themes and myths discussed in the previous chapter, television contributes to what media theorists refer to as the teleconditioning of viewers.[2] For example, if a young black male in the suburbs sees and hears through habitual television viewing that young black men enjoy hip-hop music, there is a good chance that he will soon embrace hip-hop and even understand it as representative of "his culture." Similarly, if a woman sees and hears Bishop Eddie Long pontificate about a "Strong Black Man" on Black Entertainment Television she may begin fantasizing that a sanctified Prince Charming will appear in her life. Such beliefs may be embraced and inculcated even when they are totally incongruent with the lived reality of viewers and possibly not even in their best interests.

So while we have acknowledged the positive aspects of televangelism in the previous chapter, clearly there are real dangers as well. Thus I now want to examine the possible deleterious ramifications for African Americans of the strategies and pervasive myth systems circulated by televangelism. Providing adherents a liminal space to think differently about themselves in their world is not the same as offering an intellectual challenge to fossilized regimes of truth that petrify and reproduce the material world. Is it really possible to "be loosed" from poverty and attain measures of economic wealth when one turns a blind eye to the unjust aspects of America's capitalist economy that is based on a parasitic and exploitative relationship with the underclass? Is it really feasible for African Americans to "take authority" while simultaneously affirming a plutocratic and patriarchal ordering of society that has a direct impact upon black life? And is it really probable, as Creflo Dollar would have us to believe, for moral subjects to "change their world" while leaving the larger white supremacist world that shapes and informs their daily existence unchallenged? These are the questions I am concerned with as I begin to raise serious criticisms of the three major cultural myths that underlie African American religious broadcasting.

Not the Way of the Bootstrapper

African American religious broadcasting typically displays an uncritical acceptance of the American myth of success as the defining reality of American existence. Themes of self-choice, controlling one's own destiny, and seizing economic opportunities available in the "Promised Land" of America's capitalist economy are all homiletic staples. Many preachers have come to regard the nineteenth-century economic theories of Booker T. Washington as a fitting approach to personal liberation, social transformation, and economic empowerment for the African American community in the twenty-first century. The time is right, according to many black televangelists, for African Americans to cast down their buckets and quench their thirsts from the plentiful rivers of America's opportunities.

But such an opinion does not take into account that the control over resources in America's capitalist economy today is more firmly secured in the hands of a few than ever before. It is true that during the 1980s and 1990s America celebrated a booming economy and surging stock market.[3] As the glitz of the new gilded age was displayed on the television via such shows as *Lifestyles of the Rich and Famous*, MTV's *Cribs*, and VH1's *The Fabulous Life of*, African American preachers such as Bishop Carlton Pearson and Rev. Frederick Price embraced all the hypermaterialism of the period. One has to wonder about the seemingly direct cultural correlation between the growth of religious broadcasting and the dramatic economic expansion of the economic elite in America. As Lear jets replaced limousines in corporate America and platinum supplanted gold among the hip-hop elite, African American religious broadcasters traded in their Cadillacs for Bentleys and began to franchise their congregations as "transnational corporations." (African American megachurches started the practice of what may be more soberly described as having "one church in two [or more] locations.")

The dramatic economic growth of the 1990s, however, would not correlate with economic justice in America. In fact, the gulf between the rich and poor widened during America's economic boom. Throughout the twentieth century there was a sharp contrast between the large percentage of wealth controlled by the richest 1 percent of Americans and the small percentage of wealth shared by the vast population of the poorest Americans.[4] But such economic inequality intensified over the final quarter of the twentieth century. Whereas in 1976 the top 1 percent of Americans households held 20 percent of all private wealth and the top 10 percent of households held over 50 percent, by the turn of the new millennium the top 1 percent held 33 percent of all private wealth and the top 10 percent held almost 70 percent. Within only twenty-five years the top 10 percent of America's economic elite had increased their control of the wealth in America's supposedly equitable capitalist economy by 20 percent.[5] As a result, today less than a third of America's wealth must be shared by 90 percent of its citizens. This means that America's capitalist economy looks more like a pyramid than a level playing field.

Moreover, the common saying about the rich getting richer and the poor getting poorer is a demonstrable fact. During the Reagan years the upper 1 percent of the population increased their annual income by 74 percent while the annual income for the bottom 10 percent of the population decreased by 10 percent.[6] By the mid-1990s, even during the Clinton wonder years, the United States had the smallest and fastest-shrinking middle class in the industrialized world. Though the United States is the wealthiest of the seventeen industrialized nations, it has a higher percentage of citizens living in poverty than its industrialized neighbors do.[7] With grim statistics like these it is hard to contest the argument that prosperity for a few equals injustice and inequality for many within America's capitalist economy. For the plutocrats to gain the proletariats must lose; hence, behind the curtain of America's equal opportunity are the struggling stagehands and exploited extras who must make the sacrifices offstage so that the spectacle of prosperity can continue.

For example, decreasing wage value for non-white-collar workers is a major factor contributing to the growth in wage inequality and the shrinking middle class over the past three decades in America. In 1968 the minimum hourly wage peaked at what in 1997 would have been the equivalent of $7.37. Since this time, while the real incomes of the wealthiest 5 percent of households have more than doubled, the minimum wage value has fallen 30 percent.[8] This is a deplorable reality for those finding themselves on the bottom rung of America's economic ladder; especially since the U.S. economy is 50 percent more productive today than in 1968. At this paltry pay rate, someone working fifty hours a week for the entire year will only earn $10,300.[9] So much for the payoff of hard work, saving, and thrift for those who do not even come near the bottom of America's poverty line.

Meanwhile, business executives have seen their salaries increase exponentially over this same period. In 1980 the pay of the typical CEO was forty-two times that of the average hourly worker. By 2003 the pay of a CEO was over three hundred times that of the average hourly worker, not counting the multi-million-dollar value of long-term stock options.[10]

It is likely that the gap between the undisclosed compensation of leading televangelists and megachurch pastors today and the pay of the average congregant-viewer would be just as wide.

Further, racial factors must be taken into consideration. African American private family wealth continues to lag far behind that of white households. Wealth, unlike income, develops over generations. And since with regard to income African Americans are still trying to catch up with their white counterparts in the post–civil rights era—even as the wage value of workers across the board has been dwindling—African Americans are fighting two battles at once, making up for not only the vestiges of racial discrimination and income disparity but also the declining value of labor. And while the trend among African American religious broadcasters is to deny the prevalence and prominence of race, research reveals that the racialized devil is in the details.

Racism without Racists

In the previous chapter we gave voice to those who affirm the declining significance of race in America. The myth of black victimology continues to gain ground across the racial divide, portraying racial injustice as merely a figment of black imagination.[11] With the victories of the civil rights movement, many have come to define racism according to personal prejudice as opposed to systemic or institutionalized factors. But empirical evidence concerning the state of black life in America resists such claims.

Surely, one must acknowledge the economic and social gains made by African Americans in the post–civil rights generation. This particularly pertains to black households that make up the upper-income bracket of $75,000 to $99,000. This group of "well-to-do" blacks has increased 400 percent over the past forty years.[12] But while median household income has increased within the upper echelons of black society, this relatively elite economic bracket still constitutes a mere 7 percent of African American households. The vast majority of African Americans (around 60 percent) remain in that amorphous category designated as middle class, with an income somewhere between $17,000 and $79,000.[13] And among this group the median household income for African Americans still remains around 60 percent of the white median household income. It is appropriate to assert, then, at least in economic terms, that the three-fifths compromise concerning the worth of black life remains intact.[14] Moreover, as the work of William Julius Wilson demonstrates, despite the gains of the civil rights movement, the unemployment of African American men in urban areas increased in the concluding decades of the previous century as manufacturing jobs in America's central cities were both outsourced and eradicated.[15]

In terms of wealth accumulation there is more to the story. It is important to remember that income (what one earns) and wealth (one's overall accumulated value) are not the same. As Thomas Shapiro points out in *The Hidden Cost of Being African-American: How Wealth Perpetuates Inequality*, definitions of *middle class* become even more ambiguous if one includes the accumulation of wealth in the economic equation. When we factor in accumulated wealth, African American professionals like doctors and lawyers may find themselves in the same economic class as blue-collar whites. In the post–civil rights era, the top tier of African Americans have garnered success in terms of education, professional development, and income but not in terms of attaining substantial assets. On the average, when incomes are equal between blacks and whites, there is a wealth difference of $50,000.[16] Hence, in economic terms the growing black professional class is equivalent to the white working class.

The unbalanced distribution of wealth between contemporary whites and African Americans must be situated within the historical processes that nurture racial and economic inequality and not attributed solely to the "moral virtues" of hard work, saving, and thrift. In general, each generation of African Americans begins life with fewer material assets and has been forced to confront barriers that preclude economic development. This is true because of the sedimentation of America's caste system extending from slavery as well as the economic detour of Jim Crow, which prevented African American entrepreneurs from competing in an open market.[17] Being only one generation removed from the American system of apartheid, contemporary black professionals have not been able to benefit from the accumulated assets of wealth that could help defray such expenditures as the repayment of student loans, the downpayment on a new home, and child care assistance or private school tuition for offspring. It is difficult even for married first-generation professionals to meet the rising costs of real estate and child care while attempting to reside, dress, and drive the part that their profession requires (an anxiety that racial and gender minorities tend to feel more acutely). And since

43 percent of wealth inheritance takes place among living relatives, this sort of financial assistance from parents and grandparents crucially influences young professionals' ability to forge ahead on the road to wealth attainment.[18] When generational wealth is unavailable, as often is the case among African Americans, even those making higher incomes still find themselves starting out behind the proverbial eight ball. The effects of racial injustice thus continue forty years after the signing of the Civil Rights act.

It is safe to conclude, then, that African American religious broadcasting promotes the myths of equal opportunity and black victimology at a time when black people are skating on increasingly thin economic ice as a result of both economic and continued racial injustice in America. I contend that the optimistic rhetoric of the "bootstrapper" and entrepreneurial valor has no more realistic relation to the conditions of the majority of African Americans today than it did when it was promoted by Booker T. Washington at the turn of the twentieth century.

As W. E. B. Du Bois presciently noted in 1903, a gospel of "Work and Money" represents the old attitude of adjustment and submission to injustice that undermines the realization of higher aims.[19] Du Bois understood that those who wished to promote justice should seek to establish a more open and accessible society from which succeeding generations might benefit rather than merely to create individualized pockets of prosperity. This is why I find it interesting that so many successful African American clergy today invoke their ability to pull themselves up by their own bootstraps when their boots were both provided and laced by civil rights activity that they now reject. Further, many appear to believe that "pragmatic" compromise with the societal powers that be is the answer to fighting injustice. But this is also ironic, since their success would never have been attained without the labors and sacrifices of those who were unwilling to "pragmatically" compromise with injustice. Thus the collective myths of American success and black victimology within religious broadcasting operate to the detriment of the black church in three specific ways: they promote the gilded values of conspicuous consumption and hypermaterialism among persons already in fragile financial circumstances; they foster a priestly class of black preachers to the detriment of the prophetic voice; and they can drive a political wedge between clergy and communities of faith such that the latter become less trusting of the former.

The Prosperity Ethic and the Spirit of Consumerism

The aesthetic dimension of religious broadcasting shows how the myth of American success has adjusted to the gilded sensibility of the contemporary era. Fancy clothes, luxury cars, and expansive homes all convey that a life of prosperity and commitment to God are synonymous. Further, the gaudy displays of prosperity promote, not the creation and saving of wealth, but its conspicuous consumption.

To be fair, televangelists do place some emphasis saving and various forms of wealth creation. Most notably, Bishop T. D. Jakes's latest book, *Reposition Yourself,* offers a principled critique of African American hyperconsumerism. It appears that as Bishop Jakes becomes increasingly visible and accepted in the mainstream, and as he encounters healthy public critique as raised by scholars like Cornel West and Shayne Lee, he is beginning to develop a heightened social consciousness and more mature social analysis that sets him far beyond his televangelist colleagues. Yet for most, the few messages of fiscal responsibility that are intermittently offered as ancillary points are drowned out by the far more plentiful and powerful messages promoting a crass materialism. The number of advertisements for ministerial conferences with images of mansions in the background, television broadcasts that prominently display luxury goods, and even church Web sites that feature high-end automobiles as the dominant visual focal point imply that economic empowerment is not about real wealth creation but rather about conspicuous consumption, hyperconsumerism, and commodity fetishism.

This presents an interpretive conundrum for parishioners. If the preacher is viewed as the embodiment of faith in action or as an exemplar of "what God can do," the collected luxury accoutrements of the pastor can be viewed as the end result of certain modeled or prescribed behaviors: an aesthetic of prosperity becomes an ethic of prosperity, and luxury goods may be interpreted as the tangible rewards of divine blessings. A palatial home, a diamond ring, a Rolls-Royce in the parking lot, and even the visible appearance of a "nipped and tucked" face are reified as the outward signs of an inward grace.

But what happens when through no fault of their own individuals do not receive God's blessings in tangible forms as modeled by their pastor or televangelist? How might they respond when all the indicators of a white, male, and class supremacist society cause them to raise, in the private sanctum of their soul, the question posed by William Jones in his book title *Is God a White Racist?*[20] Can the accumulation and fetishization of material goods become a means of elevating one's status with God? Do material objects give participants the opportunity to perform publicly their private spirituality of longing and self-worth vis-à-vis the divine? Many have acknowledged the viability of Max Weber's argument that New England Puritans embraced an ethic of hard work, discipline, and austerity as a way to psychologically cope with the anxiety raised by their ambiguous and uncertain status as members of God's predestined elect. So is it really implausible to think that working- and middle-class African Americans might just as readily embrace an ethic of prosperity linked to conspicuous consumption and crass materialism as a way to cope with the anxiety raised by their ambiguous and uncertain status of being in God's favor when all material conditions point out otherwise? I think not.

Rev. Ike offers insight into this line of reasoning. Speaking before a predominantly white audience, Rev. Ike shares the following story:

> I remember when I was a poor little black kid. Without shoes, without a shirt, working in a mechanic shop in S.C. during the summer. . . . And I went into a certain store and began talking to a very fancy lady in there that was the fashion-plate of the town, and I began to tell her some of my dreams. And I remember at that particular time I said, "I want a Cadillac."
>
> And she stopped what she was doing and looked at me and said, "What do you mean a Cadillac? You don't need a Cadillac."
>
> . . . I never said anything. But, I thought in my mind, "Who in the hell are you to tell me what I don't need?"[21]

Here Rev. Ike situates a poor boy who wants a Cadillac in opposition to a constructed authority figure who judges his desire as either unnecessary or improbable.[22] His visceral response can be read as a form of resistance against the status quo: a poor black boy in South Carolina dares to desire the luxuries of society that are reserved for an elite class. Could it be that Ike's silent response, "Who in the hell are you to tell me what I don't need?" is the anxiety-ridden cry of the oppressed who see others enjoy the finer things of life through the veil of economic and racial separation? Hence, whenever the opportunity presents itself, ostentatious displays of wealth, even if they are only on the surface, can visibly demonstrate African American worth in a white and class supremacist culture.

This notion is consistent with Bishop T. D. Jakes's testimony that his desire to own his own business was a response to witnessing a white man berate his father.[23] Bishop Jakes's conspicuous consumption back in Charleston may have been his way of saying to that white man and all other forms of white supremacy in West Virginia, "Who in the hell are you to tell me what I don't need?" Just the same, could Bishop Long and Pastor Dollar's downplaying of race while displaying their wealth be a way for them to emblematically become honorary white men? That is, are they seeking to become and associate with, on a symbolic level, the people they perceive to signify power, respect, and authority? If so, their denial of the importance of race may reveal that they are actually consumed by it.

This is not a far-fetched claim. Oral Roberts's attempts to cultivate connections in the business sector after World War II and to align his movement with "business principles" were his way of overcoming the stigma of being a midwestern white Pentecostal, a group often perceived as backwater yahoos,[24] as well as a way of distancing white Pentecostalism from the emotionalism and physicality of the faith that signified black religious expression in the American imagination. White Pentecostal faith movements descended from Roberts and Hagin made the transition from dusty tent revivals to swanky hotel conferences partly because their leaders were attempting to reforge their white identity as "businessmen" rather than mere revivalists and to attain a respectability defined in terms of a corporate, white male masculinity.

This is also the reason that many African American preachers today unapologetically embrace the business values of the phenomenon or the corporate ecclesiology that has come to define the Word of Faith movement. The corporate ecclesiology of the movement provides black men, who for the most part have been denied access to the corporate world, the opportunity to become "chief executive officers." For many prominent African American evangelists who were not afforded the educational opportunities to attend Wharton or the social capital and networks to reasonably compete in the business world, embracing this form of entrepreneurial evangelicalism becomes the next best thing: they do not look as if they had to settle for being a preacher because no other viable career opportunities were available, a stigma that has been associated to African American clergy for generations. (As the proverbial saying goes, "When you can't do nothing else, you can always be a preacher.")

Pastor Creflo Dollar revealed both his disdain of black preachers and his aspirations to do more in his first national interview on CNN. According to Dollar, "I didn't like preachers growing up. . . . They eat your chicken, wear a little shiny suit, and driving [sic] a little Cadillac. I didn't like them, so I was never going to be one. But, you know, God showed me I didn't have to be like the stereotype."[25] As you may recall, the Dollars have worked hard to distinguish and disassociate their ministry from what they pejoratively perceive as traditional African American religion. Like Rev. Ike, they describe neither the World Changers congregation as a black church nor themselves as black preachers, though World Changers membership is 99 percent African American. Thus it appears that for those who deny yet are deeply affected by the prevalence and persistence of race in America the image of a "little Donald Trump," as Rev. Ike described his father, is more self-affirming than the image of a "little black preacher" from which Bishop Eddie Long vehemently disassociated himself. The televisual simulacrum of being the CEO of a "multinational corporation" helps to ease the insecurity of being rendered always and already outside the mainstream due to the color of one's skin, not to mention the handicaps of limited education and the lack of access to real systems of power. A custom-tailored suit, a Rolex watch, and a fleet of luxury vehicles, however, do little to the eradicate the structural injustices that contribute to one's insecurities in the first place. Therefore, in their search for social acceptance, too many African American televangelists have mistaken vanity for dignity, pomposity for respectability, and delusions of grandeur for social capital.

But an ethic of ostentatious prosperity has dire consequences for black middle-class viewers who are only electric slide away from poverty. Though black buying power is at an all-time high ($723 billion in 2004), this figure does not translate into increased wealth in the African American community.[26] In fact, wealth is on the decline among middle-class African Americans as a result of increasing consumer debt and the current housing crisis. A study by Federal Reserve senior economist and project director Arthur B. Kennickel on the distribution of wealth in the United States between 1998 and 2001 showed that African Americans add on debt at a far greater rate of increase than their incomes. Since reports show that the majority of debt racked up by African Americans is on depreciating goods such as cars, clothes, and telecommunication services, black people are reducing their wealth-building potential with each additional dollar they earn.[27] This trend is taking place in the context of depreciating labor and housing markets that have direct consequences for African American wealth potential. As blacks pay back escalating debts, they are forced to utilize financial resources that could otherwise be used for savings and/or appreciating assets, and the increased interest rates they must pay because of their high levels of consumer debt can cut drastically into their disposable monthly income. Therefore, escalating debts, repossessions, and record rates of home foreclosures appear to be the end result of some people's prosperity ethic and "name it and claim it" spirituality.

The Priestly over the Prophetic

The collective myths of American success and black victimology also threaten African American church communities of faith by fostering a priestly class of black preachers rather than prophetic leaders. Here I am drawing on the discussion of leadership styles in the black church set forth in Peter Paris's *Black Religious Leaders: Conflict in Unity.* According to Paris, a priestly class of black preachers nurture the community according to their religious responsibilities to God and commit themselves to the preservation and expansion of the faith. Priestly leaders believe the structures of society to be fundamentally good and attribute injustice to the moral indiscretions of a few as opposed to inherent flaws in the structures of society. Rather than challenging the society at large, priestly leaders seek to integrate parishioners into the culture as productive and loyal citizens. By nurturing humility, patience, and goodwill, priests accommodate themselves to social injustice without necessarily affirming it. In other words, priests at most encourage microsocial resistance among their parishioners by helping them endure those things that cannot be readily changed. Priestly leaders, according to Paris, "make constructive use of every possible opportunity for self-development under the conditions of bondage."[28]

Priests are esteemed social figures who have the respect of the masses and the ear of the powerful. For this reason priests believe that they can appeal to the moral goodwill of the societal elite to obtain justice. Thus, historically, priestly leaders have mediated, not between humanity and God, but between the powers that be and everyday people. And whether the societal elites are right or wrong in their decision making, the priest always seeks to resist conflict, resolve disputes, and squelch massive demonstrations. Priestly types tend to fear that conflict or protest will lead to more repression and the loss of social capital. For it is true that priestly leaders often enjoy the respect of the masses and gain personal benefits from the elite classes. Demonstrable conflict can prove threatening to such a mediated social order.

Paris contrasts the priest to the prophet who is a social reformer. The prophet views society as neither fundamentally good nor bad but as fundamentally flawed. With a theological and political conception of how a just society should be structured, the prophet sets out to reform society toward this preconceived end, believing that failure to do so will lead to the inevitable destruction of society. For the prophet there is little compromise on the tenets of justice and no moral middle ground: "The prophetic struggle is one between truth and falsehood, good and evil." This is why for Paris the life and ministry of Martin Luther King Jr. are emblematic of the prophetic perspective. King's moral clarity and consistency concerning injustice put him in a position where he had no permanent allies or enemies. His aim of rooting out racial and class injustice was his guiding principle.[29]

Many African American religious broadcasters, most notably Bishop Eddie Long, understand themselves to operate according to the role of the prophet. However, their uncritical embrace of America's social structures—most obviously America's capitalist economy—and the dominant society's morals and manners reflects the nonconflictual approach of the priestly type more than the progressive posture of the prophet.

This is not to say that Bishop Long or any other evangelists are apolitical or that they do not protest white supremacy. Among the leading African American religious broadcasters, Bishop Long is unapologetically political, and Bishop Jakes does acknowledge white supremacy. But with its emphasis on the cultivation of morals and manners as a form of resistance, the priestly approach remains microsocial at best. Further, political positions that are in line with the majority of Americans cannot necessarily be considered progressive or resistant. Thus antigay marches or protests for prayer in schools, though political, should not be considered prophetic. Bishop Long, like Elder Michaux and Prophet Jones in previous generations, is the contemporary manifestation of a long tradition of political advocacy dictated by the climate of public consent. Supporting war on the heels of 9/11 or opposing gay marriage while operating in a conservative evangelical tradition does not necessarily call for moral courage or oppositional conviction. If anything, it represents a worldview and activity that almost everyone in the subculture would be comfortable with.

I believe priests have their place. They can appeal to the moral good-will of the societal elite to further the aims of justice. There is a fine line, however, between engaging in priestly forms of microsocial resistance and making the black church a hegemonic apparatus like the rural Baptist congregation of Rev. Ike's youth in Ridgeland. Black clergy's social mediation between elites and the masses can easily deteriorate into the paternalistic "gift" exchange that has defined the awkward relations between black and white evangelicals for centuries. In the world of contemporary religious broadcasting, rather than receiving building materials or protection of one's church building from white supremacists, prominent African American televangelists are receiving large honoraria, free airtime and exposure on TBN, and faith-based funding from the White House. One could justifiably argue that these gifts are in exchange for black televangelists' resounding silence around issues of social injustice that negatively affect the African American community, like the 2000 and 2004 presidential election fiascos and the federal government's failure to respond to hurricane victims on the Gulf Coast. While these are just two examples, the real danger is when the priestly class trade away social justice for white benevolence—an unfair exchange indeed.

Spiritual Authority without Political Respect

This leads us to the third way the myths of American success and black victimology harm African American Christian faith communities. As a result of the mass-mediated emergence of an elite and hegemonic class of religious leaders, one can identify a disconnect between preachers and parishioners around political issues. It is evident by the numbers that the masses confer spiritual authority on religious broadcasters. But the voting patterns of African Americans remain in sharp contrast to the political sensibilities of these leading electronic and megachurch pulpiteers.

For example, polling data show that the majority of working- and middle-class African Americans, rather than believing in the myth of black victimology, are quite clear about the prevalence of racism in America. There has been a shift over the past forty years concerning class attitudes about race in the black community. Prior to 1967 most poor African Americans expressed little trust in the American dream and blacks' ability to be fully accepted in the larger society. On the other hand, the black middle class was very optimistic. As stated earlier, many of the civil rights stalwarts viewed the breaking down of legal barriers as a necessary condition for blacks to integrate socially and economically integrate into American society. But opinions have flipped over the past forty years. Today the black poor seem more optimistic than the black working and middle classes. As Harvard political scientist Jennifer Hochschild states, "Well-off African Americans see more racial discrimination than do poor blacks, see less decline in discrimination, expect less improvement in the future, and claim to have experienced more in their own lives."[30] Thus, though the rhetoric of equal opportunity and individual responsibility is affirmed as a ritualized tool of self-affirmation and personal efficacy, it does not appear to translate to and inform the political choices African Americans make on the ground.[31]

This may explain why church members and viewers embrace the spiritual authority of persons like Bishop Jakes, Bishop Long, and Pastor Dollar but largely reject their political views.[32] Even though the vast majority of African American religious broadcasters have allowed themselves to be courted and caressed by the Bush White House in recent years, the 2004 and 2006 national elections proved that African Americans, for the most part, still reject the "party of Lincoln." The percentage of black voters supporting the Republican ticket was consistent with percentages dating back to the Reagan era.

This discrepancy between spiritual authority and political respect was evident in 2005 when radio and television personality Tavis Smiley chose to hold his annual "State of Black America" symposium at New Birth Missionary Baptist Church. When Tavis Smiley introduced Bishop Long as the Senior Pastor of New Birth, the crowd gave him a roaring ovation. But their response seemed more mixed when Mr. Smiley asked Long about his and other African American evangelical preachers' participation at a luncheon hosted by President George W. Bush at the White House. Bishop Long's curt response of "We didn't have intercourse" did not appear to register well with those gathered that morning. Further, Cornel West and Louis Farrakhan received standing ovations when West publicly challenged the bishop's moral and political courage, or lack thereof, and Farrakhan likened Bishop Long to a mannequin in a shopping mall window who looks good but is unable to speak.[33]

To be clear, the gap between the political sensibilities of spiritual leaders and the political choices of viewers is not a bad thing in itself. If anything, it reveals the critical thought of African Americans around diverse sets of issues that structure their existence. As stated from the outset of this book, we must never conflate what people do ecclesiastically with the choices they make politically. African Americans have proven to be more complicated than such a deterministic analysis could reveal. Moreover, pejorative descriptions such as *otherworldly* and *apolitical* obscure the complicated nature of African American religiosity and experience. Someone can be on a flight heading to a "Changing Your World Conference" while reading Tavis Smiley's *The Covenant with Black America*. Black religious folks are that complicated.

On the other hand, if we are to believe Frederick Harris's findings, from *Something Within: Religion in African American Political Activism,* that African Americans are more likely than other groups to be informed about political issues in church, then the dominant political themes espoused by Bishop Jakes, Bishop Long, Pastor Dollar, and others may have an impact on black political discourse and decision making over time.[34] What kind and how much? This remains to be seen. But what may be efficacious spiritually and individually may be damaging politically and socially for black people. And what may be regarded as personally empowering may prove ideologically deceptive when implemented on a mass scale. So while I do not necessarily believe that preachers have to be politically astute or aware to be effective, we must be concerned when those such as Bishop Long present their ministries as a panacea for the ills plaguing black America. When televangelists use the power of the media and the authority of their acclaim to assert that they have "the answer" to social maladies, then it becomes incumbent upon social ethicists and cultural critics to identify the shortcomings of their analysis. The political prescriptions offered by leading televangelists might be based on a social, historical, and cultural misdiagnosis. This is why, in my opinion, certain contemporary African American televangelists are guilty of political malpractice. The prescribed medicine may taste sweet, but it is powerless to heal the political and social ills that plague their constituents.

Preach, Black Man!

The final prevailing ideology fostered and reinforced by African American religious broadcasting is the myth of the Strong Black Man as savior of the race. The Strong Black Man is the imaginary hypermasculinist hero and patriarchal messiah figure of African American racial uplift discourse. Like Bishop Long's oft-repeated congregational call for "all

my 'Real Men' to stand up," the myth of the Strong Black Man is predicated on the assumption that African American socialization and progress depend on black men taking charge of the community. But, to put it
bluntly, this is a farce. The masculinist approach to social liberation does
not work and has never worked because it merely replaces one form
of oppression with another. Many cultural theorists have critiqued it as
dangerously naive.[35] This is particularly true with regard to the parochial
and patriarchal politics of the Black Power movement.

   After the 1965 Moynihan Report labeled the black family as abnor-
mal because of its alleged matriarchal structure, all of the anxieties of
black masculinity in relation to white patriarchy that dated back to preindustrial, slaveholding times were placed on full display in America.
Black men felt impelled to perform for the larger society that they were
in fact in control. In the words of Michelle Wallace, "To most of us Black
Power meant wooly heads, big black fists and stern black faces, gargantuan omnipotent black male organs, big black rifles and foot-long combat boots, tight pants over young muscular asses, dashikis, and broad
brown chests."[36] But Wallace concludes her critique with a grim reminder
of the naïveté of the movement: "When the black man went as far as the
adoration of his own genitals could carry him, his revolution stopped. A
big Afro, a rifle, and a penis in good working order were not enough to
lick the white man's world after all."[37]

   Past experiences of liberatory movements and antihegemonic resistance in America demonstrate that any single site of oppression cannot be effectively contested in isolation. Injustice anywhere is indeed
a threat to justice everywhere. White yeomen farmers in the Reconstruction era found their resistance against class exploitation thwarted
when they refused to challenge the tenets of America's racist ideology.[38] The dividing of labor along racial lines has always served as an
effective tool to thwart critical resistance to capitalist producers. Mary
Church Terrell and Frances Ellen Harper understood that the failure of
the women's movement in the late nineteenth century to include black
women would frustrate their own aims. By directing their pain as an
oppressed group against black women, white women ended up participating in both the maintenance of male supremacy and their own
continued subjugation.[39] And Martin Luther King realized that the dismantling of legalized segregation in America would be a hollow victory
in the absence of a thoroughgoing class analysis that called for a fundamental restructuring of America's capitalist economy. The ability to

sit at a lunch counter means nothing without the capacity to purchase a meal.

African American men today are repeating the mistakes of the past when they try to lead the African American community while turning women into objectified backup dancers who are to be seen and not heard. Many black men feel that to meet the benchmarks of hegemonic masculinity they must embrace antiquated views of gender. This is why, for example, Creflo Dollar cannot be a "real" man unless Taffi is a "real" woman. Power becomes a gendered zero-sum game. If Taffi is independent, forceful, and self-assured—"womanish" in black southern parlance—then Creflo must be dependent, weak, listless, and emasculated, the spirit of Ahab to her spirit of Jezebel. For Creflo to take his rightful place, he must first put Taffi in her rightful place. In a hierarchical ordering that both Bishop Long and the Dollars refer to as a divine chain of command, there can only be one head and everyone else must fall into the ranks.

But this line of reasoning is as illogical as it is antiquated. First, it assumes that there is a pure essence to male and female identity and personality, as if it were possible to be a "real" man or woman. The "realness" of our biological makeup is defined only by our sex and bodily functions. So declarations in church such as "All my Real Men stand up" don't make much sense. Moreover, one's penis has little to do with one's personality, and ovaries have little effect on one's attitudes. Gender, like race, is a social construction. And just as the racial categories of black, white, red, yellow, and brown have flattened the complexity and changing contours of ethnicity, gender is defined according to the cultural practices and social mores of a society that persons choose to embrace. A little girl no more chooses to be wrapped in a pink blanket when she is born than a little boy chooses to play with trucks. And a three-piece suit no more makes a male body "real" than a skin-tight muscle shirt.

Second, this line of reasoning buys into culturally produced and commodified images of "ideal" white femininity to which black women are expected to conform. Those who do not are negatively represented as Sapphires and Jezebels—fictive creations of a white supremacist and sexist society. According to the myth of the Strong Black Man, until men can silence Sapphire's backtalk and tame Jezebel's hypersexual and manipulative ways—as a pimp would say, "bring a bitch to her knees"—black manhood will remain elusive. Again, a gendered zero-sum game dictates that black women must become more docile, dependent, and demure so that black men can publicly perform their role of being in charge, independent, and inseminatory. To borrow from television, black women need to be more like June Cleaver and Carol Brady and less like Mabel Thomas, Willona Woods, and Pam from *Martin.*

Finally, the reasoning behind the myth of the Strong Black Man isolates both black men and women from the very real material context in which African Americans have been historically situated. The narrow view of a woman's role in society that has been expressed by Bishop Long, Pastor Dollar, and less frequently Bishop Jakes fails to acknowledge that black women's strength and resourcefulness, characteristics that the dominant society has mocked and satirized, have kept African American communities afloat during trying economic times. When African American men dealt with unjust hiring and firing practices throughout the previous century, black women's ability and willingness to work in varying domestic capacities in order to supply a steady income enabled families to survive. Leftover food brought home in the evenings and hand-me down clothes obtained from employers kept black families moving forward. And while we should never idealize the exploitation of black women who did domestic work, neither should we belittle this historical reality by not conferring the appropriate honor and respect due. Black men and women, in the best-case scenarios, have partnered together for the familial and economic good in ways that have defied the simplistic gender roles set forth by the larger society. In the vast majority of cases, black men and women were not afforded a choice. In fact, few families, regardless of race, have been able to achieve to the mythic "Leave It to Beaver" lifestyle—not that it was a just ideal to begin with. Therefore, African Americans should not be encouraged to adopt a standard of gender relations and roles that the larger society does not live up to itself.

Nevertheless, for too long the black church has propagated the myth of the Strong Black Man and supported a system of hegemonic masculinity, with three damaging results: uncritical silence in congregations concerning the public indiscretions of black male clergy; homophobia that fosters a "down low" subculture within the black church where gay black men live in an unhealthy secrecy; and the encouragement of violence against black women through the invoking of sadomasochistic themes of domination, conquest, and submission to discuss relations between the sexes. Dismantling the myth of the Strong Black Man as savior of the race requires understanding how beliefs in male dominance operate in each of these three areas within communities of faith—communities that despite their shortcomings remain critical to the resiliency of black life in America.

Don't Nobody Bring Me No Bad News

Forces of racial and economic injustice oppress both black men and black women, but in different ways. Since slavery times in America the black body has been a fetishized focus of white anxiety, insecurity, and rage. Orlando Patterson's *Rituals of Blood* offers a compelling account of the way white men's anxieties and insecurities concerning their perceived moral and physical shortcomings led them to project onto black men the fearsome image of an animalistic, sexual predator that had to be dominated and controlled for the protection of American society in general and white women in particular.[40]

Leading African Americans ranging from abolitionists to civil rights marchers worked hard to publicly challenge this distorted image of the black man as Richard Wright's fatalist protagonist Bigger Thomas. Particularly true within the church, a certain politics of respectability was embraced, by both black men and women, to present a conception of black identity and life that would counter such racist representations.[41] This motive, in part, has contributed to the prevalence of the myth of the Strong Black Man.

But to defend this more positive image of black masculinity, communities of faith have engaged in a conspiracy of silence concerning moral indiscretions among the black male clergy. Many believe that calling certain behaviors into question makes congregants guilty of participating in the same sorts of vicious and racist attacks that made the myth of the Strong Black Man necessary in the first place. Such silence fosters a willful ignorance among parishioners that enables male clergy to act with impunity. Congregations have been so concerned with not "tearing another brother down" that black male clergy have been allowed to operate without a sincere fear of incurring any consequences.

Thus it is an open secret that many male preachers "prey" in the pews and engage in exploitative sexual relations, consensual or nonconsensual: there are a plethora of extramarital affairs, undisclosed pregnancies, and abortions.[42] These and numerous cases of financial misappropriation have been either overlooked or punished with a lenient slap on the wrist. They are the dangerous results of a congregational identity constructed in relation to the leadership of a Strong Black Man. Silence is normalized and critique muffled so that parishioners, particularly women and children, can drink from the fount of symbolic masculine power. Couple this with the culturally understood and clergy-manipulated rule of "touch not God's anointed and do thine prophet no harm," and the result is a Soprano-like silencing among parishioners. Spiritual "snitches" are regarded as pariahs, and critics are treated as enemies. Pastors celebrate those they consider "team players," causing them to honor loyalty over competency. Sophomoric sayings like "Loose lips sink ships!" become rules that everyone must obey. In the end, the church loses both the intellectual challenges and the ecclesial accountability that might improve it. Such spiritual gangsterism works in the best interest of neither clergy nor congregants, since the church forfeits its standing as moral arbiter of the community and becomes viewed as little more than a bastion of hypocrisy.

Trapped in the Closet

A second harmful consequence of the myth of the Strong Black Man is homophobia. A benchmark of hegemonic masculinity is not being gay or bisexual. According to the rules of being a "real man," homosexuality is the negation of masculinity. To be perceived as effeminate, soft, a sissy, queen, or faggot—though the majority of black gay men in America do not fit such a profile—only further emasculates black males who already feel their masculinity under attack. And for the descendants of the Black Power era, blackness itself has come to be synonymous with masculinity. Therefore, rather than self-identifying as gay or bi, which of course is the cultural opposite of being masculine, an increasing number of black men who are involved in same-sex relationships consider themselves as first and foremost black—"black" being read as "man."[43] And since so many sectors of the black community have bought into the myth of the Strong Black Man to some extent (from the aggressively patriarchal and domineering husband to men who irresponsibly participate in misogynistic forms of womanizing), many black gay men have as well. Some African American gay men have elected to play by the racialized and gendered rules of manhood. As a result, race and gender ideals have produced a subculture of black men who live their sexual lives on the "down low."

The *down low* or *DL* is a term used to describe the underground subculture of black men who choose, for whatever reason, to have sex with men but maintain a public persona that is stridently heterosexual.[44]

These men date and marry women but engage sexually with men in very incognito and casual ways.[45] While this dynamic operates across racial lines, with notable examples being former New Jersey governor James McGreevy, disgraced head of the National Association of Evangelicals Ted Haggard, and Senator Larry Craig of Idaho, who has confronted allegations as a result of his lewd conduct arrest in a men's airport bathroom, some dimensions of the DL phenomenon are race specific. Living on the DL is not just a matter of being in the closet or being a self-loathing, homophobic homosexual, though that is the case in part. It is based on an internalized yet illogical belief circulating among a new generation of black men that if one is not white and effeminate, the cultural stereotype of gay men in America, one cannot be gay. Many suspect this is a social and psychological defense mechanism to cope with a homophobic society. But its causality is easy to trace to the oppressive and narrow ideal of black masculinity that circulates throughout the African American community via hip-hop culture and the black church.

Now, from a moral perspective this disconnect between public representation and private infatuation is not any more problematic than it would be for married persons who participate in heterosexual extramarital affairs. The accepted double standard is also an effect of a system of hegemonic masculinity. This is why I agree in principle with cultural critic and social activist Keith Boykin, who rejects the category of DL by defining "down low" behavior as cheating on a partner regardless of one's sexual orientation.[46] As mother wit teaches us, "Wrong is wrong; and there ain't no right way to do wrong." However, from an ethical perspective, it would be irresponsible not to point out the damaging implications of this very real sexual subculture. My goal here is not to incite homophobic fears and rhetoric but to cultivate open and honest dialogue about the sexual practices of members of the black community.

For example: though African Americans make up only 13 percent of the U.S. population, they constitute almost half of all new reported HIV cases annually. Currently the leading cause of the transmission of HIV among black men is same-sex encounters. In a recent study by the Centers for Disease Control that tested men who had sex with men in five major metropolitan cities, 46 percent of African American men were HIV positive compared to 21 percent and 17 percent of white men and Hispanic men, respectively. The test also showed that 67 percent of the black men who tested positive were unaware of their infection.[47] Further, because reportedly a characteristic of DL culture is to not think about what one is doing—lest one feel emasculated—wearing a condom is too much of a reminder that one is sexually involved with another man.[48] And while the CDC does not want to play into the "DL Boogeyman" theory that places all the burden of HIV on this subculture, specialists do acknowledge that the absence of self-identification or disclosure presents challenges to prevention programs. The same men who are participating in "high-risk" sexual activities return home at night to the bed of their female spouses and girlfriends—female partners who often believe that they are in a monogamous relationship with a Strong Black Man. Therefore, we cannot discuss or combat the pandemic of AIDS among black men and women in America until we can foster candid and critical dialogue on what motivates a subculture of African American men to participate in high-risk sexual behavior in order to preserve a hypermasculine image. So the focus should be placed less on whom men choose to sleep with than on the maintenance of a hypermasculine culture that encourages unhealthy practices and destructive lifestyle choices.

For many, it is common knowledge that the black church today is a hotbed of "down low" activity.[49] For generations it has been the unacknowledged elephant in the pews, the choir lofts, and the pulpits. Thus innuendo and rumor often swirl around the heads of prominent African American male clergy and Christian men in ways that cause many to ratchet up their hypermasculinist and homophobic rhetoric. To be sure, in many cases, the spreading of such rumors around members of the clergy is unjustified. It often amounts to little more than the attacks and gossip of a homophobic society in which the charge of homosexuality is the most salacious insult one can employ. As is the case in politics, "a dead woman or a live boy" is cause for scandal.

But every time male ministerial underlings sue a prominent televangelist or megachurch pastor for sexual harassment, the rumors through the ecclesial grapevine seem to multiply.[50] Both Rev. Ike and TBN president Paul Crouch have tried to ward off such lawsuits for years. And the audiotaped correspondence of Houston megapastor Dr. Joseph Ratliff that aired on Black Entertainment Television during a 2003 lawsuit is another prominent example. Ratliff's recorded come-on to an aspiring male minister, in which he boasted, "I'm an oral freak. I just need to lick you from head to toe," contributes to the contradictory homophobic yet homoerotic climate that the myth of the Strong Black Man has fostered within black Christian circles.[51] In many cases, the greater the insecurity about being outed, the greater the macho and masculine performance on Sunday.

As a point of clarification, large numbers of African American Christian women are not just passive victims here. They too participate in the maintenance of hegemonic masculinity that fosters DL culture within the black church. This is not just a "guy" thing. Many black women seem particularly willing to go along with the homophobic sentiments voiced within Christian circles even when they choose to identify with and befriend gay black men on their jobs and in their personal lives. It is not uncommon to hear black women comment on how gay men are "just a shame" to the African American community, but possibly for different reasons than Bishop Long might suggest. Black women, the least likely group to marry in America, may not see a "sinner" as much as they see the loss of a potential mate. This holds true particularly in major metropolitan cities such as New York, Atlanta, Houston, and Los Angeles, where gay black men make up a disproportionate amount of the black urban professional class. Hence the oft-recited declaration, "All the good men are either married or gay!" But unfortunately many black women, instead of resisting their own spiritual niggerization under a system of patriarchal dominance that relegates black Christian women to objects in need of "covering," direct their energies toward the niggerization of gay men.[52] In turn, many Christian gay men are forced to choose sides. They can be demonized and ostracized by the communities of faith in which many were raised and remain committed, or they can turn on the hypermasculine charm of a Strong Black Man.

Woman, Thou Art Lashed!

The final way the myth of the Strong Black Man as savior of the race operates to the detriment of the black church involves the connection between the expression of religious doctrine in terms of themes of domination and submission and actual physical violence against black women. What are the social and cultural implications for a community of faith that is committed to an ideal of masculinity defined by the capacity to conquer and subdue? As shown in previous chapters, Bishop Jakes's hypermasculine hunter, Bishop Long's warrior and "rhinoceros" men, and Taffi Dollar's call for women to "follow the leader" are all predicated on the ability of men to take control over something deemed weaker. "Real" manhood is thus measured by the capacity to force another into submission.

This sentiment poses real dangers. As bell hooks states, when black masculinity is constructed on the notion that to be a man one must dominate, yet the political system in which black men live precludes access to socially acceptable and viable positions of power, black men are forced to seize their manhood in socially unacceptable ways.[53] Street gangs, gun violence, and physical aggression are common means of unhealthy expression. These are frequently associated with hip-hop culture and the "thug life" of the streets. But unfortunately the "saved and sanctified" alternative for black men involves obsessive control over and violence against black women's bodies. The rhetorical tropes of authority, submission, and domination that are staples of African American religious broadcasting lend themselves to and subliminally support this type of violent behavior.

For instance, historian Nell Painter connects the long-standing ideals of obedience and submission in the American family to slavery's legacy of violence. In her essay "Soul Murder and Slavery: Toward a Fully Loaded Cost Accounting," Painter discusses how religion, democracy, and patriarchy are typically recognized for their role in shaping our ideal of the American family.[54] But she also argues that Americans should take account of the system of slavery as a constitutive influence on the ordering of the family as well. The system of slavery, according to Painter, accentuated the hierarchical as opposed to the egalitarian dimension of democracy. And the dominant themes of submission and obedience at the heart of patriarchy and religious piety were also the core values of chattel slavery. The random use of physical violence and terrorism was a fundamental means of rendering slaves wholly submissive subjects. Therefore, one cannot talk about the structure of the American family without addressing the way slavery informed its organizing basis.

This brings us back to the dominant themes of African American religious broadcasting. Could it be that despite all the talk about "loosing" the black female body, the phenomenon of religious broadcasting is actually conditioning families to adhere to an ordering of the family informed by the violence of chattel slavery? To take Painter's argument seriously, one could conclude that the "ideal" American marriage and family is based not on mutual respect, cooperation, and reciprocity but on dominance, compulsion, and social control to protect white male hegemony. And rather than promoting a vibrant space of human flourishing and egalitarian mutuality, the myth of the Strong Black Man encourages black men to embrace the violent virtues of slavery and white supremacy in order to be regarded as respectable members of society at best and to overcome a masculine inferiority complex vis-à-vis white maleness at worst. Therefore, R. Kelly and renowned pimp and pop culture icon Bishop Don Magic Juan are not the only ones who are guilty of abusing the black female body. Many Christian Strong Black Men in the name of "taking authority" may also be actively asserting their manhood by victimizing women. Here I can provide two extreme yet emblematic examples.

On January 14, 2006, the Rev. Eugene Marriot, "minister of men" at the ten-thousand-member Ebenezer A.M.E. Church in Fort Washington, Maryland, was arrested in the parking lot of the Best Western Hotel in Fairfax City, Maryland. Having received a 911 call from a bystander in the hotel parking lot, police arrived on the scene to find Marriot wrestling with an unidentified woman on the hood of his automobile. The thirty-four-year-old victim testified that Rev. Marriot had raped her, forced her to perform oral sex on him, and repeatedly whipped her with his belt. According to court documents, Rev. Marriot confessed to being involved in an "alternative lifestyle" that included sadomasochistic sexual acts such as physical domination, whipping, and other forms of torture. The victim, who had admittedly been involved with Marriot for the previous two months, acknowledged participating in this form of role play with the otherwise married Marriot but said that she had ended their sexual involvement prior to that night.[55]

This was not Marriot's first charge of physical violence against women. In 2002 the Prince George's District Court charged Marriot with assault and battery against his wife, also a minister at Ebenezer A.M.E., for throwing her on the couch and, again, whipping her with his belt. Not only were the charges dismissed after Marriot agreed to complete a court-ordered counseling program, but evidently Marriot was not removed from his ministerial responsibilities at Ebenezer, where he specialized in hosting "men only" events that focused on marriage and family life. An example of one of the men's ministry conference titles at Ebenezer A.M.E. is "Man of God, Stand Up, Unite, It's an S.O.S. (Saving Our Sons, Saving Ourselves, and Saving Our Society)."[56]

Immediately after Marriot's second arrest in January of 2006, the church placed him on paid administrative leave with full pay. But in March of 2006, after allegedly receiving the details of the attack for the first time from a local news reporter, the congregation stripped Marriot of all ecclesiastical rights and privileges. During Ebenezer's two morning worship services on the Sunday after the media coverage, the senior pastor of the church, the Rev. Grainger Browning, responded to the incident by asserting, "This is a time of prayer for our congregation."[57]

This is not the only prominent case of abuse. On August 22, 2007, famed televangelist Prophetess Juanita Bynum was also attacked in a hotel parking lot by her then-estranged husband, Bishop Thomas Weeks III. Bynum was meeting with Weeks at the Renaissance Concourse Hotel near the Atlanta airport, but the meeting ended in the parking lot with a hotel bellman pulling Bishop Weeks from atop his wife. The bellman reported to police that Weeks had been violently kicking Bynum in the stomach and groin.[58]

This was a tragic end to a reality show–like marriage in the neo-Pentecostal world. In 2002, Bynum and Week's million-dollar wedding was broadcast on Trinity Broadcasting Network and included his giving her a seven-carat diamond ring—seven being the number of completion according to televangelist lingo. Bishop Weeks, who had formerly been a D.C.-based Pentecostal pastor, joined forces with Bynum to create a conference and book series under the title *Teach Me How to Love You*. Weeks also published his own book series, which included the titles *Ladies, You Need a Man That Can Handle Your Favor* and *Men, Five Secrets You Need to Have to Handle Her Favor*. Both of these latter publications had an image on the cover of Bishop Weeks carrying Bynum on his back.

Many familiar with Bynum's ministry interpreted her highly publicized nuptials as part and parcel of her ongoing extreme image makeover. Though she had once been known for her traditional, fiery Pentecostal preaching and ascetic personal aesthetic, her blacklisting by Bishop Jakes and the newfound prominence of Paula White among black male preachers animated the emergence of a more docile, "soft," and aesthetically effeminate Juanita Bynum. She replaced her tightly cropped hair with an abundance of weave, her surgically altered facial features became accented by makeup, and she now sat supportively in the audience as her husband Bishop Weeks ministered to women about "how to love." In 2004, Bynum even reconciled with her former mentor and business partner Bishop Jakes. At the MegaFest conference inside Atlanta's Georgia Dome, Prophetess Bynum literally crawled on her hands and knees toward the bishop, who sat approvingly on stage in his chair, while begging for his forgiveness. During her plea in front of a capacity crowd of women, Bynum profusely apologized to Bishop Jakes while attributing her previous actions to "the spirit of Jezebel."

In the weeks following the violent incident, Bishop Weeks immediately returned to the pulpit of his Global Destiny Ministries, where he blamed the alleged attack on Satan, and Prophetess Bynum, to the chagrin of many activists against domestic violence, hit the media circuit providing an account of the attack that many considered to be overly spiritualized, sensationalist, and self-serving.[59] Bishop Jakes, however, withheld public comment. When he did respond, it was with a generic statement released to the *Atlanta and Journal and Constitution* that provided statistics on as well as practical steps employed at the Potter's House to respond to domestic violence cases. Under the heading "Domestic Violence Is Unholy: Church Must Fight against, Not as Judge but as Protector," he warned that the church should not take a definitive stand against abusers and argued that "the church's job is not a judicial one."[60] And though Bishop Jakes described himself as "a longtime advocate and tireless fighter against domestic violence," some found it odd that he did not support organizations such as the National Black Church Initiative, which had called for Bishop Weeks to either voluntarily step down or be suspended while the facts of the case were sorted through the justice system.

Bishop Jakes, then, like Rev. Grainger Browning, offered only a veiled and ambiguous response. Just as Rev. Browning described the moment as "a time of prayer" without addressing Rev. Marriott or the case directly, Bishop Jakes said about Weeks and Bynum only that he was "deeply saddened and concerned."[61] This causes me to ask: What was Rev. Browning asking his congregation to pray for? And what was Bishop Jakes deeply concerned about? Are we to pray for and be concerned about male preachers who commit such heinous acts against women? Are we to pray for the woman who was raped, sodomized, and physically abused by this congregation's minister of men? Are we to be concerned about a woman televangelist who was stomped in a parking lot by her husband? Or should we pray for and be deeply concerned and saddened about an unhealthy culture of hypermasculinity and a patriarchal savior complex that possibly helps to cultivate sadomasochistic and misogynistic tendencies? For the sake of the black church, black family, and black community, I hope it is all three equally.

BENEDICTION

Blest Be the Tie That Binds

We share each other's woes,
Each other's burdens bear;
And often for each other flows
The sympathizing tear.

— "Blest Be the Tie That Binds,"
in *African American Heritage Hymnal*

In 2006, the scheduled commencement ceremony at the Inter-denominational Theological Center in Atlanta revealed the complicated times in which African American theological education finds itself. ITC President Michael Battle created a firestorm of controversy by inviting alum and former board member Bishop Eddie Long to serve as commencement speaker. It just so happens that the predominantly black consortium of seminaries elected to award prominent theologian James Cone an honorary doctorate degree during the same ceremony. A large portion of the graduating class protested the invitation of Bishop Long, citing his theological stances on gays and women and his embrace of a "prosperity" ethic. These students believed that Bishop Long contradicted the institution's mission of extending the prophetic legacy of the black church into the twenty-first century. Yet many students welcomed his invitation as a fresh and relevant change. How could ITC be serious about its commitment and call to the black church, they argued, if it distanced itself from the most prominent and popular black preachers of the current generation?

Professor Cone thus found himself in an ethical dilemma. Predictably, he sided with those who were opposed to Bishop Eddie Long's invitation. So it became a matter of whether he should attend and remain conspicuously quiet about the theological and ideological controversy or whether he should voice his objections and possibly draw attention away from the graduates by turning the ceremony into a clash between famed televangelist and prominent theologian. Noting that graduation should be a time for graduates and family members to celebrate their academic accomplishments, Professor Cone elected to avert further controversy by opting out of the ceremony.

To be sure, I can respect Professor Cone's reasoning even as I disagree with his decision. He was correct insofar as a commencement ceremony is neither the time nor place for a knockdown, drag-out theological fight. But this yet raises some important questions: When is the right time or place? And more importantly, what are the necessary conditions to facilitate both the time and place for leading televangelists like Bishop Long and African American theologians like James Cone to meet, converse, and deliberate? These are the questions that emerging generations of African American theologians must confront in an age of evangelicalism fueled by advanced media technologies.

Times have changed since the days of F. W. McGee and Benjamin Elijah Mays. Early African American religious scholars and radio preachers were in some ways separated by social and class barriers that hindered any type of meaningful exchange. I am certain E. Franklin Frazier would never have had to worry about sharing the stage with Prophetess Rosa Horn at Howard University's commencement. But this is no longer the case. In recent years, students and faculty on the campus of Princeton University warmly welcomed Bishop T. D. Jakes. And such occurrences as the conflictual partnering of Bishop Long and Professor Cone will occur with greater frequency as televangelists and megachurch pastors continue to have a consistent and critical impact on persons pursuing advanced theological education. So rather than having one side constantly be forced to cancel their speaking engagements, or having persons from opposing sides simply sit next to each other silently like Bloods and Crips at a gang violence summit, we must find a means to foster productive dialogue and critical exchange.

With this in mind, I end this book the way it begins: citing the prophetic and prescient reflections of W. E. B. Du Bois. Du Bois concludes "Of the Faith of the Fathers," with a critique of what he regards as the diverging ethical tendencies of African American religious race politics—"the first tending toward radicalism, the other toward hypocritical compromise." Unfortunately, these tendencies are two sides of the same detrimental coin and provide insight into the dilemma black theologians face. The former, often displayed by educated elites, emphasizes the radicalism of African American resistance to the point of excess. In Du Bois's words, the spirit of "radical complaint, radical remedies, bitter denunciation or angry silence" among "the better classes" of black people leads them to "segregate themselves . . . and form an aristocracy, cultured but pessimistic, whose bitter criticism stings while it points to no way of escape."[1]

On the other hand, those who merely seek an economic opening act out the tendency to compromise. In search of financial gain, they sacrifice frank speech for wariness, principle for practicality, and courage for amenability. Such a person, Du Bois argues, "shuts his eyes to wrong; in too many cases he sees positive personal advantage in deception and lying. His real thoughts, his real aspirations, must be guarded in whispers; he must not criticize, he must not complain." Compromisers understand themselves to be employing the tools of deception in order to dismantle the strong but in the process become trapped in their own illusions.

Du Bois's statement, I believe, sums up the condition of African American Christian theological reflection over the past forty years. The two competing camps of the podium theorists and pulpit practitioners are as divided as the Hatfields and McCoys. Though they are kissing cousins that largely emerged out of the same faith community, we have allowed disagreement over their diverging ethical tendencies to escalate to a point that their few encounters are characterized by insecure silence and political ineptitude.

For instance, there appears to be an inclination among Christian scholars of black religion to gather the intellectual wagons around narrow conceptions of black religious identity, sacred stories concerning the "high moments" of protest activity, and nostalgic understandings of the form and function of black religious life in America. As academicians, we become the elite arbiters of all that is the "true black church," pessimistically evaluating every minister of the Gospel by to this mythic ethical standard of religious and racial authenticity. But we are quickly frustrated when our projected understanding of what black religion is and does fails to produce a legion of Martin Luther Kings and Fannie Lou Hamers. Though our anger is in some ways justified, and our courage to speak truth to power should be commended, we often expect African Americans to drink from an intellectual and academic cup that the masses are unable to recognize. Therefore, sensing disillusionment and rejection, some of us have become bitter. And as Du Bois puts it, "The very fact that this bitterness is natural and justifiable only serves to intensify it and make it more maddening."[2]

Then there are the pulpit practitioners that have used the advanced tools of mass media to orchestrate the otherwise inconceivable and the seemingly unattainable. Through this process they have created a mythic world of racial harmony and economic justice in the television studios of megachurches and Christian networks across this country. A contemporary class of preachers appears to believe that by creating that world on television they will not have to courageously confront the very real world of white supremacy, class exploitation, and gender discrimination. Yes, these preachers stand tall as exemplars of success and achievement. Moreover, they have a proven track record of encouraging the disillusioned and downtrodden to valiantly "run on and see what the end is going to be." They do indeed inspire. But the price of inspiration is a lie. Their silence concerning injustice is deafening. Their lack of courage in the face of controversy is disheartening. And their fairy-tale understanding of American society is woefully inadequate for those who need more than simplistic homiletic formulations to confront the complexity of their existential circumstances.

Between these two competing camps and extreme ethical attitudes, however, lie the majority of African American Christians: people whose spiritual strivings are bound up with a quest for justice for generations that have passed and those yet to come. They show both complexity in their religious beliefs and sophistication in their political choices. In a way they are like the man in the 1976 movie *Car Wash*, who has photographs of three men hanging up inside his shoeshine stand: Martin Luther King Jr., President John F. Kennedy, and the Reverend Daddy Rich, a prosperity preacher who is meant to be a spoof on Rev. Ike. This shoeshine man reflects the diversity of thought demonstrated by ordinary people. Many of those who discovered a message of hope in Martin Luther King also packed into the Cathedral to hear Rev. Ike on Saturday night. Indeed, some women may attend Bishop T. D. Jakes's MegaFest conference one week and enthusiastically engage Emilie Townes's writings in class the next week. And as stated earlier, some may even fly down to Atlanta to hear Pastor Dollar while reading a book by Tavis Smiley on the flight.

These people are the reason why I have provided this ethical analysis. I wanted to challenge the erudite but isolating tendencies of the religious academy as well as the insular and illusory world of the African American pulpit. The former, at its worst, is inclined to be elitist to the point of irrelevance, and the latter capriciously relevant to the extent of being relativistic. One is too concerned with a static notion of what is right, and the other is too concerned with its arbitrary understanding of what is good. This book seeks to spark a dialogue between the two camps so that they do not merely ignore, glibly dismiss, or fear each other. But for this to happen, black scholars of religion and religious broadcasters must be as courageous, complex, and astute as the people they claim to represent.

As scholars of black religion, we must expand the stories we tell about black religious life in America. Rev. Ike, Bishop T. D. Jakes, Bishop Eddie Long, and Pastor Creflo Dollar are indeed representatives of the black church. Their individual traditions, theological orientations, and political sensibilities are squarely situated within a narrative that can largely be traced back to their antebellum ancestors. At the same time, like all African Americans, they are informed by the cultural air that they breathe. This is why scholars of black religion who engage varying forms of Christian practice, as well as those who ascribe to the black theology of liberation project, can ill afford to willfully ignore this religious phenomenon. By excavating the traditions, ecclesial perspectives, and theological sources that inform these pop culture icons, scholars can explore understudied intellectual terrains that will offer both clues and clarity in explaining the complex nature of black religious life in America.

Moreover, we ought to engage and take seriously those who can gain the ear and pierce the hearts of the masses. These popular preachers possess a spiritual genius that must be recognized. If anything, they can teach academicians a language, a rhythmic sensibility, and an imaginative insight into the human condition that can help reconnect the life of the mind with the heart of the community. For what does it profit scholars to *talk about* black Christians when they cannot *talk to* black Christians?

At the same time, leading religious broadcasters must resist becoming a kingdom unto themselves. They cannot be allowed to operate on spiritual and cultural islands, hemmed in by their own sense of intellectual insecurity. Rather than merely assuming spiritual authority, leading evangelists must remain accountable to their individual constituency and larger community. These preachers ought to equip themselves with the intellectual resources and analytical tools to engage the world in which their faith must operate —not simply the fictive world created by their spiritual imaginations and acted out on safe pulpit stages and inside television studios but rather the real world, which has a proven record of trying to bind physically, socially, economically, and politically the people that they aim to "loose." For what does it profit a preacher to gain financial largesse and a new Rolls-Royce but lose his community to bankruptcy, foreclosure, joblessness, and discrimination?

I pray the positive end result of this book will be to move toward answering these questions by sparking dialogue in African American Christian communities across the philosophical divide of theory and praxis. We do not have to agree on theology, nor must we see eye to eye on political orientation. We must, however, be willing to open ourselves to challenge and critique for the betterment of all. If not, we are all guilty of selling empty promises, and we have become as sounding brass and tinkling cymbals.

Notes

PRELUDE

1. Cornel West, "The Dilemma of the Black Intellectual," in *The Cornel West Reader*, ed. Cornel West (New York: Basic Books, 1999), 312.
2. See Jacquelyn Grant, *White Women's Christ and Black Women's Jesus: Feminist Christology and Womanist Response* (Atlanta: Scholars Press, 1989).
3. For an important essay on the language describing African American women in our culture, see Hortense J. Spillers, "Mama's Baby, Papa's Maybe," in *Black, White, and in Color: Essays on American Literature and Culture* (Chicago: University of Chicago Press, 2003). "God's leading lady," "anointed woman of God," and "Daddy's little girl" are appellations commonly employed by T. D. Jakes (two of the three are titles of his books) to describe God's relationship with African American women. Obviously, the infantilization and hyperfeminization of black women and the upholding of patriarchal systems of dominance that are inherent in Jakes's designations should be criticized. To raise such criticism is, in part, the purpose of this book.

INVOCATION

1. W. E. B. Du Bois, "The Souls of Black Folk," in *Du Bois: Writings,* ed. Nathan Huggins (New York: Penguin, 1996), 494.
2. For a comprehensive introduction to the electronic church phenomenon in America, see Robert Abelman and Stewart M. Hoover, eds., *Religious Television: Controversies and Conclusions* (Norwood, NJ: Ablex, 1990), esp. Quentin J. Schultze's "Defining the Electronic Church," 41–52; Stewart M. Hoover, *Mass Media Religion: The Social Sources of the Electronic Church* (Beverly Hills, CA: Sage Publications, 1988); Quentin J. Schultze, *Televangelism and American Culture: The Business of Popular Religion* (Grand Rapids, MI: Baker Book House, 1991); Peter G. Horsfield, *Religious Television: The American Experience* (New York: Longman, 1984); Jeffrey K. Hadden and Anson D. Shupe, *Televangelism: Power and Politics on God's Frontier* (New York: Henry Holt, 1988); Quentin J. Schultze, *Christianity and the Mass Media in America: Toward a Democratic Accommodation* (East Lansing: Michigan State University Press, 2003).

3. Gustav Niebuhr, "Where Religion Gets a Big Dose of Shopping-Mall Culture," *New York Times*, April 16, 1995; Tamelyn Tucker-Worgs, "Get on Board, Little Children, There's Room for Many More: The Black Megachurch Phenomenon," *Journal of the Interdenominational Theological Center* 29, nos. 1 and 2 (2001–2): 177–203.

4. Schultze, *Televangelism and American Culture*, 220.

5. The *Taking Authority* broadcast airs throughout the country but also in Denmark and daily in the Philippines. The broadcast schedule is at www.new-birth.org/broadcast_schedule.asp.

6. Du Bois, "The Souls of Black Folk," 494.

7. Ibid., 495.

8. More than simply offering descriptive categories, Du Bois actually points to this form of religious expression in "Of the Faith of Our Fathers." He writes of the black church of the North and South, "Their churches are differentiating,—now into groups of cold, fashionable devotees, in no way distinguishable from similar white groups save in color of skin; now into large social and business institutions catering to the desire for information and amusement of their members, warily avoiding unpleasant questions both within and without the black world, and preaching in effect if not in word: Dum vivimus, vivamus [While we live, let us live]" (W. E. B. Du Bois, "Of the Faith of Our Fathers," in *Du Bois: Writings*, 504–5).

9. Max Weber, *The Theory of Social and Economic Organization*, trans. A. M. Henderson and Talcott Parsons (New York: Oxford University Press, 1947), 329.

10. Schultze, *Televangelism and American Culture*, 30.

11. C. Eric Lincoln and Lawrence H. Mamiya, *The Black Church in the African American Experience* (Durham: Duke University Press, 1990), 6.

12. Sermon titles are derived from Rev. Jamal Harrison-Bryant, as found on www.jamalbryant.org.

13. Carlos Watson, *Off Topic with Carlos Watson*, Cable News Network (CNN), January 23, 2005.

14. I challenge anyone to identify a Christian movement today that rivals the black electronic church phenomenon in terms of popularity and influence within African American Christian communities of faith.

15. Author Shayne Lee titles a chapter in his work on T. D. Jakes "the new black church" and describes all of the preachers in it as "neo-Pentecostal." Shayne Lee, *T. D. Jakes: America's New Preacher* (New York: New York University Press, 2005), 158–77. Also see Marc Lamont Hill, "I Bling Because I'm Happy," *PopMatters*, August 5, 2005, http://popmatters.com/columns/hill/050805.html.

16. Lincoln and Mamiya, *Black Church*, 275.

17. See "The New Megachurches," *Ebony*, December 2001.

18. Jeffrey Stout, *Democracy and Tradition* (Princeton: Princeton University Press, 2004), 178.

19. Roland Barthes, *Mythologies*, trans. Annette Lavers (New York: Hill and Wang, 1972).

CHAPTER 1. WE TOO SING AMERICA

1. The term *evangelical* connotes typically conservative Christian traditions that are represented by such terms as *fundamentalist, Pentecostal,* and *Charismatic.* Robert H. Krapohl and Charles H. Lippy, *The Evangelicals: A Historical, Thematic, and Biographical Guide* (Westport, CT: Greenwood Press, 1999), 77.

2. Heather Hendershot, *Shaking the World for Jesus: Media and Conservative Evangelical Culture* (Chicago: University of Chicago Press, 2004), 1.

3. Examples include Quentin Schultze's "Evangelical Radio and the Rise of the Electronic Church," *Journal of Broadcasting and Electronic Media* 32 (1988): 289–306; Dennis N. Voskuil's "The Power of the Air," in *American Evangelicals and the Mass Media,* ed. Quentin J. Schultze (Grand Rapids, MI: Zondervan, 1990); and Horsfield's seminal and essential text *Religious Television.*

4. Schultze, "Evangelical Radio"; Horsfield, *Religious Television;* Hoover, *Mass Media Religion.*

5. George M. Marsden, *Fundamentalism and American Culture,* 2nd ed. (New York: Oxford University Press, 2006), 188–91.

6. Voskuil, "Power of the Air," 72.

7. Schultze, "Evangelical Radio," 293.

8. Horsfield, *Religious Television,* 3.

9. Voskuil, "Power of the Air," 76.

10. Ibid., 89.

11. Jeffrey K. Hadden and Charles E. Swann, *Prime Time Preachers: The Rising Power of Televangelism* (Reading, MA: Addison-Wesley, 1981), 80–81.

12. Hadden and Shupe, *Televangelism,* 51.

13. Voskuil, "Power of the Air," 90.

14. Razelle Frankl, *Televangelism: The Marketing of Popular Religion* (Carbondale: Southern Illinois University Press, 1987), 27–32.

15. Bobby Chris Alexander, *Televangelism Reconsidered: Ritual in the Search for Human Community* (Atlanta: Scholars Press, 1994); Hadden and Swann, *Prime Time Preachers.*

16. Charles Grandison Finney, *Lectures on Revivals of Religion* (Cambridge, MA: Harvard University Press, 1960), 9.

17. Steve Bruce, *Pray TV: Televangelism in America* (New York: Routledge, 1990), 241.

18. Ibid., 180.

19. Hendershot, *Shaking the World*, 10.

20. Benjamin Elijah Mays and Joseph William Nicholson, *The Negro's Church* (New York: Institute of Social and Religious Research, 1933); Benjamin Elijah Mays, *The Negro's God as Reflected in His Literature* (Boston: Chapman and Grimes, 1938).

21. Randall Burkett and David W. Wills, "Afro-American Religious History, 1919–1939: Bibliographic Essay and Research Guide," 1986, www.amherst. edu/~aardoc/Biblio.html, 4.

22. Arthur Huff Fauset, *Black Gods of the Metropolis: Negro Religious Cults of the Urban North* (Philadelphia: University of Pennsylvania Press, 1971); Joseph R. Washington, *Black Sects and Cults* (Lanham, MD: University Press of America, 1984), 114.

23. By *first generation* I mean persons such as Benjamin Elijah Mays, Howard Thurman, and George Kelsey. The second generation includes the early voices of black theology of liberation and balance such as J. Deotis Roberts, James Cone, Albert Cleage, Gayraud Wilmore, and Peter Paris. Also, when I say *black scholars of religion,* this includes theologians, historians, philosophers, and sociologists.

24. Stuart Hall, "New Ethnicities," in *Black British Cultural Studies: A Reader,* ed. Houston A. Baker, Manthia Diawara, and Ruth H. Lindeborg (Chicago: University of Chicago Press, 1996), 164.

25. Cheryl Townsend Gilkes, "Plenty Good Room: Adaptation in a Changing Black Church," *Annals of the American Academy of Political and Social Science* 558 (1998): 101–21.

26. Omar M. McRoberts, *Streets of Glory: Church and Community in a Black Urban Neighborhood* (Chicago: University of Chicago Press, 2003); Milmon F. Harrison, *Righteous Riches: The Word of Faith Movement in Contemporary African American Religion* (New York: Oxford University Press, 2005); Marla Faye Frederick, *Between Sundays: Black Women and Everyday Struggles of Faith* (Berkeley: University of California Press, 2003).

27. See the introduction to James H. Cone's *Risks of Faith: The Emergence of a Black Theology of Liberation, 1968–1998* (Boston: Beacon Press, 1999).

28. See Victor Anderson, *Beyond Ontological Blackness: An Essay on African American Religious and Cultural Criticism* (New York: Continuum, 1995), and "'We See through a Glass Darkly': Black Narrative Theology and the Opacity of African American Religious Thought," in *The Ties That Bind: African American and Hispanic American/Latino/a Theologies in Dialogue,* ed. Anthony B. Pinn and Benjamin Valentin (New York: Continuum, 2001).

29. Eddie S. Glaude, *In a Shade of Blue: Pragmatism and the Politics of Black America* (Chicago: University of Chicago Press, 2007), 77.

30. Dwight N. Hopkins, *Heart and Head: Black Theology—Past, Present, and Future* (New York: Palgrave, 2002), 19.

31. Ibid., 20.

32. Paul Oliver, *Songsters and Saints: Vocal Traditions on Race Records* (Cambridge: Cambridge University Press, 1984), 140.

33. See William T. Dargan and Isaac Watts, *Lining out the Word: Dr. Watts Hymn Singing in the Music of Black Americans* (Berkeley: University of California Press, 2006).

34. Michael W. Harris, *The Rise of Gospel Blues: The Music of Thomas Andrew Dorsey in the Urban Church* (New York: Oxford University Press, 1992), 156.

35. Thomas Dorsey, quoted in ibid., 68.

36. Rev. A. W. Nix, "Black Diamond Express to Hell, Part I," in *Complete Recorded Works in Chronological Order*, vol. 1, *1927–1928* (CD) (Document Records, 2005).

37. P. Oliver, *Songsters and Saints*, 151.

38. Ibid., 153.

39. Rev. Leora Ross, "Dry Bones in the Valley," in *Preachers and Congregations*, vol. 6, *1924–36* (CD) (Document Records, 2005).

40. P. Oliver, *Songsters and Saints*, 146.

41. Evelyn Brooks Higginbotham, "Rethinking Vernacular Culture: Black Religion and Race Records in the 1920s and 1930s," in West and Glaude, *African American Religious Thought*.

42. James H. Cone, *A Black Theology of Liberation*, 2nd ed. (Maryknoll, NY: Orbis Books, 1986), P. Oliver, *Songsters and Saints*, 160.

43. Rev. J. M. Gates, "Pay Your Policy Man," in *Are You Bound for Heaven or Hell? The Best of Reverend J. M. Gates* (CD) (Original recording 1930; remastered, Sony Music Entertainment, 2004).

44. Richard Schragger, "The Anti-Chain Store Movement, Localist Ideology, and the Remnants of the Progressive Constitution, 1920–1940," *Iowa Law Review* 90 (2005): 1011.

45. Bruce, *Pray TV*, 24–25.

46. Rev. J. M. Gates, "Good Bye to Chain Stores, Pt. 2," in *Are You Bound for Heaven*.

47. Rev. J. M. Gates, "Kinky Hair Is No Disgrace," in *Are You Bound for Heaven*.

48. See "The 'Happy-Am-I' Preacher as Seen in His Radio Pulpit on the Potomac," *New York Times*, September 9, 1934.

49. "Happy Am I," *Time*, June 11, 1934.

50. Lillian Ashcraft Webb, *About My Father's Business: The Life of Elder Michaux* (Westport, CT: Greenwood Press, 1981), 44.

51. "President Praises Negroes at Fair," *New York Times*, October 21, 1940.

52. Grant Wacker, "The Pentecostal Tradition," in *Caring and Curing: Health and Medicine in the Western Religious Traditions*, ed. Ronald L. Numbers and Darrel W. Amundsen (Baltimore: Johns Hopkins University Press, 1986), 519.

53. For more biographical information on Mother Rosa Horn, and for three of her printed sermons, see Bettye Collier-Thomas, *Daughters of Thunder: Black Women Preachers and Their Sermons, 1850–1979* (San Francisco: Jossey-Bass, 1998), 175–76.

54. Nick Salvatore, *Singing in a Strange Land: C. L. Franklin, the Black Church, and the Transformation of America* (New York: Little, Brown, 2005), 188.

55. "Dr. King to Press New Voter Drive," *New York Times*, April 2, 1965.

56. Salvatore, *Singing in a Strange Land*, 170.

57. One such moment came when Franklin was forced to choose between the National Baptist Convention under the leadership of Rev. J. H. Jackson and the denunciation and expulsion of Martin Luther King Jr. from the convention over Jackson's anti–civil rights demonstration posture. A longtime friend of King, C. L., like the vast majority of preachers, chose to remain affiliated with Jackson and the National Baptist Convention rather than to leave the organization, whose constituency was critical to Franklin's fan base. To be sure, Franklin actively supported King and his efforts for the rest of King's life, but this, again, was a freedom afforded only by his vast popularity.

CHAPTER 2. SOMETHING WITHIN

1. According to Rev. Ike, his parents were involved in an "on and off" relationship his entire life. When they separated for good in 1940, his father's position toward child support was, "You [Ike's mother] took my son away from me, so you are going to have to support him." Rev. Frederick J. Eikerenkoetter, interview, Bel Harbor, FL, 2005.

2. Milton C. Sernett, *Bound for the Promised Land: African American Religion and the Great Migration* (Durham: Duke University Press, 1997). Also see Albert J. Raboteau, *Canaan Land: A Religious History of African Americans* (New York: Oxford University Press, 2001), 82.

3. Clayton Riley, "The Golden Gospel of Rev. Ike," *New York Times Magazine*, March 9, 1975.

4. Ibid.

5. See Michael Eric Dyson's discussion of the sexual subculture of black Christian practice to contextualize the alleged sexual indiscretions of Martin Luther King Jr. in *I May Not Get There with You: The True Martin Luther King, Jr.* (New York: Free Press, 2000).

6. This desire for crossover appeal is glaringly apparent in Rev. Ike's *New York Times* advertisements for the church (see, e.g., *New York Times*, November 28, 1972). Besides denouncing the tag "black preacher" (Rev. Ike is a self-professed "green preacher"), he deliberately distinguishes himself from other

black ministers of the city by emphasizing the congregation's geographic locale. The bottom of each advertisement reads, "The Church is NOT [sic] located in Harlem, but in the Washington Heights section of Manhattan."

7. Rev. Ike, "Rev. Ike Speaks On," in United Christian Evangelistic Association Publicity Packet, United Christian Evangelistic Association, Boston, n.d. (received in 2005).

8. Quoted in Riley, "Golden Gospel."

9. Rev. Frederick J. Eikerenkoetter, interview, Bel Harbor, FL, 2005.

10. Rev. Ike, "Evangelism in the Church," *New York Amsterdam News,* Summer 1976.

11. James K. Cazalas, "Rev. Ike Wows 'Em with 'Get It Now' Philosophy," *Pittsburgh Press,* May 6, 1973.

12. A few scholars, most notably Milmon Harrison, Darnise Martin, and Stephanie Mitchem, have called Rev. Ike a proto-prosperity preacher or New Thought adherent, but Gallatin's dissertation is the only work primarily focused on Rev. Ike to date. Martin Gallatin, "Reverend Ike's Ministry: A Sociological Investigation of Religious Innovation" (PhD diss., New York University, 1979).

13. For a more nuanced treatment of African American conversionist and thaumaturgical forms of religion and the ways in which Pentecostal practices have been integrated with varying forms of Religious Science, including New Thought, see Darnise C. Martin, *Beyond Christianity: African Americans in a New Thought Church* (New York: New York University Press, 2005), ch. 2.***

14. Albert J. Raboteau, *Slave Religion: The "Invisible Institution" in the Antebellum South* (New York: Oxford University Press, 1978); Orlando Patterson, *Slavery and Social Death: A Comparative Study* (Cambridge, MA: Harvard University Press, 1982).

15. Benjamin Elijah Mays, *Born to Rebel: An Autobiography* (New York: Scribner, 1971), 13.

16. Edward Franklin Frazier and C. Eric Lincoln, *The Negro Church in America and The Black Church since Frazier* (New York: Schocken Books, 1974), 35.

17. Mays and Nicholson, *Negro's Church,* 278.

18. David W. Wills, "The Cultural Themes of American Religious History," in West and Glaude, *African American Religious Thought* (Louisville, KY: Westminster John Knox, 2003), 215–16.

19. S. P. Fullinwider, "Racial Christianity," in West and Glaude, *African American Religious Thought,* 479–80.

20. James Baldwin, *The Fire Next Time* (New York: Dial Press, 1963), 18.

21. Raboteau, *Canaan Land,* 66.

22. Rosa Young, "What Induced Me to Build a School in the Rural District," in *Afro-American Religious History: A Documentary Witness,* ed. Milton C. Sernett (Durham: Duke University Press, 1985), 325.

23. Baer and Singer, "Religious Diversification," 506.

24. Zora Neale Hurston's term describes influential whites who supported the "New Negro" artistic movement as a result of their interest in African American life in the early twentieth century. Since their humanitarian efforts had a distinctly racial angle, she referred to such benefactors as Negrotarians. Valerie Boyd, *Wrapped in Rainbows: The Life of Zora Neale Hurston* (New York: Scribner, 2003), 100.

25. Harry Richardson, *Dark Glory: A Picture of the Church among Negroes in the Rural South* (New York: Friendship Press, 1947), 152–53.

26. Ibid., 157–58.

27. Rev. Frederick J. Eikerenkoetter, interview, Bel Harbor, FL, 2005.

28. Baer and Singer, "Religious Diversification," 509.

29. Hans A. Baer and Merrill Singer, *African-American Religion in the Twentieth Century: Varieties of Protest and Accommodation* (Knoxville: University of Tennessee Press, 1992), 62.

30. While I in no way desire to downplay the participation of African Americans in the healing revivalist movement, I am more concerned here with Pentecostalism as practiced by whites during the period. As stated in the text, with regard to mass media attention, white Pentecostals became the dominant face of Pentecostalism to the larger society. Thus, as Rev. Ike admits in his own writings, persons such as Oral Roberts became the standard-bearers of success. But Ike's theological double-consciousness surely informs whom and what he validates as an influence and theological interlocutor—so much so that he often fails to be equally critical of theological beliefs and practices across racial lines. While Ike will castigate a black Pentecostal preacher for being concerned with "pie in the sky" and conversion, he seemingly ignores this dimension of Roberts's theology.

31. See Robert Mapes Anderson, *Vision of the Disinherited: The Making of American Pentecostalism* (New York: Oxford University Press, 1979); I. M. Lewis, *Ecstatic Religion: A Study of Shamanism and Spirit Possession*, 2nd ed. (New York: Routledge, 1989).

32. Raboteau, *Slave Religion* and "The Afro-American Traditions," in *Caring and Curing: Health and Medicine in the Western Religious Traditions*, ed. Ronald L. Numbers and Darrel W. Amundsen (Baltimore: Johns Hopkins University Press, 1986).

33. Iain MacRobert contends that the Pentecostal movement has always been about much more than glossolalic manifestations and that descriptions of it that emphasize glossolalia reflect later developments in the white Pentecostal movement. Black and early Pentecostals have always considered glossolalia as just one of many fruits of a total experience of the Spirit. For additional critiques of and challenges to the white supremacist bias that has impeded the production

of a fair history of Pentecostalism in America, see Iain MacRobert, *The Black Roots and White Racism of Early Pentecostalism in the USA* (New York: St. Martin's Press, 1988).

34. David Edwin Harrell, *All Things Are Possible: The Healing and Charismatic Revivals in Modern America* (Bloomington: Indiana University Press, 1975).

35. Wacker contends that the practices of speaking in tongues and divine healing are the "enduring backbone of the Pentecostal tradition." Wacker, "Pentecostal Tradition," 515.

36. Vinson Synan notes that the postwar economic prosperity that moved many Pentecostals out of poverty served as an efficient cause of their subsequent expansion as a community of faith. Such growth contradicts the then-popular deprivation theories that directly associated ecstatic, conversionist forms of religion such as Pentecostalism with poverty. Vinson Synan, *The Holiness-Pentecostal Tradition: Charismatic Movements in the Twentieth Century*, 2nd ed. (Grand Rapids, MI: W. B. Eerdmans, 1997), 122.

37. The elder Rev. Roberts took his son to a tent revival meeting in Ada, Oklahoma, led by Rev. Geo W. Moncey, "evangelist, divine healer." David Edwin Harrell, *Oral Roberts: An American Life* (Bloomington: Indiana University Press, 1985), 5.

38. Ibid., 159.

39. Ibid., 92.

40. Every edition of the *Healing Waters* magazine is full of praise from local pastors testifying to the success of a particular campaign in the region.

41. Harrell, *Oral Roberts*, 95–96.

42. Oral Roberts, "100 Radio Stations for Healing Waters Broadcast in 12 Months," *Healing Waters: The Magazine of Bible Deliverance*, September 1949, 12.

43. Ibid., 119.

44. Lee Braxton, "Oral Roberts Goes on ABC Network October 4," *America's Healing Magazine*, October 1953, 13.

45. Harrell, *Oral Roberts*, 128.

46. Ibid., 94.

47. Ibid., 96–97.

48. Rev. G. Hanson, "Instructions for Those Who Seek Healing in Roberts Campaign," *Healing Waters: The Magazine of Bible Deliverance*, May 1948, 8.

49. As quoted in Harrell, *Oral Roberts*, 168.

50. Oral Roberts, "Do You Want God to Return Your Money Seven Times?" *America's Healing Magazine*, April 1954, 10.

51. M. Harrison, *Righteous Riches*, 12; Harrell, *Oral Roberts*, 141–43.

52. Rev. Frederick J. Eikerenkoetter, interview, Bel Harbor, FL, 2005.

53. Harrell, *Oral Roberts,* 66; Oral Roberts, *My Story* (Tulsa, OK: Summitt, 1961), 77.

54. Baer and Singer, "Religious Diversification," 513.

55. To demonstrate the magnitude of this phenomenon, E. Franklin Frazier notes that in the 1920s, at the height of the southern migration into Harlem, only 54 out of 140 churches gathered in traditional edifices. J. A. Harrison, "The Storefront Church as a Revitalization Movement," in *The Black Church in America,* ed. Anne Kusener Nelsen and Hart M. Nelsen (New York: Basic Books, 1971); Edward Franklin Frazier, *Negro Church in America* (New York: Schocken Books, 1963).

56. Jill Watts, *God, Harlem U.S.A.: The Father Divine Story* (Berkeley: University of California Press, 1992), 21; Frazier, *Negro Church in America,* 71.

57. Wallace D. Best, *Passionately Human, No Less Divine: Religion and Culture in Black Chicago, 1915–1952* (Princeton: Princeton University Press, 2005), 40.

58. Hans A. Baer, *The Black Spiritual Movement: A Religious Response to Racism,* 2nd ed. (Knoxville: University of Tennessee Press, 2001), 9.

59. It is believed that blacks used the terms *Spiritual* rather than *Spiritualist* to distinguish the movement from the larger Spiritualist orientation in America. See ibid., 7.

60. See Baer, *Black Spiritual Movement.*

61. Allan H. Spear, *Black Chicago: The Making of a Negro Ghetto, 1890–1920* (Chicago: University of Chicago Press, 1967), 176.

62. Washington, *Black Sects and Cults,* 113.

63. Ibid., 114.

64. Best, *Passionately Human,* 41.

65. Ibid., 43.

66. Baer and Singer, *African-American Religion,* 62–63.

67. For more on Prophet James F. Jones, see "Prophet Jones: Bizarre Detroit Evangelist Builds Himself a $2 Million Kingdom in Slums in Six Years," *Ebony,* April 1950, 67–72; "The Prophet Jones," *Newsweek,* January 12, 1953, 73; Herbert Brean, "Prophet Jones: Detroit Evangelist Preaches Good Faith and Gleans Its Happy Rewards," *Life,* November 27, 1944, 57–63; John Kobler, "Prophet Jones: Messiah in Mink," *Saturday Evening Post,* March 2, 1955, 20–21, 74–77; "Morals and Manners: Preview for the Prophet," *Time,* March 2, 1953, 17; Tim Retzloff, "Seer or Queer? Postwar Fascination with Detroit's Prophet Jones," *GLQ: A Journal of Gay and Lesbian Studies* 8, no. 3 (2002): 271–96; Zena Simmons, "Detroit's Flamboyant Prophet Jones," *Detroit News,* September 13, 1997, http://info.detnews.com/history/story/index.cfm?id=182&category=people.

68. Z. Simmons, "Detroit's Flamboyant Prophet Jones."

69. Ibid.

70. Kobler, "Prophet Jones."

71. Retzloff, "Seer or Queer?" 276–77.

72. "Rev. C. L. Franklin Continues Attack on Prophet Jones," *Michigan Chronicle*, June 1955, 18.

73. Retzloff, "Seer or Queer?" 287.

74. Ibid.

75. Teresa Hairston, "Rev. Ike: The Prosperity Pioneer," *Gospel Today*, September–October 2004.

CHAPTER 3. STANDING ON THE PROMISES

1. Lincoln and Mamiya, *Black Church*, 386.

2. Quoted in Adrienne Gaines, "Revive Us, Precious Lord: A New Pentecostal Fervor Is Stirring America's Black Mainline Churches. Leaders of the Movement Say the Holy Spirit Is Breaking Centuries-Old Traditions," *Charisma Magazine*, May 2003.

3. Stanley M. Burgess and Eduard M. van der Maas, *The New International Dictionary of Pentecostal and Charismatic Movements*, rev. and expanded ed. (Grand Rapids, MI: Zondervan, 2002), xix.

4. Ibid.

5. Cheryl Jeanne Sanders, *Saints in Exile: The Holiness-Pentecostal Experience in African American Religion and Culture* (New York: Oxford University Press, 1996), 6.

6. Harrell, *All Things Are Possible*, 8–9.

7. I agree with Shayne Lee in this regard, though I think his broad description of neo-Pentecostalism as primarily a worship style that appropriately describes nondenominational and mainline denominations alike is too far-reaching. While such a definition may be appropriate to describe the changes among the dominant society, expressive and demonstrative worship is more the norm than the exception among traditional African American Christian practices. Hence, if we were to use the term *neo-Pentecostalism* so broadly, it would mean so much that it would not mean anything at all. Lee, *T. D. Jakes*, 34.

8. T. D. Jakes, *Can You Stand to Be Blessed? Insights to Help You Survive the Peaks and Valleys* (Shippensburg, PA: Treasure House, 1994), 49.

9. Lauren Winner, "T.D. Jakes Feels Your Pain," *Christianity Today*, February 7, 2000, 52–59.

10. Biographical information derived from Bishop Carlton Pearson, interview, Tulsa, OK, December 7–9, 2005.

11. Unless otherwise noted, information on Pearson is derived from Bishop Carlton Pearson, interview, Tulsa, OK, December 7–9, 2005.

12. By this time Rev. Ike was largely viewed as a pariah in Christian broadcasting. Most black evangelists were extremely careful distance themselves from Ike or his ministry. Therefore, it was nearly impossible to raise the sort of fund-

ing from black viewers for black evangelists to independently broadcast their own television shows.

13. Lee, *T. D. Jakes*, 44.

14. Today the following six associations constitute the two black mainline denominations: the National Baptist Convention; the National Baptist Convention of America; the Progressive National Convention; the African Methodist Episcopal Church; the African Methodist Episcopal Zion Church; and the Christian Methodist Episcopal Church.

15. To be sure, there are examples of Baptist bishops in African American religious history. The Primitive Baptists once ordained their own bishops. But this recent emergence of Baptist bishops cannot be divorced from the increasingly hierarchical power structure of the black church that is a result of the megachurch phenomenon.

16. Cornel West, "The Prophetic Tradition in Afro-America," in West and Glaude, *African American Religious Thought*, 1042.

17. Evelyn Brooks Higginbotham, *Righteous Discontent: The Women's Movement in the Black Baptist Church, 1880–1920* (Cambridge, MA: Harvard University Press, 1993), 44.

18. Lawrence Patrick Jackson, *Ralph Ellison: Emergence of Genius* (New York: John Wiley, 2002), 28.

19. Higginbotham, "Rethinking Vernacular Culture," 984.

20. Baer and Singer, *African-American Religion*, 59.

21. Lincoln and Mamiya, *Black Church*, 385.

22. Quoted in Gaines, "Revive Us, Precious Lord."

23. Such a culture of despotic nepotism eventually came to a head in 1997 with the downfall of then–convention president Rev. Henry Lyons. Lyons was eventually charged and found guilty of multiple counts of fraud, extortion, money laundering, and tax evasion.

24. To be sure, the catchphrase of the newfound fellowship, "The Right to Choose," was not lost on National Baptist Convention stalwarts. Then-president Henry Lyons was quoted as saying, "My personal opinion is that my friend Bishop Morton is trying to put me out of business." Jacqueline Trussell, "The Full Gospel Baptist Church Fellowship: Giving Baptists a Choice," Black and Christian.com, December 2000, www.blackandchristian.com/articles/academy/trussell-12-00.shtml.

25. Full Gospel Baptist Church Fellowship, "About Us," November 21, 2007, www.fullgospelbaptist.org/html/aboutus.html.

26. Kenneth Copeland and Gloria Copeland, *Prosperity Promises* (Fort Worth, TX: Kenneth Copeland, 1997), 57.

27. M. Harrison, *Righteous Riches*, 10.

28. Ibid., 97.

29. Kenneth Copeland, *Managing God's Mutual Funds—Yours and His: Understanding True Prosperity* (Fort Worth, TX: Kenneth Copeland, 1996), 7.

30. Creflo A. Dollar, *The Color of Love: Understanding God's Answer to Racism, Separation, and Division* (Tulsa, OK: Harrison House, 1997), 187–90.

31. McRoberts, *Streets of Glory,* 52.

32. D. R. McConnell, *A Different Gospel,* updated ed. (Peabody, MA: Hendrickson, 1995), 3–14.

33. Dale H. Simmons, *E. W. Kenyon and the Postbellum Pursuit of Peace, Power, and Plenty* (Lanham, MD: Scarecrow Press, 1997), 1.

34. Ibid., 14.

35. Essek William Kenyon, *The Two Kinds of Faith: Faith's Secret Revealed,* 10th ed. (Seattle: Kenyon's Gospel Publishing Society, 1969), 60.

36. Harrell, *Oral Roberts,* 423.

37. Ibid., 424.

38. Ibid., 425.

CHAPTER 4. COME, YE DISCONSOLATE

1. T. D. Jakes, *The Ten Commandments of Working in a Hostile Environment* (New York: Berkley Books, 2005).

2. Jakes, *Can You Stand to Be Blessed?* 23.

3. It is important to note that Jakes's congregations have never been rooted in any particular community or locale. His ministry has always sought to transcend a local congregation of believers with the aim of positioning the ministry (i.e., T. D. Jakes) where it has the broadest audience possible. Serving as the pastor of a local congregation appears to be just a stepping-stone toward this greater end.

4. Sarah Jordan Powell, interview, Tulsa, OK, 2005. Shayne Lee also provides a thorough account of Bishop Jakes relationship with Sarah Jordan Powell and initial meeting with Bishop Carlton Pearson in his chapter "Jakes Receives His Big Break" in *T. D. Jakes.*

5. T. D. Jakes, *Behind Closed Doors* (Tulsa, OK: Higher Dimensions Ministries, 1992).

6. T. D. Jakes, *The Pride of Life* (Tulsa, OK: Higher Dimensions Ministries, 2000); Bishop Carlton Pearson, interview, Tulsa, OK, 2005.

7. Bishop Carlton Pearson, interview, Tulsa, OK, 2005.

8. See, for example, Ken Ward Jr., "Successful Book, TV Exposure Allow Kanawha Minister to Live in Style," *Charleston Gazette,* April 5, 1995; "TV Preachers: Being Called a Bishop Does Not Mean That You Can Live Like a King," *Charleston Gazette,* April 21, 1995; Dan Radmacher, "Liberal Offerings Minister Lives Good Life," *Charleston Gazette,* April 10, 1995, 4A.

9. T. D. Jakes, *Naked and Not Ashamed: We've Been Afraid to Reveal What God Longs to Heal* (Shippensburg, PA: Treasure House, 1995), 107.

10. T. D. Jakes, *Reposition Yourself: Living Life without Limits* (New York: Atria Books, 2007), 54.

11. Lee, *T. D. Jakes*, 98–122.

12. T. D. Jakes, *The Great Investment: Faith, Family, and Finance* (New York: G. P. Putnam's Sons, 2000), 13–14.

13. Ibid., 14.

14. Jakes, *Ten Commandments*.

15. Jakes, *Great Investment*, 20.

16. Jakes, *Can You Stand to Be Blessed?* 49.

17. T. D. Jakes, *Reposition Yourself*, 178.

18. Lee, *T. D. Jakes*, 28–31.

19. Jakes, "Domestic Abuse Is Unholy," 117.

20. "We don't drink poison because we like the taste of the antidote. If life has, through no fault of our own, landed us in a crisis situation, we know that He [sic] is the Christ over the crisis." Jakes, *Great Investment*, 16.

21. You can learn about T. D. Jakes's recent activities and products when the sanctuary goes dark and church announcements are played on the large sanctuary screens. A white male anchorman sitting at a desk informs the congregation via the "Potter's House News." This newsbreak is divided into two segments by commercials for Jakes's latest sermon tape series while parishioners proudly applaud their pastor.

22. For a helpful examination of the larger culture of "seeker-friendly" congregations and their characteristics, see Richard P. Cimino and Don Lattin, *Shopping for Faith: American Religion in the New Millennium* (San Francisco: Jossey-Bass; Donald E. Miller, *Reinventing American Protestantism: Christianity in the New Millennium* (Berkeley: University of California Press, 1997).

23. Potter's House, "Mission Statement," November 19, 2002, www.thepottershouse.org/PH_mission.html.

24. T. D. Jakes, *The Lady, Her Lover, and Her Lord* (New York: G. P. Putnam's Sons, 1998), 176.

25. Potter's House, "Mission Statement."

26. In 1998 Deion Sanders donated a million dollars to the Potter's House Ministry.

27. "Jakes: No Political Party Can Contain Us," CNN.com, October 20, 2006, www.cnn.com/2006/US/07/05/jakes.commentary/.

28. T. D. Jakes and Cornel West, "Preachers, Profits and the Prophetic: The New Face of American Evangelicalism," lecture and public dialogue, Princeton University, October 26, 2005.

29. Jakes, *Reposition Yourself*, 216.

30. Ed Gordon, "Bishop T. D. Jakes on African Aid and President Bush," National Public Radio, *News and Notes*, June 23, 2005.

31. "Jakes: No Political Party."

32. "The New Black Spirituality," *Ebony*, December 2004, 24.

33. Max Weber, *The Protestant Ethic and the Spirit of Capitalism*, 3rd ed. (Los Angeles: Roxbury, 2001), 109.

34. Jakes, *Reposition Yourself*, 38.

35. Jakes and West, "Preachers, Profits."

36. T. D. Jakes, *God's Leading Lady: Out of the Shadows and into the Light* (New York: G. P. Putnam's Sons, 2002), 227–28.

37. Ibid., 41.

38. T. D. Jakes, *Loose That Man and Let Him Go!* (Minneapolis: Bethany House, 1995), 46, 47, 51.

39. T. D. Jakes, *Woman, Thou Art Loosed!* (Shippensburg, PA: Destiny Images, 1993), 98.

40. T. D. Jakes, *Daddy Loves His Girls* (Lake Mary, FL: Charisma House, 1996), 35.

41. Jakes, *Loose That Man*, 41, 42.

42. Jakes, *The Lady, Her Lover*, 58.

43. Ibid.

44. Jakes, *Daddy Loves His Girls*, 36.

CHAPTER 5. WE ARE SOLDIERS!

1. Though Dr. King is the only nonpresident with the distinction of having a federal holiday named in his honor, and though he was first and foremost a Christian minister, on the third Monday of each January TBN chooses to refrain from formally recognizing the King holiday. One can only speculate why, but I am confident that it has something to do with the network's Christian conservative viewing base. To be sure, this is the same network that aired Ronald Reagan's funeral in its entirety and commonly airs tributes extolling the Christian witness of both Presidents Reagan and George W. Bush.

2. Eddie L. Long, *Taking Over: Seizing Your City for God in the New Millennium* (Lake Mary, FL: Charisma House, 1999), 60.

3. John Blake, "God's 'Scarred Leader' Has Transformed a Metro Atlanta Church into a Christian Colossus; Long View at New Birth," *Atlanta Journal and Constitution*, July 10, 1999.

4. Though father and son reconciled before Floyd Long's death in 1995, Bishop now believes that his father did not know how to show love because his own father (Bishop Long's paternal grandfather) had been so distant.

5. Long, *Taking Over*, 59.

6. Blake, "God's 'Scarred Leader.'"

7. Long, *Taking Over*, 19.

8. Eddie L. Long, *I Don't Want Delilah, I Need You!* (Minneapolis: Bethany House, 1998), 42.

9. Ibid., 111.

10. Long, *Taking Over,* 41.

11. Ibid., 63.

12. Long, *I Don't Want Delilah,* 113.

13. Ibid., 111.

14. Ibid., 42.

15. Ibid., 113.

16. Long, *Taking Over,* 61.

17. B.E.L.L. Ministries is the independent entity established by Eddie L. Long to package and promote his many ministry-related products and activities. These include his books, videos, annual conferences, and urban education initiative, as well as the Father's House for pastors who desire to submit to the "prophetic vision and apostolic authority of Bishop Eddie L. Long." See www.bellministries.org.

18. "Black Preachers," History Channel, February 5, 2005.

19. Depending upon the occasion, different wall-sized banners of Bishop Eddie Long's image hang down on each side of the stage. For example, at New Birth's annual pastors' and ministers' conference, two wall-sized banners of the bishop were hung with the conference theme "Spirit & Truth" etched upon the bishop's chest.

20. John Blake, "Pastor Inspiration: Divine or Online? Surfing for Sermons: Sometimes Desperate Ministers Lift Texts from Web," *Atlanta Journal-Constitution,* May 12, 2007.

21. Blake, "God's 'Scarred Leader.'"

22. Long, *Taking Over,* 51.

23. Ibid., 54.

24. Ibid., 49.

25. Ibid., 47–52.

26. Ibid., 127.

27. *Holy Bible, New Revised Standard Version: Containing the Old and New Testaments, with the Apocryphal-Deuterocanonical Books,* Ref. ed. (Grand Rapids, MI: Zondervan, 1993).

28. Long, *Taking Over,* 154.

29. Ibid., 153.

30. Ibid., 20.

31. Ibid.

32. Ernest Holsendolph, "Praying for the Flat Tax; Steve Forbes Receives a Rousing Reception from a Black Dekalb Audience," *Atlanta Journal and Constitution,* March 14, 1999.

33. John Blake, "Pastors Choose Sides over the Direction of the Black Church," *Atlanta Journal and Constitution,* February 15, 2005.

34. Long, *Taking Over,* 44.

35. I use the term *randomly* rather loosely here. In actuality, on the video Bishop Long asks parishioners how much of a balance that they have on the card before volunteering payment. And when certain credit card balances are revealed to be well into the thousands, Bishop Long begins seeking volunteers from the congregation to pay.

36. John Blake, "Bishop's Charity Generous to Bishop: New Birth's Long Received 3 Million," *Atlanta Journal and Constitution,* August 28, 2005.

37. Bishop Eddie L. Long, "Martin Luther King Jr. Annual Holiday Celebration," WAGA–Fox 5, January 14, 2002.

38. Ibid.

39. Ibid.

40. See the following videos: Bishop Eddie L. Long, *Stop the Silence March* (Atlanta: B.E.L.L. Ministries, 2004) and *Conquer and Subdue* (Atlanta: B.E.L.L. Ministries, 2004).

41. Long, *Taking Over,* viii–ix.

42. Eddie L. Long, *One Nation under God* (Atlanta: B.E.L.L. Ministries, 2001).

43. Bishop Eddie L. Long, *First the Natural Then the Spiritual* (Atlanta: B.E.L.L. Ministries, 2003).

44. Long, *Stop the Silence March.*

45. Long, *I Don't Want Delilah,* 60.

46. Ibid., 70.

CHAPTER 6. FILL MY CUP, LORD

1. Within the traditional black Baptist denominations, seminary training is not required for ordination. The autonomous nature of congregational authority allows each independent ordination committee to determine whether theological education is necessary for ministerial credentials.

2. Creflo Dollar, "My Partners and Me," *Changing Your World,* August 2002, 79.

3. For a roster of Kenneth Copeland–led World of Faith conferences from 2002 to 2008, see www.bvov.tv/kcm/ondemand/index.php.

4. In 2005, Harrison House completed a deal with Time Warner and Warner Faith Publishing for Time Warner to acquire all backlist titles of Creflo Dollar's publications. "Dr. Creflo Dollar to Time Warner and Faith Publishing," Harrison House, news release, October 27, 2005, www.harrisonhouse.com/news.aspx?newsId=8.

5. Michael Luo, "Preaching a Gospel of Wealth in a Glittery Market, New York," *New York Times,* January 15, 2006.

6. C. Dollar, *Color of Love,* 191.

7. Creflo Dollar, *Not Guilty: Experience God's Gift of Acceptance and Freedom* (New York: Warner Faith, 2006), 105.

8. Creflo Dollar, "Made after His Kind," Archived Audio and Video Messages, September 15 and 22, 2002, Creflo Dollar Ministries, http://interactive. creflodollarministries.org/broadcasts/archives2002_t.asp?site=CDM.

9. Kenneth Copeland, quoted in Robert M. Bowman Jr., *The Word of Faith Controversy: Understanding the Health and Wealth Gospel* (Grand Rapids, MI: Baker Books, 2001), 126.

10. Kenneth Copeland, *Walking in the Realm of the Miraculous* (Fort Worth, TX: Kenneth Copeland, 1987), 15–16.

11. For more information on New Thought in the African American church, see Martin, *Beyond Christianity,* ch. 2.

12. C. Dollar, *Not Guilty,* 148.

13. Ibid.

14. Creflo Dollar, "Jesus Growth into Sonship," Archived Audio and Video Messages, December 8 and 15, 2002, Creflo Dollar Ministries, http://interactive. creflodollarministries.org/broadcasts/archives2002_t.asp?site=CDM.

15. Dollar, *Color of Love,* 188.

16. See the chapter "Release Words out of Your Mouth to Unleash Prosperity," in Creflo Dollar, *Total Life Prosperity: 14 Practical Steps to Receiving God's Full Blessing* (Nashville, TN: Thomas Nelson, 1999), 45.

17. Pastor Creflo Dollar, "Remarks Made at Southwest Believers Convention, Tuesday, August 5, 2003, Fort Worth Convention Center," www.bvov.tv/asx/2003swbc/tueevh.asx.

18. Creflo Dollar, *No More Debt: God's Strategy for Debt Cancellation* (Atlanta: Creflo Dollar Ministries, 2000), 31.

19. Ibid., 76.

20. C. Dollar, *Total Life Prosperity,* 63.

21. Carlos Watson, *Off Topic with Carlos Watson,* Cable News Network (CNN), 2005.

22. Though Dollar's Web site states that he earned a Master of Divinity degree and a PhD in counseling, Dollar, like Rev. Frederick J. Eikerenkoetter, does not disclose the institution.

23. Watson, *Off Topic.*

24. Kalefah Sanneh, "Pray and Grow Rich," *New Yorker,* October 2004.

25. Creflo Dollar's "United We Stand, Divided We Fall," 2004, is no longer available on his Web site, but a lengthy excerpt is quoted on the TimBookTu Discussion Board at b2.timbooktu.com/viewtopic.php?t=1027& sid=bcb01ff9e 16cc88e44759c4faefo8132.

26. C. Dollar, *Color of Love.*

27. Watson, *Off Topic.*

28. Isabel Wilkerson, "A Dollar and a Dream," *Essence,* December 2005, 166–70.

29. Creflo Dollar and Taffi Dollar, *The Successful Family: Everything You Need to Know to Build a Stronger Family* (College Park, GA: Creflo Dollar Ministries, 2002), 81.

30. Ibid., 75.

31. Ibid., 74.

32. Ibid.

33. Ibid., 77.

34. Ibid., 78.

35. Taffi Dollar, *A Woman after God's Own Heart: Fulfilling the Will of God for Your Life and Empowering Those around You* (Nashville, TN: Thomas Nelson, 2000), 115.

36. Ibid., 120.

37. C. Dollar and T. Dollar, *The Successful Family,* 81.

CHAPTER 7. THE REASONS WHY WE SING

1. Stephanie Y. Mitchem, *Name It and Claim It? Prosperity Preaching in the Black Church* (Cleveland, OH: Pilgrim Press, 2007), 31.

2. Ibid., 32.

3. Stuart Hall, "Encoding/Decoding," in *Culture, Media, Language,* ed. Center for Contemporary Cultural Studies (London: Hutchinson, 1980).

4. One of the key purposes of Harrison's book is to demonstrate how African Americans adapt and appropriate the tenets of the Word of Faith movement to respond to their particular condition as African Americans. M. Harrison, *Righteous Riches.*

5. Victor Witter Turner, *From Ritual to Theatre: The Human Seriousness of Play* (New York: Performing Arts Journal, 1982), 44.

6. Frederick, *Between Sundays,* 135.

7. M. Harrison, *Righteous Riches,* 25.

8. Ibid.

9. Riley, "Golden Gospel."

10. Michael Eric Dyson, quoted in Deborah Potter, "Prosperity Gospel," *Religion and Ethics Newsweekly: An Online Companion to the Weekly Television Program,* Public Broadcasting Service, August 17, 2007, www.pbs.org/wnet/religionandethics/week1051/feature.html.

11. Quoted in Jonathan L. Walton, "Empowered: The Entrepreneurial Ministry of T. D. Jakes," *Christian Century,* July 10, 2007, 26.

12. Lee, *T. D. Jakes,* 126–27.

13. Like Bobby Alexander, I use the term *empowerment* to connote not only political power and influence but also the enlargement of opportunities and freedoms made possible by social inclusion or human community. Alexander, *Televangelism Reconsidered*, 5.

14. Turner, *From Ritual to Theatre*, 47.

15. Ibid.

16. Robert Wuthnow, *American Mythos: Why Our Best Efforts to Be a Better Nation Fall Short* (Princeton: Princeton University Press, 2006), 3.

17. For example, Bishop T. D. Jakes's suggestion that entrepreneurship is a viable means of economic empowerment for African Americans operates from the assumption, like the myth of American success, that the possession of a frontier spirit is enough to overcome the unjust structuring of America's capitalist economy.

18. Harold Vanderpool, "The American Success Syndrome," *Christian Century*, September 24, 1975, 820–23.

19. Alger remains one of the most famous authors in American history. Certainly his formulaic and accessible style of writing would not earn him the distinction of being considered a "man of letters" by the emerging American literati class of his time. But in popularity Alger once rivaled Mark Twain; one would have been hard pressed to find a library in an American home that did not contain a Horatio Alger book.

20. Richard Weiss's *American Myth of Success* traces the way in which the success myth has been transformed with each generation. This is particularly important as it relates to the paradoxical relationship between thrift and conspicuous consumption in American culture. Richard Weiss, *The American Myth of Success: From Horatio Alger to Norman Vincent Peale* (New York: Basic Books, 1969).

21. Jennifer L. Hochschild, *Facing up to the American Dream: Race, Class, and the Soul of the Nation* (Princeton: Princeton University Press, 1995), 168.

22. Sydney E. Ahlstrom, *A Religious History of the American People* (New Haven: Yale University Press, 1972), 789.

23. Conrad Cherry, *God's New Israel: Religious Interpretations of American Destiny*, rev. and updated ed. (Chapel Hill: University of North Carolina Press, 1998), 220.

24. See "What Is the American Dream?" in Hochschild, *Facing Up*.

25. Jakes and West, "Preachers, Profits."

26. Lee, *T. D. Jakes*, 6–7, 186.

27. C. Dollar, *No More Debt*, 9.

28. Floyd Flake, *The Way of the Bootstrapper* (San Francisco: Harper Collins, 1999); Joy Bennett, "The Rev Dr. Jamal-Harrison Bryant: From G.E.D. To Ph.D. and a Global Mission," *Ebony*, September 2007.

29. Henry Louis Gates and Cornel West, *The Future of the Race* (New York: Alfred A. Knopf, 1996), 84.

30. Shelby Steele, *The Content of Our Character: A New Vision of Race in America* (New York: St. Martin's Press, 1990); John H. McWhorter, *Losing the Race: Self-Sabotage in Black America* (New York: Free Press, 2000), 49.

31. Riley, "Golden Gospel."

32. Ibid.

33. C. Dollar, *Color of Love,* 6–7.

34. Michael Dyson, *I May Not Get There,* 291.

35. Mark Anthony Neal, *New Black Man* (New York: Routledge, 2005), 21.

36. Steve Estes, *I Am a Man! Race, Manhood, and the Civil Rights Movement* (Chapel Hill: University of North Carolina Press, 2005).

37. See Patricia Hill Collins, *Black Sexual Politics: African Americans, Gender, and the New Racism* (New York: Routledge, 2004), ch. 6.

38. Neal, *New Black Man,* 24. See Tyler Perry's Web site at www.tylerperry.com/.

39. Neal, *New Black Man,* 24.

40. By *early work* I particularly mean the 1995 book *Loose That Man and Let Him Go!* for Jakes has appeared to problematize the myth of the Strong Black Man in his recent book *He-Motions: Even Strong Men Struggle* (New York: Putnam's, 2004). Not to posit Jakes as a paragon of progressive black male sensibilities, but he does now to some extent critique the rhetoric of hypermasculinity that can be found in his earlier work and in the writings of his peers such as Bishop Long.

41. Bishop T. D. Jakes, *Loose That Man and Let Him Go!* 2nd ed. (Bethany House, 2003), 29.

42. Ibid., 42.

43. Jakes, *Lady, Her Lover,* 62.

44. Ibid., 58; Lee, *T. D. Jakes,* 132.

45. Quoted in Walton, "Empowered," 27–28.

46. Long, *I Don't Want Delilah,* 70.

47. Ibid., 69.

48. Emilie Maureen Townes, *Womanist Ethics and the Cultural Production of Evil* (New York: Palgrave Macmillan, 2006).

49. C. Dollar and T. Dollar, *Successful Family,* 50.

50. Ibid., 55.

51. Townes, *Womanist Ethics,* 61.

52. C. Dollar and T. Dollar, *Successful Family,* 52.

53. Ibid., 81.

CHAPTER 8. LIFT EVERY VOICE

1. David Van Biema, "Spirit Raiser: America's Best," *Time,* September 17, 2001, 55.

2. William F. Fore, *Television and Religion: The Shaping of Faith, Values, and Culture* (Minneapolis: Augsburg Publishing House, 1987), 57–61. Also see Conrad Phillip Kottak, *Prime-Time Society: An Anthropological Analysis of Television and Culture* (Belmont, CA: Wadsworth, 1990); Gregor T. Goethals, *The TV Ritual: Worship at the Video Altar* (Boston: Beacon Press, 1981).

3. Richard W. Stevenson, "In a Time of Plenty, the Poor Are Still Poorer," *New York Times*, January 23, 2000.

4. See ch. 3, "Millennial Plutographics: American Fortunes and Misfortunes at the Turn of the Century," in Kevin P. Phillips, *Wealth and Democracy: A Political History of the American Rich* (New York: Broadway Books, 2002), 108–68. Also see Kevin P. Phillips, *The Politics of Rich and Poor: Wealth and the American Electorate in the Reagan Aftermath* (New York: Random House, 1990).

5. Chuck Collins and Felice Yeskel, *Economic Apartheid in America: A Primer on Economic Inequality and Insecurity*, rev. and updated 2nd ed. (New York: New Press, 2005), 51.

6. Mark L. Taylor, *The Executed God: The Way of the Cross in Lockdown America* (Minneapolis: Augsburg Publishing House, 2001), 54.

7. Ibid., 55; Stevenson, "In a Time of Plenty."

8. Minimum wage is currently set at $5.15 in America. Robert Pollin and Stephanie Luce, *The Living Wage: Building a Fair Economy*, rev. ed. (New York: New Press, 2000), 167.

9. Ibid., 2.

10. Collins and Yeskel, *Economic Apartheid in America*, 44–45.

11. Eduardo Bonilla-Silva, *Racism without Racists: Color-Blind Racism and the Persistence of Racial Inequality in the United States* (Lanham, MD: Rowman and Littlefield, 2003), 8.

12. Michael Eric Dyson, *Is Bill Cosby Right? Or Has the Black Middle Class Lost Its Mind?* (New York: Basic Books, 2005), 62.

13. Thomas M. Shapiro, *The Hidden Cost of Being African-American: How Wealth Perpetuates Inequality* (New York: Oxford University Press, 2004), 87.

14. The median household income of a black family in 2003 was $29,026, whereas that of a white family was $46,900. Michael Dyson, *Is Bill Cosby Right?*

15. William J. Wilson, ed., *The Ghetto Underclass: Social Science Perspectives*, updated ed. (Newbury Park, CA: Sage Publications, 1993); William J. Wilson, *When Work Disappears: The World of the New Urban Poor* (New York: Alfred A. Knopf, 1996) and *The Truly Disadvantaged: The Inner City, the Underclass, and Public Policy* (Chicago: University of Chicago Press, 1987).

16. Shapiro, *Hidden Cost*, 92.

17. Melvin L. Oliver and Thomas M. Shapiro, *Black Wealth/White Wealth: A New Perspective on Racial Inequality* (New York: Routledge, 1995), 45–50.

18. Shapiro, *Hidden Cost*, 65.

19. As in W. E. B. Du Bois, "Of Booker T. Washington and Others," from "The Souls of Black Folk," 398.

20. William Ronald Jones, *Is God a White Racist? A Preamble to Black Theology* (Garden City, NY: Anchor Press, 1973).

21. Rev. Ike, *The Master of Money,* video (Boston: Thinkonomics, n.d. [ca. late 1980s/early 1990s]), available from https://store.revike.org/index.asp?pageAction=VIEWPROD&ProdID=43.

22. It is of note that Rev. Ike chooses to omit the race of the woman in the story, as overtly revealing this (if the woman had been white) could have overcomplicated the narrative based upon time and place. Injecting the racial dimension could have also evoked feelings of anxiety and guilt among his predominantly white audience that would have trumped his own race-effacing philosophy and offended his listeners. However, he still effectively uses the story covertly. Placing an emphasis on his race, contrasted against the authority of the woman, affords Rev. Ike the ability to get his point across in a palatable way.

23. Jakes and West, "Preachers, Profits."

24. The *Healing Waters* magazine is full of testimonies from "businessmen" testifying to the business acumen demonstrated by Oral Roberts in his varying campaigns.

25. Watson, *Off Topic with Carlos Watson.*

26. Tamara E. Holmes, "No Parallels between Buying Power and Wealth," *Black Enterprise,* June 2005, 50.

27. Aissatou Sidime, "Credit Use Strangles Wealth: African American Debt Is Increasing Faster Than Income," *Black Enterprise,* November 2004, 38; Holmes, "No Parallels."

28. Peter J. Paris, *Black Religious Leaders: Conflict in Unity,* 2nd ed. (Louisville, KY: Westminster John Knox, 1991), 19.

29. To be sure, moral leadership like that found in the life and ministry of Martin Luther King, Jr. is far from the norm and represents an exceptional personality. Insofar as I make this claim concerning the prophetic type, I affirm Cornel West's contention that the prophetic strand of a faith community is always the minority perspective. Cornel West, *Democracy Matters: Winning the Fight against Imperialism* (New York: Penguin, 2004).

30. Hochschild, *Facing Up,* 73.

31. Jeremy Levitt, "Most African Americans Perceive the GOP to Be Racist and Working against Their Interests," *Chicago Sun-Times,* December 5, 2004; Ben Smith, "GOP Lured Few Black Voters; Traditional Party Lines Still Define County's African American Precincts," *Atlanta Journal and Constitution,* November 16, 2000.

32. Levitt, "Most African Americans"; Smith, "GOP Lured Few"; Ben Smith, "Black Republicans Make No Headway in Dekalb," *Atlanta Journal and Constitution,* November 23, 2000.

33. *State of the Black Union: Defining the Agenda,* video, C-Span Archives, February 26, 2005.

34. Fredrick C. Harris, *Something Within: Religion in African-American Political Activism* (New York: Oxford University Press, 1999).

35. Michele Wallace, *Black Macho and the Myth of the Superwoman* (New York: Dial Press, 1979); bell hooks, *We Real Cool: Black Men and Masculinity* (New York: Routledge, 2004); Audre Lorde, "Sexism: An American Disease in Blackface," in *Sister Outsider: Essays and Speeches* (Trumansburg, NY: Crossing Press, 1984); Hill Collins, *Black Sexual Politics* and *From Black Power to Hip Hop: Racism, Nationalism, and Feminism* (Philadelphia: Temple University Press, 2006).

36. Wallace, *Black Macho,* 44.

37. Ibid., 69.

38. W. E. B. Du Bois, *Black Reconstruction in America* (New York: Atheneum, 1992), 27.

39. Paula Giddings, *When and Where I Enter: The Impact of Black Women on Race and Sex in America* (New York: William Morrow, 1984), 87–89.

40. Orlando Patterson, *Rituals of Blood: Consequences of Slavery in Two American Centuries* (Washington, DC: Civitas/CounterPoint, 1998).

41. See Estes, *I Am a Man!*

42. Marcia Dyson, "When Preachers Prey: Minister's Wife Marcia Dyson Speaks of Sexual Interaction between Ministers and Church Women," *Essence,* May 1, 1998.

43. Kelly Brown Douglas, *Sexuality and the Black Church: A Womanist Perspective* (Maryknoll, NY: Orbis Books, 1999), 103.

44. J. L. King, *On the Down Low: A Journey into the Lives of Straight Black Men Who Sleep with Men* (New York: Broadway Books, 2004).

45. Benoit Denizet-Lewis, "Double Lives on the Down Low," *New York Times,* August 3, 2003.

46. Black gay activist and author Keith Boykin rejects the category of DL, defining it as cheating on a partner regardless of sexual orientation. Keith Boykin, *Beyond the Down Low: Sex and Denial in Black America* (New York: Carroll and Graf, 2005).

47. Centers for Disease Control and Prevention, "HIV/AIDS among African Americans," CDC HIV/AIDS Fact Sheet, June 2007, www.cdc.gov/hiv/topics/aa/resources/factsheets/pdf/aa.pdf.

48. Denizet-Lewis, "Double Lives."

49. King, *On the Down Low,* 77–84. For further details, see the chapter entitled "The Black Church."

50. "Rev. Ike Hit with Sex Harassment Suit by Former Male Employee," *Jet,* October 30, 1995; "Man Files Sexual Assault Lawsuit against Pastor; Police Investigation under Way into Alleged Assault," *Click2Houston.com,* August

29, 2003; Alan Bernstein, "Suit Accuses Pastor of Sexual Assault," *Houston Chronicle*, August 30, 2003.

51. "Tapes Released in Pastor's Alleged Sexual-Assault Case, Criminal Charges Not Filed against Pastor," *Click2Houston.com*, September 30, 2003. Ratliff's case can also be viewed as another example of the way African American clergy can be given a pass on unethical behavior. No charges were filed, as Ratliff settled out of court only after the tapes were made public. The congregation approved a two-month paid leave of absence for their pastor. Richard Vara, "Pastor Accused of Assault Given 2-Month Paid Leave," *Houston Chronicle*, October 29, 2003.

52. Lesbianism is rarely, if ever, brought up or challenged by African American religious broadcasters.

53. Hooks, *We Real Cool*, 57–58.

54. Nell Irvin Painter, "Soul Murder and Slavery: Toward a Fully Loaded Cost Accounting," in *Southern History across the Color Line*, ed. Nell Irvin Painter (Chapel Hill: University of North Carolina Press, 2002), 18.

55. Tom Jackman and Hamil R. Harris, "Ministry Leader Accused of Raping Woman," *Washington Post*, March 8, 2006; Tom Jackman, "Minister's Ex-Girlfriend Tells VA Judge of Protracted Rape," *Washington Post*, March 15, 2006.

56. Derived from the congregation's Web site at www.ebenezerame.org.

57. Jackman and Harris, "Ministry Leader Accused."

58. Saeed Ahmed, "Juanita Bynum Allegedly Attacked by Husband," *Atlanta Journal and Constitution*, August 23, 2007.

59. S. A. Reid, "Bishop Accused in Beating Blames Satan for His Woes," *Atlanta Journal and Constitution*, August 27, 2007.

60. Jakes, "Domestic Abuse Is Unholy."

61. Ibid.

BENEDICTION

1. W. E. B. Du Bois, "Of The Faith of Our Fathers," in *The Selected Writings of W. E. B. Du Bois* (New York: New American Library, 1970), 503–4.

2. Ibid.

Bibliography

Abelman, Robert, and Stewart M. Hoover. *Religious Television: Controversies and Conclusions.* Norwood, NJ: Ablex, 1990.

African American Heritage Hymnal. Chicago: GIA Publications, 2001.

Ahlstrom, Sydney E. *A Religious History of the American People.* New Haven: Yale University Press, 1972.

Ahmed, Saeed. "Juanita Bynum Allegedly Attacked by Husband." *Atlanta Journal and Constitution,* August 23, 2007.

Alexander, Bobby Chris. *Televangelism Reconsidered: Ritual in the Search for Human Community.* Atlanta: Scholars Press, 1994.

Anderson, Robert Mapes. *Vision of the Disinherited: The Making of American Pentecostalism.* New York: Oxford University Press, 1979.

Anderson, Victor. *Beyond Ontological Blackness: An Essay on African American Religious and Cultural Criticism.* New York: Continuum, 1995.

———. "'We See through a Glass Darkly': Black Narrative Theology and the Opacity of African American Religious Thought." In *The Ties That Bind: African American and Hispanic American/Latino/a Theologies in Dialogue,* edited by Anthony B. Pinn and Benjamin Valentin. New York: Continuum, 2001.

Baer, Hans A. *The Black Spiritual Movement: A Religious Response to Racism.* 2nd ed. Knoxville: University of Tennessee Press, 2001.

Baer, Hans A., and Merrill Singer. *African-American Religion in the Twentieth Century: Varieties of Protest and Accommodation.* Knoxville: University of Tennessee Press, 1992.

———. "Religious Diversification during the Era of Advanced Industrial Capitalism." In *African American Religious Thought: An Anthology,* edited by Cornel West and Eddie S. Glaude. Louisville, KY: Westminster John Knox, 2003.

Baldwin, James. *The Fire Next Time.* New York: Dial Press, 1963.

Barthes, Roland. *Mythologies.* Translated by Annette Lavers. New York: Hill and Wang, 1972.

Bennett, Joy. "The Rev Dr. Jamal-Harrison Bryant: From G.E.D. to Ph.D. and a Global Mission." *Ebony,* September 2007.

Bernstein, Alan. "Suit Accuses Pastor of Sexual Assault." *Houston Chronicle,* August 30, 2003.

Best, Wallace D. *Passionately Human, No Less Divine: Religion and Culture in Black Chicago, 1915–1952.* Princeton: Princeton University Press, 2005.

Biema, David Van. "Spirit Raiser: America's Best." *Time,* September 17, 2001.

"Black Preachers." History Channel, February 5, 2005.

Blake, John. "Bishop's Charity Generous to Bishop: New Birth's Long Received 3 Million." *Atlanta Journal and Constitution,* August 28, 2005.

———. "God's 'Scarred Leader' Has Transformed a Metro Atlanta Church into a Christian Colossus; Long View at New Birth." *Atlanta Journal and Constitution,* July 10, 1999.

———. "Pastor Inspiration: Divine or Online? Surfing for Sermons: Sometimes Desperate Ministers Lift Texts from Web." *Atlanta Journal-Constitution,* May 12, 2007.

———. "Pastors Choose Sides over the Direction of the Black Church." *Atlanta Journal and Constitution,* February 15, 2005.

Bonilla-Silva, Eduardo. *Racism without Racists: Color-Blind Racism and the Persistence of Racial Inequality in the United States.* Lanham, MD: Rowman and Littlefield, 2003.

Bowman, Robert M., Jr. *The Word of Faith Controversy: Understanding the Health and Wealth Gospel.* Grand Rapids, MI: Baker Books, 2001.

Boyd, Valerie. *Wrapped in Rainbows: The Life of Zora Neale Hurston.* New York: Scribner, 2003.

Boykin, Keith. *Beyond the Down Low: Sex and Denial in Black America.* New York: Carroll and Graf, 2005.

Braxton, Lee. "Oral Roberts Goes on ABC Network October 4." *America's Healing Magazine,* October 1953, 13.

Brean, Herbert. "Prophet Jones: Detroit Evangelist Preaches Good Faith and Gleans Its Happy Rewards." *Life,* November 27, 1944, 57–63.

Bruce, Steve. *Pray TV: Televangelism in America.* New York: Routledge, 1990.

Burgess, Stanley M., and Eduard M. van der Maas. *The New International Dictionary of Pentecostal and Charismatic Movements.* Rev. and expanded ed. Grand Rapids, MI: Zondervan, 2002.

Burkett, Randall, and David W. Wills. "Afro-American Religious History, 1919–1939: Bibliographic Essay and Research Guide." 1986. www.amherst.edu/~aardoc/Biblio.html.

Cazalas, James K. "Rev. Ike Wows 'Em with 'Get It Now' Philosophy." *Pittsburgh Press,* May 6, 1973.

Centers for Disease Control and Prevention. "HIV/AIDS among African Americans." CDC HIV/AIDS Fact Sheet. June 2007. www.cdc.gov/hiv/topics/aa/resources/factsheets/pdf/aa.pdf.

Cherry, Conrad. *God's New Israel: Religious Interpretations of American Destiny.* Rev. and updated ed. Chapel Hill: University of North Carolina Press, 1998.

Cimino, Richard P., and Don Lattin. *Shopping for Faith: American Religion in the New Millennium*. San Francisco: Jossey-Bass.

Collier-Thomas, Bettye. *Daughters of Thunder: Black Women Preachers and Their Sermons, 1850–1979*. San Francisco: Jossey-Bass, 1998.

Collins, Chuck, and Felice Yeskel. *Economic Apartheid in America: A Primer on Economic Inequality and Insecurity*. Rev. and updated 2nd ed. New York: New Press, 2005.

Cone, James H. *A Black Theology of Liberation*. 2nd ed. Maryknoll, NY: Orbis Books, 1986.

———. *Risks of Faith: The Emergence of a Black Theology of Liberation, 1968–1998*. Boston: Beacon Press, 1999.

Copeland, Kenneth. *Managing God's Mutual Funds—Yours and His: Understanding True Prosperity*. Fort Worth, TX: Kenneth Copeland, 1996.

———. *Walking in the Realm of the Miraculous*. Fort Worth, TX: Kenneth Copeland, 1987.

Copeland, Kenneth, and Gloria Copeland. *Prosperity Promises*. Fort Worth, TX: Kenneth Copeland, 1997.

Dargan, William T., and Isaac Watts. *Lining out the Word: Dr. Watts Hymn Singing in the Music of Black Americans*. Berkeley: University of California Press, 2006.

Denizet-Lewis, Benoit. "Double Lives on the Down Low." *New York Times*, August 3, 2003.

Dollar, Creflo A. *The Color of Love: Understanding God's Answer to Racism, Separation, and Division*. Tulsa, OK: Harrison House, 1997.

———. *How Faith Is Released. Part I*. Atlanta: Creflo Dollar Ministries, 2005.

———. "Jesus Growth into Sonship." Archived Audio and Video Messages, December 8 and 15, 2002, Creflo Dollar Ministries. http://interactive.creflodollarministries.org/broadcasts/archives2002_t.asp?site=CDM.

———. "Made after His Kind." Archived Audio and Video Messages, September 15 and 22, 2002, Creflo Dollar Ministries. http://interactive.creflodollarministries.org/broadcasts/archives2002_t.asp?site=CDM.

———. "My Partners and Me." *Changing Your World*, August 2002.

———. *No More Debt: God's Strategy for Debt Cancellation*. Atlanta: Creflo Dollar Ministries, 2000.

———. *Not Guilty: Experience God's Gift of Acceptance and Freedom*. New York: Warner Faith, 2006.

———. "Remarks Made at Southwest Believers Convention, Tuesday, August 5, 2003, Fort Worth Convention Center." www.bvov.tv/asx/2003swbc/tueevh.asx.

———. *Total Life Prosperity: 14 Practical Steps to Receiving God's Full Blessing*. Nashville, TN: Thomas Nelson, 1999.

Dollar, Creflo, and Taffi Dollar. *The Successful Family: Everything You Need to Know to Build a Stronger Family*. College Park, GA: Creflo Dollar Ministries, 2002.

Dollar, Taffi. *A Woman after God's Own Heart: Fulfilling the Will of God for Your Life and Empowering Those around You*. Nashville, TN: Thomas Nelson, 2000.

Douglas, Kelly Brown. *Sexuality and the Black Church: A Womanist Perspective*. Maryknoll, NY: Orbis Books, 1999.

"Dr. Creflo Dollar to Time Warner and Faith Publishing." Harrison House, news release, October 27, 2005. www.harrisonhouse.com/news.aspx?newsId=8.

"Dr. King to Press New Voter Drive." *New York Times*, April 2, 1965.

Du Bois, W. E. B. *Black Reconstruction in America*. New York: Atheneum, 1992.

———. *Du Bois: Writings*. Edited by Nathan Huggins. New York: Penguin, 1996.

———. "Of the Faith of Our Fathers." In *Du Bois: Writings*, edited by Nathan Huggins. New York: Penguin, 1996.

———. *The Selected Writings of W. E. B. Du Bois*. Edited by Walter Wilson. New York: New American Library, 1970.

———. "The Souls of Black Folk." In *Du Bois: Writings*, edited by Nathan Huggins. New York: Penguin, 1996.

Dyson, Marcia. "When Preachers Prey: Minister's Wife Marcia Dyson Speaks of Sexual Interaction between Ministers and Church Women." *Essence*, May 1, 1998.

Dyson, Michael Eric. *I May Not Get There with You: The True Martin Luther King, Jr*. New York: Free Press, 2000.

———. *Is Bill Cosby Right?: Or Has the Black Middle Class Lost Its Mind?* New York: Basic Books, 2005.

Estes, Steve. *I Am a Man! Race, Manhood, and the Civil Rights Movement*. Chapel Hill: University of North Carolina Press, 2005.

Fauset, Arthur Huff. *Black Gods of the Metropolis: Negro Religious Cults of the Urban North*. Philadelphia: University of Pennsylvania Press, 1971.

Finney, Charles Grandison. *Lectures on Revivals of Religion*. Cambridge, MA: Harvard University Press, 1960.

Flake, Floyd. *The Way of the Bootstrapper*. San Francisco: HarperCollins, 1999.

Fore, William F. *Television and Religion: The Shaping of Faith, Values, and Culture*. Minneapolis: Augsburg Publishing House, 1987.

Frankl, Razelle. *Televangelism: The Marketing of Popular Religion*. Carbondale: Southern Illinois University Press, 1987.

Frazier, Edward Franklin. *The Negro Church in America*. New York: Schocken Books, 1963.

Frazier, Edward Franklin, and C. Eric Lincoln. *The Negro Church in America and The Black Church since Frazier*. New York: Schocken Books, 1974.

Frederick, Marla Faye. *Between Sundays: Black Women and Everyday Struggles of Faith*. Berkeley: University of California Press, 2003.

Full Gospel Baptist Church Fellowship. "About Us." November 21, 2007. www.fullgospelbaptist.org/html/aboutus.html.

Fullinwider, S. P. "Racial Christianity." In *African-American Religious Thought: An Anthology*, edited by Cornel West and Eddie S. Glaude. Louisville, KY: Westminster John Knox, 2003.

Gaines, Adrienne. "Revive Us, Precious Lord: A New Pentecostal Fervor Is Stirring America's Black Mainline Churches. Leaders of the Movement Say the Holy Spirit Is Breaking Centuries-Old Traditions." *Charisma Magazine*, May 2003.

Gallatin, Martin. "Reverend Ike's Ministry: A Sociological Investigation of Religious Innovation." PhD diss., New York University, 1979.

Gates, Henry Louis, and Cornel West. *The Future of the Race*. New York: Vintage Books, 1996.

Gates, Rev. J. M. *Are You Bound for Heaven or Hell? The Best of Reverend J. M. Gates* (CD). Original recording 1930, remastered. Sony Music Entertainment, 0002199B8, 2004.

Giddings, Paula. *When and Where I Enter: The Impact of Black Women on Race and Sex in America*. New York: William Morrow, 1984.

Gilkes, Cheryl Townsend. "Plenty Good Room: Adaptation in a Changing Black Church." *Annals of the American Academy of Political and Social Science*, 558 (July 1998): 101–21.

Glaude, Eddie S. *In a Shade of Blue: Pragmatism and the Politics of Black America*. Chicago: University of Chicago Press, 2007.

Goethals, Gregor T. *The TV Ritual: Worship at the Video Altar*. Boston: Beacon Press, 1981.

Gordon, Ed. "Bishop T. D. Jakes on African Aid and President Bush." National Public Radio, *News and Notes*, June 23, 2005.

Grant, Jacquelyn. *White Women's Christ and Black Women's Jesus: Feminist Christology and Womanist Response*. Atlanta: Scholars Press, 1989.

Hadden, Jeffrey K., and Anson D. Shupe. *Televangelism: Power and Politics on God's Frontier*. New York: Henry Holt, 1988.

Hadden, Jeffrey K., and Charles E. Swann. *Prime Time Preachers: The Rising Power of Televangelism*. Reading, MA: Addison-Wesley, 1981.

Hairston, Teresa. "Rev. Ike: The Prosperity Pioneer." *Gospel Today*, September/October 2004.

Hall, Stuart. "Encoding/Decoding." In *Culture, Media, Language*, edited by Center for Contemporary Cultural Studies. London: Hutchinson, 1980.

———. "New Ethnicities." In *Black British Cultural Studies: A Reader*, edited by Houston A. Baker, Manthia Diawara, and Ruth H. Lindeborg. Chicago: University of Chicago Press, 1996.

Hanson, Rev. G. "Instructions for Those Who Seek Healing in Roberts Campaign." *Healing Waters: The Magazine of Bible Deliverance*, May 1948, 8.

"Happy Am I." *Time*, June 11, 1934.

"The 'Happy-Am-I' Preacher as Seen in His Radio Pulpit on the Potomac." *New York Times*, September 9, 1934.

Harrell, David Edwin. *All Things Are Possible: The Healing and Charismatic Revivals in Modern America*. Bloomington: Indiana University Press, 1975.

———. *Oral Roberts: An American Life*. Bloomington: Indiana University Press, 1985.

Harris, Fredrick C. *Something Within: Religion in African-American Political Activism*. New York: Oxford University Press, 1999.

Harris, Michael W. *The Rise of Gospel Blues: The Music of Thomas Andrew Dorsey in the Urban Church*. New York: Oxford University Press, 1992.

Harrison, J. A. "The Storefront Church as a Revitalization Movement." In *The Black Church in America*, edited by Anne Kusener Nelsen and Hart M. Nelsen. New York: Basic Books, 1971.

Harrison, Milmon F. *Righteous Riches: The Word of Faith Movement in Contemporary African American Religion*. New York: Oxford University Press, 2005.

Hendershot, Heather. *Shaking the World for Jesus: Media and Conservative Evangelical Culture*. Chicago: Chicago University Press, 2004.

Higginbotham, Evelyn Brooks. "Rethinking Vernacular Culture: Black Religion and Race Records in the 1920s and 1930s." In *African American Religious Thought: An Anthology*, edited by Cornel West and Eddie S. Glaude. Louisville, KY: Westminster John Knox, 2003.

———. *Righteous Discontent: The Women's Movement in the Black Baptist Church, 1880–1920*. Cambridge, MA: Harvard University Press, 1993.

Hill Collins, Patricia. *Black Sexual Politics: African Americans, Gender, and the New Racism*. New York: Routledge, 2004.

———. *From Black Power to Hip Hop: Racism, Nationalism, and Feminism*. Politics, History, and Social Change. Philadelphia: Temple University Press, 2006.

Hill, Marc Lamont. "I Bling Because I'm Happy." *PopMatters*, August 5, 2005, http://popmatters.com/columns/hill/050805.html.

Hochschild, Jennifer L. *Facing Up to the American Dream: Race, Class, and the Soul of the Nation*. Princeton: Princeton University Press, 1995.

Holmes, Tamara E. "No Parallels between Buying Power and Wealth." *Black Enterprise*, June 2005, 50.

Holsendolph, Ernest. "Praying for the Flat Tax; Steve Forbes Receives a Rousing Reception from a Black Dekalb Audience." *Atlanta Journal and Constitution,* March 14, 1999.

Holy Bible, New Revised Standard Version: Containing the Old and New Testaments, with the Apocryphal-Deuterocanonical Books. Ref. ed. Grand Rapids, MI: Zondervan, 1993.

hooks, bell. *We Real Cool: Black Men and Masculinity.* New York: Routledge, 2004.

Hoover, Stewart M. *Mass Media Religion: The Social Sources of the Electronic Church.* Beverly Hills, CA: Sage Publications, 1988.

Hopkins, Dwight N. *Heart and Head: Black Theology—Past, Present, and Future.* New York: Palgrave, 2002.

Hopkins, Dwight N., and George C. L. Cummings. *Cut Loose Your Stammering Tongue: Black Theology in the Slave Narratives.* 2nd ed. Louisville, KY: Westminster John Knox, 2003.

Horsfield, Peter G. *Religious Television: The American Experience.* New York: Longman, 1984.

Ike, Rev. "Evangelism in the Church." *New York Amsterdam News,* Summer 1976.

———. *The Master of Money.* Video. Boston: Thinkonomics, n.d. (ca. late 1980s/early 1990s). Available from https://store.revike.org/index.asp?PageAction=VIEWPROD&ProdID=43.

Jackman, Tom. "Minister's Ex-Girlfriend Tells VA Judge of Protracted Rape." *Washington Post,* March 15, 2006.

Jackman, Tom, and Hamil R. Harris. "Ministry Leader Accused of Raping Woman." *Washington Post,* March 8, 2006.

Jackson, Lawrence Patrick. *Ralph Ellison: Emergence of Genius.* New York: John Wiley, 2002.

"Jakes: No Political Party Can Contain Us." CNN.com, October 20, 2006. www.cnn.com/2006/US/07/05/jakes.commentary/.

Jakes, T. D. *Behind Closed Doors.* Tulsa, OK: Higher Dimensions Ministries, 1992.

———. *Can You Stand to Be Blessed? Insights to Help You Survive the Peaks and Valleys.* Shippensburg, PA: Treasure House, 1994.

———. *Daddy Loves His Girls.* Lake Mary, FL: Charisma House, 1996.

———. "Domestic Abuse Is Unholy: Church Must Fight against It, Not as a Judge but as a Protector." *Atlanta Journal and Constitution,* September 4, 2007.

———. *God's Leading Lady: Out of the Shadows and into the Light.* New York: G. P. Putnam's Sons, 2002.

———. *The Great Investment: Faith, Family, and Finance.* New York: G. P. Putnam's Sons, 2000.

———. *He-Motions: Even Strong Men Struggle*. New York: Putnam's, 2004.
———. *The Lady, Her Lover, and Her Lord*. New York: G. P. Putnam's Sons, 1998.
———. *Loose That Man and Let Him Go!* Minneapolis: Bethany House, 1995.
———. *Loose That Man and Let Him Go!* 2nd ed. Minneapolis: Bethany House, 2003.
———. *Naked and Not Ashamed: We've Been Afraid to Reveal What God Longs to Heal*. Shippensburg, PA: Treasure House, 1995.
———. *The Pride of Life*. Tulsa, OK: Higher Dimensions Ministries, 2000.
———. *Reposition Yourself: Living Life without Limits*. New York: Atria Books, 2007.
———. *The Ten Commandments of Working in a Hostile Environment*. New York: Berkley Books, 2005.
———. *Woman, Thou Art Loosed!* Shippensburg, PA: Destiny Images, 1993.
Jakes, T. D., and Cornel West. "Preachers, Profits and the Prophetic: The New Face of American Evangelicalism." Lecture and public dialogue, Princeton University, October 26, 2005.
Jones, William Ronald. *Is God a White Racist? A Preamble to Black Theology*. Garden City, NY: Anchor Press, 1973.
Kenyon, Essek William. *The Two Kinds of Faith: Faith's Secret Revealed*. 10th ed. Seattle: Kenyon's Gospel Publishing Society, 1969.
King, J. L. *On the Down Low: A Journey into the Lives of Straight Black Men Who Sleep with Men*. New York: Broadway Books, 2004.
Kobler, John. "Prophet Jones: Messiah in Mink." *Saturday Evening Post*, March 2, 1955, 20–21, 74–77.
Kottak, Conrad Phillip. *Prime-Time Society: An Anthropological Analysis of Television and Culture*. Belmont, CA: Wadsworth, 1990.
Krapohl, Robert H., and Charles H. Lippy. *The Evangelicals: A Historical, Thematic, and Biographical Guide*. Westport, CT: Greenwood Press, 1999.
Lee, Shayne. *T. D. Jakes: America's New Preacher*. New York: New York University Press, 2005.
Levitt, Jeremy. "Most African Americans Perceive the GOP to Be Racist and Working against Their Interests." *Chicago Sun-Times*, December 5, 2004.
Lewis, I. M. *Ecstatic Religion: A Study of Shamanism and Spirit Possession*. 2nd ed. New York: Routledge, 1989.
Lincoln, C. Eric, and Lawrence H. Mamiya. *The Black Church in the African American Experience*. Durham: Duke University Press, 1990.
Long, Bishop Eddie L. *Conquer and Subdue*. Atlanta: B.E.L.L. Ministries, 2004.
———. *First the Natural Then the Spiritual*. Atlanta: B.E.L.L. Ministries, 2003.

———. *I Don't Want Delilah, I Need You!* Minneapolis: Bethany House, 1998.
———. "Martin Luther King Jr. Annual Holiday Celebration." WAGA–Fox 5, January 14, 2002.
———. *One Nation under God.* Atlanta: B.E.L.L. Ministries, 2001.
———. *Stop the Silence March.* Atlanta: B.E.L.L. Ministries, 2004.
———. *Taking Over: Seizing Your City for God in the New Millennium.* Lake Mary, FL: Charisma House, 1999.
Lorde, Audre. "Sexism: An American Disease in Blackface." In *Sister Outsider: Essays and Speeches.* Trumansburg, NY: Crossing Press, 1984.
Luo, Michael. "Preaching a Gospel of Wealth in a Glittery Market, New York." *New York Times,* January 15, 2006.
MacRobert, Iain. *The Black Roots and White Racism of Early Pentecostalism in the USA.* New York: St. Martin's Press, 1988.
"Man Files Sexual Assault Lawsuit against Pastor; Police Investigation under Way into Alleged Assault." *Click2Houston.com,* August 29, 2003.
Marsden, George M. *Fundamentalism and American Culture.* 2nd ed. New York: Oxford University Press, 2006.
Martin, Darnise C. *Beyond Christianity: African Americans in a New Thought Church.* New York: New York University Press, 2005.
Mays, Benjamin Elijah. *Born to Rebel: An Autobiography.* New York: Scribner, 1971.
———. *The Negro's God as Reflected in His Literature.* Boston: Chapman and Grimes, 1938.
Mays, Benjamin Elijah, and Joseph William Nicholson. *The Negro's Church.* New York: Institute of Social and Religious Research, 1933.
McConnell, D. R. *A Different Gospel.* Updated ed. Peabody, MA: Hendrickson, 1995.
McRoberts, Omar M. *Streets of Glory: Church and Community in a Black Urban Neighborhood.* Chicago: University of Chicago Press, 2003.
McWhorter, John H. *Losing the Race: Self-Sabotage in Black America.* New York: Free Press, 2000.
Miller, Donald E. *Reinventing American Protestantism: Christianity in the New Millennium.* Berkeley: University of California Press, 1997.
Mitchem, Stephanie Y. *Name It and Claim It? Prosperity Preaching in the Black Church.* Cleveland, OH: Pilgrim Press, 2007.
"Morals and Manners: Preview for the Prophet." *Time,* March 2, 1953, 17.
Neal, Mark Anthony. *New Black Man.* New York: Routledge, 2005.
"The New Black Spirituality." *Ebony,* December 2004, 135–66.
"The New Megachurches." *Ebony,* December 2001.
Niebuhr, Gustav. "Where Religion Gets a Big Dose of Shopping-Mall Culture." *New York Times,* April 16, 1995, 1.

Nix, Reverend A. W. "Black Diamond Express to Hell, Part I." In *Complete Recorded Works in Chronological Order,* vol. 1, *1927–1928* (CD). Document Records, 2005.

Oliver, Melvin L., and Thomas M. Shapiro. *Black Wealth/White Wealth: A New Perspective on Racial Inequality.* New York: Routledge, 1995.

Oliver, Paul. *Songsters and Saints: Vocal Traditions on Race Records.* New York: Cambridge University Press, 1984.

Painter, Nell Irvin. "Soul Murder and Slavery: Toward a Fully Loaded Cost Accounting." In *Southern History across the Color Line,* edited by Nell Irvin Painter, 15–39. Chapel Hill: University of North Carolina Press, 2002.

Paris, Peter J. *Black Religious Leaders: Conflict in Unity.* 2nd ed. Louisville, KY: Westminster John Knox, 1991.

Patterson, Orlando. *Rituals of Blood: Consequences of Slavery in Two American Centuries.* Washington, DC: Civitas/Counterpoint, 1998.

———. *Slavery and Social Death: A Comparative Study.* Cambridge, MA: Harvard University Press, 1982.

Phillips, Kevin P. *The Politics of Rich and Poor: Wealth and the American Electorate in the Reagan Aftermath.* New York: Random House, 1990.

———. *Wealth and Democracy: A Political History of the American Rich.* New York: Broadway Books, 2002.

Pollin, Robert, and Stephanie Luce. *The Living Wage: Building a Fair Economy.* Rev. ed. New York: New Press, 2000.

Potter, Deborah. "Prosperity Gospel." *Religion and Ethics Newsweekly: An Online Companion to the Weekly Television Program,* Public Broadcasting Service, August 17, 2007.

Potter's House, "Mission Statement," November 19, 2002, www.thepottershouse.org/PH_mission.html.

"President Praises Negroes at Fair." *New York Times,* October 21, 1940.

"The Prophet Jones." *Newsweek,* January 12, 1953, 73.

"Prophet Jones: Bizarre Detroit Evangelist Builds Himself a $2 Million Kingdom in Slums in Six Years." *Ebony,* April 1950, 67–72.

Raboteau, Albert J. "The Afro-American Traditions." In *Caring and Curing: Health and Medicine in the Western Religious Traditions,* edited by Ronald L. Numbers and Darrel W. Amundsen. Baltimore: Johns Hopkins University Press, 1986.

———. *Canaan Land: A Religious History of African Americans.* New York: Oxford University Press, 2001.

———. *Slave Religion: The "Invisible Institution" in the Antebellum South.* New York: Oxford University Press, 1978.

Radmacher, Dan. "Liberal Offerings Minister Lives Good Life." *Charleston Gazette,* April 10, 1995, 4A.

Reid, S. A. "Bishop Accused in Beating Blames Satan for His Woes." *Atlanta Journal and Constitution*, August 27, 2007.

Retzloff, Tim. "Seer or Queer? Postwar Fascination with Detroit's Prophet Jones." *GLQ: A Journal of Gay and Lesbian Studies* 8, no. 3 (2002): 271–96.

"Rev. C. L. Franklin Continues Attack on Prophet Jones." *Michigan Chronicle*, June 1955, 18.

"Rev. Ike Hit with Sex Harassment Suit by Former Male Employee." *Jet*, October 30, 1995, 24–5.

Richardson, Harry. *Dark Glory: A Picture of the Church among Negroes in the Rural South*. New York: Friendship Press, 1947.

Riley, Clayton. "The Golden Gospel of Rev. Ike." *New York Times Magazine*, March 9, 1975.

Roberts, Oral. "Do You Want God to Return Your Money Seven Times?" *America's Healing Magazine*, April 1954, 10.

———. *My Story*. Tulsa, OK: Summitt, 1961.

———. "100 Radio Stations for Healing Waters Broadcast in 12 Months." *Healing Waters: The Magazine of Bible Deliverance*, September 1949, 12.

Ross, Reverend Leora. "Dry Bones in the Valley." In *Preachers and Congregations*, vol. 6, *1924–36* (CD). Document Records, 2005.

Salvatore, Nick. *Singing in a Strange Land: C. L. Franklin, the Black Church, and the Transformation of America*. New York: Little, Brown, 2005.

Sanders, Cheryl Jeanne. *Saints in Exile: The Holiness-Pentecostal Experience in African American Religion and Culture*. New York: Oxford University Press, 1996.

Sanneh, Kalefah. "Pray and Grow Rich." *New Yorker*, October 2004.

Schragger, Richard. "The Anti-Chain Store Movement, Localist Ideology, and the Remnants of the Progressive Constitution, 1920–1940." *Iowa Law Review* 90 (2005): 1011.

Schultze, Quentin J. *Christianity and the Mass Media in America: Toward a Democratic Accommodation*. East Lansing: Michigan State University Press, 2003.

———. "Defining the Electronic Church." In *Religious Television: Controversies and Conclusions*, edited by Robert Abelman and Stewart M. Hoover. Norwood, NJ: Ablex, 1990.

———. "Evangelical Radio and the Rise of the Electronic Church 1921–1948." *Journal of Broadcasting and Electronic Media* 32 (1988): 289–306.

———. *Televangelism and American Culture: The Business of Popular Religion*. Grand Rapids, MI: Baker Book House, 1991.

Sernett, Milton C. *Bound for the Promised Land: African American Religion and the Great Migration*. Durham: Duke University Press, 1997.

Shapiro, Thomas M. *The Hidden Cost of Being African-American: How Wealth Perpetuates Inequality*. New York: Oxford University Press, 2004.

Sidime, Aissatou. "Credit Use Strangles Wealth: African American Debt Is Increasing Faster Than Income." *Black Enterprise*, November 2004, 38.

Simmons, Dale H. E. W. *Kenyon and the Postbellum Pursuit of Peace, Power, and Plenty.* Lanham, MD: Scarecrow Press, 1997.

Simmons, Zena. "Detroit's Flamboyant Prophet Jones." *Detroit News*, September 13, 1997. http://info.detnews.com/history/story/index.cfm?id=182&category=people.

Smith, Ben. "Black Republicans Make No Headway in Dekalb." *Atlanta Journal and Constitution*, November 23, 2000.

———. "GOP Lured Few Black Voters; Traditional Party Lines Still Define County's African American Precincts." *Atlanta Journal and Constitution*, November 16, 2000.

Spear, Allan H. *Black Chicago: The Making of a Negro Ghetto, 1890–1920.* Chicago: University of Chicago Press, 1967.

Spillers, Hortense J. "Mama's Baby, Papa's Maybe." In *Black, White, and in Color: Essays on American Literature and Culture.* Chicago: University of Chicago Press, 2003.

State of the Black Union: Defining the Agenda. Video, C-Span Archives, February 26, 2005.

Steele, Shelby. *The Content of Our Character: A New Vision of Race in America.* New York: St. Martin's Press, 1990.

Stevenson, Richard W. "In a Time of Plenty; the Poor Are Still Poorer." *New York Times*, January 23, 2000.

Stout, Jeffrey. *Democracy and Tradition.* Princeton: Princeton University Press, 2004.

Synan, Vinson. *The Holiness-Pentecostal Tradition: Charismatic Movements in the Twentieth Century.* 2nd ed. Grand Rapids, MI: W. B. Eerdmans, 1997.

"Tapes Released in Pastor's Alleged Sexual-Assault Case, Criminal Charges Not Filed against Pastor." *Click2Houston.com*, September 30, 2003.

Taylor, Mark L. *The Executed God: The Way of the Cross in Lockdown America.* Minneapolis: Augsburg Publishing House, 2001.

Townes, Emilie Maureen. *Womanist Ethics and the Cultural Production of Evil.* New York: Palgrave Macmillan, 2006.

Trussell, Jacqueline. "The Full Gospel Baptist Church Fellowship: Giving Baptists a Choice." Black and Christian.com, December 2000. www.blackandchristian.com/articles/academy/trussell-12-00.shtml.

Tucker-Worgs, Tamelyn. "Get on Board, Little Children, There's Room for Many More: The Black Megachurch Phenomenon." *Journal of the Interdenominational Theological Center* 29, nos. 1 and 2 (2001-2): 177–203.

Turner, Victor Witter. *From Ritual to Theatre: The Human Seriousness of Play.* Performance Studies Series. New York City: Performing Arts Journal, 1982.

"TV Preachers: Being Called a Bishop Does Not Mean That You Can Live Like a King." *Charleston Gazette*, April 21, 1995, 820–23.

Vanderpool, Harold. "The American Success Syndrome." *Christian Century,* September 24, 1975.

Vara, Richard. "Pastor Accused of Assault Given 2-Month Paid Leave." *Houston Chronicle*, October 29, 2003.

Voskuil, Dennis N. "The Power of the Air: Evangelicals and the Rise of Religious Broadcasting." In *American Evangelicals and the Mass Media*, edited by Quentin J. Schultze. Grand Rapids, MI: Zondervan, 1990.

Wacker, Grant. "The Pentecostal Tradition." In *Caring and Curing: Health and Medicine in the Western Religious Traditions*, edited by Ronald L. Numbers and Darrel W. Amundsen, 514–38. Baltimore: Johns Hopkins University Press, 1986.

Wallace, Michele. *Black Macho and the Myth of the Superwoman*. New York: Dial Press, 1979.

Walton, Jonathan L. "Empowered: The Entrepreneurial Ministry of T. D. Jakes." *Christian Century*, July 10, 2007.

Ward, Ken, Jr. "Successful Book, TV Exposure Allow Kanawha Minister to Live in Style." *Charleston Gazette*, April 5, 1995.

Washington, Joseph R. *Black Sects and Cults*. Lanham, MD: University Press of America, 1984.

Watson, Carlos. *Off Topic with Carlos Watson*. Cable News Network (CNN), January 23, 2005.

Watts, Jill. *God, Harlem U.S.A.: The Father Divine Story*. Berkeley: University of California Press, 1992.

Webb, Lillian Ashcraft. *About My Father's Business: The Life of Elder Michaux*. Westport, CT: Greenwood Press, 1981.

Weber, Max. *The Protestant Ethic and the Spirit of Capitalism*. 3rd ed. Los Angeles: Roxbury, 2001.

———. *The Theory of Social and Economic Organization*. Translated by A. M. Henderson and Talcott Parsons. New York: Oxford University Press, 1947.

Weiss, Richard. *The American Myth of Success: From Horatio Alger to Norman Vincent Peale*. New York: Basic Books, 1969.

West, Cornel. *Democracy Matters: Winning the Fight against Imperialism*. New York: Penguin, 2004.

———. "The Dilemma of the Black Intellectual." In *The Cornel West Reader*, edited by Cornel West. New York: Basic Books, 1999.

———. "The Prophetic Tradition in Afro-America." In *African American Religious Thought*, edited by Cornel West and Eddie S. Glaude, 1037–50. Louisville, KY: Westminster John Knox, 2003.

West, Cornel, and Eddie S. Glaude, eds. *African American Religious Thought: An Anthology*. Louisville, KY: Westminster John Knox, 2003.

Wilkerson, Isabel. "A Dollar and a Dream." *Essence*, December 2005, 166–70.

Wilson, William J. *The Ghetto Underclass: Social Science Perspectives*. Updated ed. Newbury Park, CA: Sage Publications, 1993.

———. *The Truly Disadvantaged: The Inner City, the Underclass, and Public Policy*. Chicago: University of Chicago Press, 1987.

———. *When Work Disappears: The World of the New Urban Poor*. New York: Alfred A. Knopf, 1996.

Winner, Lauren. "T. D. Jakes Feels Your Pain." *Christianity Today*, February 7, 2000, 52–59.

Wuthnow, Robert. *American Mythos: Why Our Best Efforts to Be a Better Nation Fall Short*. Princeton: Princeton University Press, 2006.

Young, Rosa. "What Induced Me to Build a School in the Rural District." In *Afro-American Religious History: A Documentary Witness*, edited by Milton C. Sernett. Durham: Duke University Press, 1985.

Index

About the Author

JONATHAN L. WALTON is Assistant Professor of Religious Studies at the University of California, Riverside.